Are You the Foie Gras Correspondent?

ARE YOU THE FOIE GRAS CORRESPONDENT?

(Another slow news day
in South West France)

Chris Bockman

Matador
9 Priory Business Park,
Wistow Road, Kibworth Beauchamp,
Leicestershire. LE8 0RX
Tel: 0116 279 2299
Email: books@troubador.co.uk
Web: www.troubador.co.uk/matador
Twitter: @matadorbooks

ISBN 978 1788034 654

British Library Cataloguing in Publication Data.
A catalogue record for this book is available from the British Library.

Printed and Bound in the UK by 4Edge Limied
Typeset in 11pt Minion Pro by Troubador Publishing Ltd, Leicester, UK

Matador is an imprint of Troubador Publishing Ltd

Contents

Preface

I t was a visit to the local police station in the department of the Tarn in rural south-west France that had me thinking there was a goldmine of opportunity in off-beat broadcast journalism in this region, just waiting to be tapped into.

While working in London, I had succumbed to that desire to own a crumbling ancient home in the rural bliss of southern France. So I did it, buying a cheap cottage in the medieval village of Penne, about 90 kilometres from Toulouse, and then spending a small fortune over the next two decades trying to make it actually inhabitable (including, naturally, suing the original builders for shoddy work and having to do it all over again).

During those early days, I received a letter inviting me to the nearest police station (called 'Gendarmerie' in the countryside) in Vaour, about 7 kilometres away, 'to fill in some paperwork'. Actually, it's just a clever way for the authorities to keep tabs on whoever is new to the area.

But what really amazed me was that the local station was manned by a team of 7 officers who all lived in the village of Vaour with a mission to protect three villages, including mine, Penne, so that was a total population of 1,500 residents in all.

It got me wondering — had I finally discovered the easiest job in the world? I had a lot of time to do some thinking, because all my important personal information had to be filled in on a manual typewriter by an officer who clearly had no idea what he was doing and had to start all over again each time he made a mistake.

The walls of the station were in a peeling yellow paint, bought no doubt - along with the ribbon in the typewriter - during a budget windfall back at the time of the liberation of the region by the Maquis during World War II.

But one thing caught my attention: a highly detailed map of the region on a wall, with lots of drawing pins in different colours dotted around it. I asked the policeman what they stood for, and he explained that each drawing pin represented a crime committed at that location, and the colours represented the type of crime - burglaries and drunk-driving made up the majority. But one stood out, one lone colour, and when I asked him what that was, he told me with some enthusiasm – it was a double homicide!

Wow, I thought, even here! And was the killer caught?

Monsieur's eyes froze for a few seconds, then he squinted, put his hand to his forehead and squeezed hard, and then came the answer – "I can't remember...".

And I guess that answer provided both the inspiration and confirmation that I needed: I was indeed in a landscape oozing with quirky stories. I decided to move down full time.

To be honest, it wasn't a difficult decision to make. I had been working on the breakfast show GMTV in London. I had no idea why they had hired me - I was a misfit from day one. My out-loud remarks seemed to make the 'Week's Most Outrageous Quotes' list every Friday morning. For example on one overnight, after being given my assignment by the night editor, I said to no-one in particular:

"I think I am working on the wrong show - I have been asked to write about some gay guy called Drew Barrymore (it was in fact Michael Barrymore) behaving badly, and about the battle of the bands with some group called Blur that I have never heard of..."

But apparently it was my doorstepping the Transport Minister Brian Mawhinney at 6:30am outside the BBC Today radio programme offices and asking in relation to the train service cuts, why he was "screwing rail passengers" that really underlined the fact that my career in breakfast television was coming to an end. Another hint came when the irate news editor Peter McHugh gathered us in his office at 9:30am at end of the show and started by pointing at the Thames skyline behind him and saying: "There are a million stories out there, except none of them are in our fucking rundown!"

I knew it was time to go. The usual things - the news boss avoiding eye contact; suddenly not being invited to certain meetings to discuss the news agenda for the next day... So I jumped ship, or to put it more precisely, took one of the last low cost flights from London to Toulouse on the French airline Air Lib, just hours before it collapsed, making my return flight – well, like me – redundant.

A Frivolous Opportunity

Many people will remember the moving pictures of Chris Patten, the last governor of Hong Kong weeping as he prepared to to set foot on the Royal Yacht Britannia as the last British colony that really mattered was handed over to the Chinese... But does anyone remember Whisky and Soda?

They were Patten's Norfolk terriers, who had had the run of the place in the governor's colonial mansion, but faced six months in quarantine as soon as they arrived back in the UK, thanks to antiquated rabies laws.

It turns out Chris Patten – like around half of the cabinet ministers in office during his time – had bought a second home in the countryside around Toulouse. His, in the Tarn, came with the obligatory swimming pool and tennis court.

Later he made rather a lot of money in a glamorous shiny ad for Eurostar in the upmarket magazines where he alluded to the Orient Express sleeper experience he went through each time he took the night train from Brussels to his home in the Tarn. I have met Chris a few times and have been meaning to ask him about this luxury train that he refers to taking to get to his home in southern France. No-one I know has ever taken it. Is it a special secret perk for EU grandees? I have certainly taken the overnight sleeper from Paris which takes about 10 hours and is staffed by surly and threatening employees surely trained by the people running the prison camps in Guantanamo and North Korea. As for the sleeping arrangements, generally they consist of six bunks in the tiniest of spaces – to accomodate both travellers and their luggage – and they make hikers' mountain refuges (normally the most sparse facilities on earth) appear business class in comparison.

Anyway, I digress. Word had reached me that Chris Patten felt humiliated that, having faced off with the Chinese on behalf of the British Empire, he couldn't bring his dogs home. So he decided they would go into exile instead.

Personally, I thought being appointed in quick succession EU Foreign Relations Commissioner and Chancellor of Oxford University was a reasonable pay back for his service, and certainly enough to sweeten the pill of having to comply with quarantine rules like the rest of us. But apparently Chris didn't feel that way.

The Reuters news desk in London went wild – track down Whisky and Soda immediately! You knew there was real urgency because usually every conversation with the Reuters TV news desk also ended with the question 'How much will it cost?' but not this time.

As it happened, I was in Lyon when I was asked to do the story and decided to take a night train (again) to Toulouse and meet my cameraman there. I didn't know my French geography very well back then, but I did know when I woke up and saw cliffs and waves that I was nowhere near Toulouse.

In fact, the train had split in two somewhere overnight – one half headed to Toulouse, the other to Spain – and I was about to reach the border. Of course the inspector had never bothered to tell me that after checking my ticket, but he was happy to ask me to pay the extra fee for travelling to the border and then taking the next train back the other way, to Toulouse.

Anyway, the story doesn't get much more exciting than that, although I did produce the goods – my world exclusive (yes these were very much pre 9/11 days) consisted of finding Chris Patten's house.

None of the locals had heard of him but the local randy young men had definitely heard of his three gorgeous daughters.

Having found the house and trampled illegally on Chris Patten's property (one day months later in Brussels, he said to me: "So that was you after my dogs!"), I went across the road to a rundown peasant shack and there they were, Whisky and Soda, clearly much happier here, a comfortable distance away from both the humidity of Hong Kong and the unpleasantness of some damp Dover kennel.

The conclusion from my first story in France was that there was a market for frivolous, pointless stories and I was in business! In fact, the number of frivolous and highly popular stories that I was able to cover over the years knew no limits, but a few really stand out.

Rugby

otherwise known as

the Local Mafia or Shakedown Artists

I often used to joke there were three people in Toulouse that I must never piss off if I wanted to live peacefully in this town: the manager of Le Stade Toulousain, Guy Novès (more on him later); the head of the Airbus press office, Barbara Kracht (yes it is indeed pronounced 'crashed'), and city mayor, Philippe Douste-Blazy. More on those last two later.

I've written and said this too many times to remember, but south-west France is probably the only part of Europe (except some Welsh valleys) where young boys dream of becoming the next Vincent Clerc or Stephen Jones rather than the next David Beckham.

Nobody seems to know how rugby became so popular in this corner of France. There are plenty of theories, one is that locals in Bordeaux took to the game when they saw English sailors playing with a rugby ball in the port. Others say the region's rural peasant roots, the muddy winter terrain and collegial atmosphere in the villages made the sport a perfect fit.

Calling rugby a religion might seem excessive, but the sport does have its very own pilgrimage destination: a church dedicated to the world of the sport called *Notre Dame de Rugby*, in the Landes region. The once abandoned chapel was restored in memory of several members of a local rugby team killed in a car crash after a game. The stained glass windows depict the Virgin Mary with a baby Jesus in her arms holding a rugby ball, or scrum scenes; there are boots hanging up near the altar and rugby shirts of players from around the world signed and framed, on the walls.

The local priest holds one service a year in the chapel and it always gets a big media turnout. He prays for players worldwide but never prays for a French victory, saying God believes it's up to the team to do the hard work. Here is one of the stories I did on it for the BBC during the Six Nations Tournament.

From Our Own Correspondent
BBC Radio 4
February 2013

The French had been really looking forward to this year's 6 Nations Rugby Championship and felt their 'favourites to win' status made sense. But now there is a sense of dismay and shell shock, nowhere more so than in the south-west of the country where rugby is king. Most of the top clubs and most players on the national side come from the region; local cafés in beautiful villages have names like 'Le Fair Play' or the 'Le Ballon Oval'.

This year, the French said they had a generation of new players who would dazzle on the international stage like Wesley Fofana, and comeback kids at the top of their game like Fred Michalak.

But it's all gone so horribly wrong for the team that has a cockerel as its national symbol. However, not all is lost – as the

French prepare to play England in 'Le Crunch', there is still hope for them, a powerful force they can count on: divine intervention.

Rugby is a religion in this corner of France and to prove it, all you have to do is head to La Chapelle Notre Dame du Rugby (literally: 'The Chapel of Our Lady of Rugby').

Perched on a hillside surrounded by forest on the outskirts of the small village of Larrivière-Saint- Savin, about two hours south of Bordeaux, the small, simple but elegant chapel gives little away at first.

But as you approach the entrance, in an exterior alcove below the bell tower is a statue of the Virgin Mary being handed a rugby ball by a small boy. But it's when you go inside the chapel (which, unlike most rural churches these days is always open) that you quickly realise this is no ordinary place of worship.

The beautiful stained glass windows show rugby scenes: a scrum, the Virgin Mary holding a baby Jesus in her arms as he prepares to throw a rugby ball into a line-out. In another, the Virgin Mary cradles an injured player in her arms. Old rugby boots dangle by their laces next to the altar. And along the walls, proof that a Who's Who of the world of rugby through the decades have flocked here. There are photos and newspaper articles of players displayed alongside jerseys worn by the stars of the past such as Serge Blanco or Fabien Pelous, with simple messages of support for the volunteers who look after the chapel.

To understand the chapel's connection with the sport you have to go back to a tragic event in 1964. Three young players with the well known local club Dax were killed in a car crash after a game. The community grieved. A local priest, Father Michel Devert, convinced everyone that the forgotten, ruined chapel should become a place of remembrance for the young players and a centre of worship for the world of rugby.

These days the restored chapel is in a beautiful state, largely thanks to a busy committee called the 'Friends of Notre Dame du Rugby' raising funds and getting players around the world to send *in mementos. One of the committee members is Benoît Dauga, a former captain of the French side who played for his country 60 times.*

Several priests in the diocese take turns holding masses at the chapel, including one who once played for the most successful club in French rugby – Le Stade Toulousain.

There are fewer than a dozen simple wooden pews and just one regularly scheduled official service a year, at Pentecost, which is always packed and spills over outside, especially when the weather is good and the local rugby clubs bring along brass bands. Often an additional mass is held ahead of particularly important international games or tournaments when French honour is at stake. The events are usually filmed and broadcast on the French news channels.

But one priest, Father Gilbert Lavigne, told me that while he prays for all the players, he never prays for a French victory. He says God believes it's up to the Quinze de France (the French squad) to do the hard work. Alas, you won't see so much fair play in the comments left in the visitors' book on the altar: Absolute pride and admiration for the chapel; rather less for foreign teams, especially England.

Most of the visitors are men who visit during the 6 Nations, or over the summer when on holiday in the area, taking a break from the beach to make a special pilgrimage to the site.

Sifting through the pages of written comments left over the years, there are amusing quips: "This team will need nothing less than a miracle to win anything", "Forgive them their sins on the pitch" or "Please, when will the Virgin Mary bear a fly-half worthy of the name?"

One thing is certain: even if you don't like rugby, you are best off not admitting to it. In fact ex-rugby players down here have a similar secret code when describing their club days as English public school old boys do when they ask each other which school they went to and when…

Men will nod wisely and reflect on past glories as they reveal to each other that they played say for small town clubs like Moissac or Castelnaudary in 1974. Of course it goes without saying those were the glory years of the club and it won everything back then. Fortunately there is no-one to check and no desire to, because rugby is associated with an era of team spirit, people pulling together, playing hard and then partying hard (at sessions known here as the 'troisième mi-temps', the 'third half').

Go to any rugby stadium and berets, long moustaches, drums and trumpets are part of the supporter's survival kit. And the fans are nearly all white. You could say rugby comforts a section of the population who remember France with rose-tinted glasses… And the France they think back to is the one in the 1950s and early 60s, before mass immigration, before crime and rough housing estates, when the country was prosperous and had a generous welfare system to actively promote big families and early retirement. And in the rugby stadiums today, many of the supporters come to games to seek solace and rekindle fond memories of French life before it all changed… as if the 'cultural revolution' of 1968 had never happened, nor the painful war in Algeria before it, etc.

Of course in the crowd not everyone is there for nostalgia. Some are rather successful business types accompanied by much younger, very sexy women. It's often said that to Saturday afternoon games men bring their mistresses; the trade-off being that the wives take the credit card shopping.

Before rugby went professional, the game gave small towns in particular prestige and standing if the teams played well. Since they couldn't be paid for being on the team, players were given 'fictional' jobs, often by the councils of the towns where they played. That way you could say the local political structure and the world of rugby were bound to be attached together for good.

It's not surprising that with so much generosity from local mayors, many rugby players, when they thought about hanging up their boots, saw municipal politics as their ticket to post-retirement new careers.

I learnt this early on to my great shame and momentary mortification (I repeatedly shamed myself over the years). I had called up the Toulouse town hall press office asking to do a story on the latest crackdown on urban delinquency and whether I could follow the city police around. I hope they captured criminals more rapidly than they followed up on reporters' requests because weeks must have gone by and I had forgotten about the story. Then one day I get a call out of the blue, it went something like this:

- "What do you want?"

Me: "Who is calling?"

- "Walter Spanghero, what do you want?"

– "Who? I didn't call you!"

- "Yes you did, you want to see the police or something…"

- "Oh yes, sorry, what's your name again?"

- "Walter Spanghero, former captain of the French rugby team."

- "Now you are joking

– head of the police and former French rugby captain? For a start, that's an Italian name!"

- "My name is Walter Spanghero, former French rugby captain. What exactly do you want?"

Anyway, only later did my total slinking embarrassment sink in and highlight the fact that a minimum of background research is useful in this business! This is for any journalism students out there reading this – for me of course, it's way too late.

Walter Spanghero is indeed one of the most well-known former rugby players in France, coming from a large family of players, all with marked and scarred faces from years embedded in the rough sport, and in Walter's case, with hands so big the rugby ball must have almost disappeared when he clasped it in his heyday.

It's been said that he was absolutely brutal on the pitch. When I finally met up with him, he was running a car crushing company, which seemed to me to be a perfect fit. Incidentally, he told me later that going into politics and working under the then mayor Philippe Douste-Blazy was the worst single mistake in his life. He had indeed bowed out pretty quickly. Fabien Pelous, another former French captain – with cauliflower ears from his time in the scrum and no angel himself – went briefly into local politics too and said it was the only time he ever received death threats.

In any case, the umbilical cord between the world of rugby and local politics in south-west France is nearly impossible to cut. I remember the President of the Stade Toulousain, René Bouscatel campaigning side by side at a street market with the outgoing centre-right mayor of Toulouse, Jean-Luc Moudenc during local elections.

His rival was the unknown socialist candidate Pierre Cohen, clearly seen as an outsider by the local establishment – Jewish sounding name and born in Tunisia. Bouscatel turned to me and said: "Who is Cohen? What is he doing in a place like this? For a start, he doesn't even like rugby!"

It's true, Pierre Cohen was one of the rare politicians in the region to say even before he was elected that he preferred football. A taboo had been broken – suddenly it seemed politicians were free from the 'friendly' hand of the rugby world, constantly on the look out for new subsidies, new grounds, stadiums, jobs from elected officials and so on.

Well, that brave new world didn't quite work out – as soon as he was elected as the new mayor, Pierre Cohen quickly revealed in his weekly agenda distributed to the media that he would be going to all the Stade Toulousain home games. The big problem is that rugby is a big sport in a relatively small region, the Southwest. Here is where most of the first division or Top 14 clubs are based and from where most of the star players emerge as well, which isn't surprising because it's also home to most of the grass roots popular support.

That means the sport is constantly on the look out for new revenue from a relatively small base and even money from national television rights is totally dwarfed by that available in the world of football.

So that means town mayors and business leaders constantly face and dread the knock on the door, the back-slapping phone call inviting them to a rugby match with seating in the VIP tribune and a chance to eat and drink with the players afterwards – in other words, a shakedown.

In the US, and especially since 9/11, any town council that tries to reduce the costs of the local fire service is dicing with political suicide. Facing down the rugby brotherhood here in south-west France is almost as risky.

Sometimes the rugby world can be pretty boardroom shrewd. I remember doing a story on Sir Christopher Gent, one of the big names of British capitalism. When I met him, he was president of the UK drug company GlaxoSmithKline. But during his heyday at the turn of the century he had turned the nimble Vodafone into a giant, masterminding one of the biggest mergers in European history at that time, buying the German company Mannesmann.

Anyway like many men of his status, he discreetly bought a big pile in the countryside – his was near the town of Agen. The countryside around the town is extremely attractive. But Agen isn't. With a population of 70,000, halfway between Bordeaux and Toulouse, it has known better days. Once an industrial hotspot that attracted immigration from Italy in the 1950s when there were plenty of jobs around, but now a backwater, its decline is similar to that of many other urban centres too small and unappealing to entrepreneurs and big business. It's had much of the life sucked out of it as decision-makers move to be as close to major hubs as possible.

Like the town itself, Agen rugby club has an illustrious history with huge success at the time of the economic boom in the 1960s.

But that was a long time ago. The club's current owners, with an entrepreneurial spirit and big ambitions, were keen to recruit stars, and they have to be paid for of course. When one of the club bosses heard about a certain English gentleman, Chris Gent, living in the area, they paid him a visit with an offer he couldn't turn down.

And the deal made a lot of sense – they wanted to tap him up for his business and sponsorship contacts especially in New York, and in return for a personal investment of €50,000, he would become one of the official 'Musketeers' of the club and be able to sit in the VIP section of the stadium on match day, next to the mayor and other grandees.

In other words, it was a way for Chris Gent to introduce himself to local French notables and be part of their community and not just another wealthy Brit with a home in southern France yet separated by culture and language from the population around him... And it worked!

Agen after relegation returned to the top flight (but later it went down again). Anyone else looking to become part of the French community in this part of France could be encouraged to take this route: join the friends of/association of whichever local rugby club is nearby (or become a volunteer fireman in the local brigade – probably the next fastest route to acceptance into French rural life in the Southwest).

Believe me, not all rugby games are fun to watch. I remember the first one I saw was Toulouse against Bourgoin (who? where? Yep, I said the same thing). I remember the temperature on the scoreboard said -1°C and the score was something like 80 – 3 to the host team, so it's not like there was a lot of suspense to help me overlook the fact that my toes were getting frostbite. But if the game itself is often hit or miss, most of the fun has come from some of the characters associated with it.

Over the years I have been lucky enough to work for a TV programme called *Total Rugby*, re-named recently *World Rugby*, which at times has been sponsored, backed, and is these days financed by World Rugby, the rugby world's governing body.

The show has been produced by various different production companies, but fortunately I have managed to stay with it for a number of years.

***

Bernard Laporte

One of the most fun stories for the show that I ever did was a day out on a Friday ahead of a long weekend, during an extremely hot spell in June when no-one with any sense would have emerged from their homes after 10am.

But the day out was with Bernard Laporte who at the time I liked to compare with the mad scientist Dr Strangelove. He also had a granite southern accent and spoke in machine gun bursts which I am sure most of his compatriots don't understand either. (I often wonder why on the flagship evening TV news on France 2 for example, when someone – say a teacher from Senegal – is speaking French slowly and correctly and has obviously learnt the language thoroughly, they subtitle them, when it is in fact people like Laporte or the head of the fishermen's union at the communist inspired CGT in Marseille who should be subtitled, as they brutalise the language... although with the CGT you have a pretty good idea what they are going to say).

"Bernie le Dingue" or 'Bernie the madman' as he was often called, has calmed down a lot since then, when he took over managing Toulon and won nearly everything going and then launched an underdog campaign to run French rugby. He criss-crossed the country for months, claiming he was part of the genuine world of authentic rugby lovers, while he was actually taking on the elite in their warm VIP boxes. Running on the anti-elite ticket is a trendy campaign theme these days but at the time it was quite a novelty. Anyway it worked.

To those who don't remember, Bernard Laporte was the French national rugby coach, with the bald head and owl eyes with rimmed glasses. He was outspoken with his own players – when he coached Le Stade Français in Paris there is a video of him dressed in black, jumping up and down in anger in front of his players at half time in the changing room – priceless. His accent is extremely thick south-western, difficult for anyone to understand and, as I said, he should be subtitled each time he appears on French TV. He has also always been a handler's nightmare, not least when he became sports minister under Nicolas Sarkozy and referred to upset rugby fans at the Stade de France in Paris as 'bourgeois crap'. Fortunately he loved to be in the glare of the media too, and that's where I came in.

I had his mobile phone number, I can't remember how, but I called up and said I wanted to do a profile of him and his business interest in the wine industry. Bernard Laporte's passion for rugby is only just ahead of – or on a par with – his enthusiasm for doing business, often mixing the two when he sees a financial opportunity.

He has a part ownership in a winery in his hometown of Gaillac, about an hour north of Toulouse, so we agreed to meet at a bodega owned by a friend of his. I arrived with my cameraman well on time, as did a crew from the French channel TF1 that was doing a sort of 'lifestyle of the rich and famous' story on him. A couple of other Laporte acolytes had also turned up.

But there was no sign of him. About an hour later he shows up with a rather attractive blonde woman in tow, the two looking a little sheepish and flush (but as I said earlier, it had been an unseasonably hot morning...). Needless to say, TF1 didn't get any shots of the blonde and their programme focused on Bernard Laporte the loving family man who once away from the brutal world of rugby had just one wish – to snuggle up at home in Paris with his adored wife.

There was no snuggling up during our day out – it started with heavy red wine and tripe. Bearing in mind it was about 10am and already a searing heat to turn a dog mad. But in that virile atmosphere, the offal was washed down with the wine, no questions asked, followed by a trip to the nearby vineyard, the one partly owned by Bernard Laporte himself. The wine label even had his face on the bottle. I have no idea whether that helped with sales or not, but throughout his career Laporte has been accused of mixing his personal business interests and sports well too closely.

Anyway, visiting his winery meant a lot of wine tasting was required and by the time we ended up in the backroom at a restaurant owned by another long time friend of his, we were all well cooked. And when we had finished the long liquid lunch, I admit I was hardly capable of driving.

Bernard on the other hand, was on the phone discussing which bar he would be meeting his mates at, later that same evening in Lyon, as he was heading there to watch a rugby game the next day. You certainly can't deny his stamina.

I have met Bernard Laporte several times since that day.

During his time as manager of the French national side, his worst mistake was to go on holiday in the beautiful resort of Arcachon, just west of Bordeaux, a sort of French Cape Cod. Because while out jogging there, he bumped into the French President Nicolas Sarkozy, also out running. Naturally, they went for lunch and of course as was only to be expected, Sarkozy offered Laporte the job of Sports Minister there and then, with his work to begin after the end of the 2007 World Cup which France was co-hosting with Wales.

The World Cup ended up being a disaster for France – they lost their opening game to Argentina and were knocked out in the semis by England. Who was to blame? There are many suspects but I can't help feeling that the knowledge that he was to become Sports Minister rattled Laporte throughout the preparations for the World Cup.

I was at Pyrenees ski resort Font Romeu, where the team were carrying out high altitude training ahead of the World Cup. I saw Laporte handed a big pile of documents at the team hotel. He had instructions from the Sports Ministry to go through them, to help him prepare for the transition to power.

I remember him saying to an assistant after a brief look at the pile: "Bin it". Maybe a wise decision at the time, but clearly knowing he had looming ministerial duties to handle while also managing the immediate huge expectations from the home crowd which expected France to win the World Cup on home soil must have derailed his concentration.

After that, he did take up the job as Sports Minister, but his role in government fizzled out rapidly as expected.

I next caught up with him at Toulon, his latest comeback into rugby management. In a strange twist, he had become manager of one Johnny Wilkinson – who had helped eliminate France from the World Cup twice. He chuckles at that but he also says that if he had had players available with the same drive as Wilkinson, winning the world cup would have come easily.

With such an all-star list, I headed to Toulon often and whatever the weather, the first person I usually saw there was Johnny Wilkinson, alone, kicking penalties, no different from a lone kid kicking a ball against a wall with an imaginary goalkeeper. As Bernard Laporte told me, Wilkinson was often the first to arrive in the morning and the last to leave. He was frequently dismissed as boring because he didn't talk in soundbites. Just like David Beckham in fact. But unlike Beckham, it was because he was highly intelligent and thought things through, because he didn't see things in black and white and wanted to answer questions with honesty even if that exposed vulnerability. When I carried out a very long format interview with him, he had turned to buddhism both to help heal his physical injuries and tackle the deep depression he suffered from after THAT last minute winning drop goal in the World Cup finals against Australia. He felt guilty that he got all the glory as opposed to the team and it weighed on him for years. There aren't many around like him…

***

Toulon itself is a mixture of Glasgow, Naples and Marseille, in miniature. A naval headquarters; rough, tough; lots of poor housing; immigrants of North African origin and one of the first cities in France to elect a National Front mayor.

Yet the richest person in an otherwise poor port city is a self-made man of Algerian origin, who made his money in the comic book publishing business.

Mourad Boudjellal grew up in Toulon with a chip on his shoulder and a desire to get revenge on the town that voted for the far right. Toulon is sandwiched between two football towns, Marseille and Nice. Maybe for that reason, it's always had one of the most passionate rugby crowds in France, and they knew years of glory in the 1970s. But then came obscurity, teetering towards bankruptcy in the late 1990s.

So, what if a local millionaire, an Arab to boot, bought the club and turned it around? How would the far right supporters react then? Boudjellal told me that story for BBC World News as we zoomed through the narrow roads of the old town in his Maserati. Whenever we came across young kids from Arabic backgrounds, they would shout out in respect: "Boudjellal – richest Arab in Toulon!"

He also told me he never loses points for speeding because he gets his foreign players with foreign driving licences to own up to driving the car and in return he pays their fines.

Boudjellal is paranoid, sees conspiracies everywhere and loves being a flame thrower in the staid, conservative world of rugby, which is not surprising considering where he has come from. When he first got involved, he was questioned extensively by the French Secret Service about his intentions – not in rugby but in politics, especially local politics. They wanted to know if saving the club was a stepping stone to running for mayor. Wisely, he has avoided the political world, concentrating on his team. He immediately went on a spending spree, bringing in stars such as former All Black legends Tana Umaga or Anton Oliver or Australians like George Gregan, often on six month contracts worth hundreds of thousands of euros, until then unheard of in the world of rugby. Now of course, household names like Wilkinson, Michalak, Bryan Habana are all part of the Toulon Rugby Club DNA.

The team quickly got promoted to the first division and stayed there. For a long time they even became the best team in France and in Europe by doing the double – winning both the European Cup and home championship – the 'Top 14' – in the same season. That also meant they quickly became the most despised club by every other rugby owner and the whole rugby establishment. But a day out with the president of Toulon Rugby Club is an unforgettable experience, and with Bernard Laporte there as manager, you could never come across a more combustible odd couple. When Bernard Laporte left to run a (successful) presidential style insurgent campaign across France to become the new head of French rugby at the FFR, Toulon became a slightly quieter place.

***

Guy Novès

"I know people. If I see you here again I will get them to break your legs." That is Guy Novès, the most successful rugby club manager in France, warning a journalist who dared return to the training ground to cover the Stade Toulousain, after having been banned.

Just about any self-respecting French rugby journalist has been banned from at least three rugby club grounds in the course of their career, which at least shows how influential the rugby sports press is… or how thin-skinned its readers.

However, few journalists have to take out restraining orders against club managers! But then with Guy Novès, everything is a little excessive. He's a former rugby international who then became a school sports teacher before turning to rugby management. With rugged, wild-man handsome looks, a thin skin when it comes to criticism and a distinct tendency to constantly see plots too in the rugby world, Novès is not a man you should cross in a hurry. On the other hand, like many insecure leaders no matter how talented, he is very open to flattery.

One of the first times I met him was just before a semi-final Heineken Cup match and I asked whether I could film the training session. "No."

"But I wont give any secrets away and anything you don't want me to film, I'll put the camera down." "No, no press is allowed." "But Guy, everyone in England is saying 'who is this Guy chap, doing these amazing things in southern France?! They can't get enough of you!"

"Ok be there that at 2pm."

My working relationship with Guy Novès has been more or less like that since I got here. When he got into a fist fight in the tunnel ahead of a game against arch-rival, the Stade Français, it was caught on tape by a Canal Plus cameraman. It was never broadcast of course – Novès told the cameraman if it saw the light of day he would never work in rugby again.

Guy Novès has two very attractive daughters, one married Vincent Clerc, the poster child of French rugby – a bit like France's Dan Carter, the son every mother wants their daughter to marry, etc. ... you get the idea.

The other daughter went out with the former 'bad boy', All-Black Byron Kelleher. Nicknamed 'the bison' with his messy dark brown hair and aggressive playing style, he had previously had well publicised affairs with an Asian porn star in Las Vegas and a reputation for bringing lots of women back to his loft/lair in Toulouse[1].

So suddenly, when it became known he was going out with the manager's daughter, some said 'wow he has settled down at last', others said 'boy is he in trouble'. It was when he was involved in a car crash in the early hours of one Sunday morning with some nightclub owner friends that his rugby career came to an end. They crashed into a Porsche and even the blind drunk bison met his match: the Porsche owner was a professional boxer who knocked him out. I don't think it was that which Novès took offence to – badly behaving rugby players is not exactly a headline – what he was upset about was that the girl with Kelleher wasn't his daughter and it was clear that the two had been doing more than just heavy drinking together.

For the rest of the season, Kelleher was officially 'injured' and never played for the Stade Toulousain again. Yet he still had to turn up for training and was officially a pariah in the weight

---

1   Kelleher is one of the only people I've ever scheduled a TV interview with who didn't show up for it. When I called him to ask where he was, he replied in a whisper he had some girl draped over his body – his arm was trapped under her and he couldn't remember her name and anyway he wouldn't be able to make it.

room – nobody dared talk to him for fear that Novès would interpret conversation as collusion with the enemy.

It was a humiliating end to a great career. He tried to relaunch in Paris, but the damage to morale had been done. They say sleeping with work colleagues is dangerous, but going out with the boss's daughter is surely even riskier...

The rise and rise of money in French rugby and the number of international stars, especially from the southern hemisphere, has made French club rugby the richest league in the world by far. But not everyone is happy with that, especially as it's become harder for younger French players to make their mark in the top flight. Fans moan that they have to pay more and more to watch the games and they complain that managers are so scared of making mistakes that the flair has gone out of the game.

This is a story I did tackling the issue for the BBC.

From Our Own Correspondent
BBC Radio 4
January 2010

Fast moving storm clouds over the Bay of Biscay scooped up a fresh pail of water making landfall and then burst. The region generously drenched kept the local population shivering and indoors. But not quite everyone. Around a dozen kids from the ages of five to seven are out practising their rugby skills. They are learning to pass accurately and do dummies – a trick way of swerving past their opponents. The white lines of the pitch have been washed out. Their rubber studded boots are invisible, sunk well below ankle level in the mud, and yet there's not a complaint.

They are youngest members of Castanet Rugby Club. There are 28 five-year-olds that play in this club. In fact around 150 try to get in each year.

Christine Arcangeli, an unflappable rugby mum, organises the junior teams. She is finding fresh shirts for the Saturday game, press-ganging volunteers to do the driving and to referee. Castanet, with five hundred players, has 50 volunteers to keep it all going.

She says it's not the kids themselves who want to take up rugby. It comes from their parents, especially their fathers. In this region of France, the passion is handed down one generation at a time.

Of the 28 new recruits, Christine says only five will drop out. Every year thousands of parents try to get their young boys into after-school rugby academies. The most sought-after are those run by the Stade Toulousain, Biarritz and Colomiers. Around a third of the French team squad for this Six Nations Cup come from the Stade Toulousain alone.

During the open days, it's the parents who are the most nervous, pacing the touchlines. Fathers desperate to see their sons succeed, mothers worried about the over-aggressive tackle.

One of the Stade Toulousain selectors, a former star player, Michel Marfaing, told me the competition is so tough and the let-down so hard if their boy is not picked, that the club sends parents their pass or fail slips by post several weeks later so no one feels shamed on the spot.

In Britain the sport may be associated with elite private schools but in this part of France, its roots are farm based. Players say farming and rugby go hand in hand — both involve hard work in all types of weather, toiling in the soil. And nurturing a small vine or lamb is similar to bringing out the best in a new player.

Didier Esperes is a village postman about to retire. He spends three days a week volunteering at Castanet. He says he doesn't know why rugby has proven so popular in the region but ever since he was a boy every village has always had its church and its rugby pitch. Castanet is no different. It was a village when the club was created forty years ago.

Jean-Jacques Sadolou has been a member since the club started and he fits the bill. A farmer's son, he once had the stocky build men down here tend to have. Now he has a bulge, the result of the local diet of duck liver and cassoulet washed down with red wine.

He says the club is as popular as ever, the trouble is finding money to keep it running – difficult when there are 170 other clubs with 34,000 players in the region also looking for financing.

Castanet's top team have reached the third division for the first time and are now semi-professionals. They don't have to travel far for away games because nearly every club in France's top three divisions is based in the south-west of France. The top clubs that aren't, such as Paris' Stade Français, are now packed with players from the Southwest, hired on big salaries. And that, along with the arrival of stars from abroad, is creating a lot of tension in the clubby French game. There are now worries that globalisation has caught up with rugby, that it's going the same way as football, with too many mercenaries in the game.

That's the kind of thing you will hear from the fans. If you want to know what they are thinking, you have to turn up for the famous 'troisième mi-temps' or 'third half'. That's the post-game get-together.

One of the most popular is the standing room only, zinc counter wine bar Chez Vincent, surrounded by glistening full-shell fresh scallops, oysters and hanging wild boar sausage, in the heart of the Victor Hugo indoor food market in Toulouse.

Several of the Stade Toulousain team staff go too – it might seem an exercise in masochism as the rosé flows and the conversations become louder, but the team get to hear first hand what's being said in the stands.

It's usually pretty simplistic – 'Why spend a fortune on players who can't hold a slippery ball?' Or 'we seem to see half naked players spending more time advertising hair gel on TV than in training'.

For a more sober opinion, I turn to a policeman, Alain Pietau, who spends much of his time training new recruits to patrol in the high crime urban housing projects. He trains an amateur rugby team and played at a decent level himself too. He believes the famous 'French flair' is disappearing from the game. France has never won the World Cup and is now trying to copy England and southern hemisphere teams with a playing style that is boring, suffocating, but that ultimately wins cups.

Before the game went professional over a decade ago, players had a job and a skill to fall back on when they hung up their boots. Now rugby is a full time occupation but in which few earn enough to retire on. So towns down here have found a novel if potentially illegal way of keeping good players in their local clubs: fake jobs with real salaries. In other words, a job on the town hall payroll for life in return for loyalty to the local club... But good luck getting local mayors to talk about it publicly.

In fact local politics and rugby go hand in hand. The former French manager Bernard Laporte became, briefly, Sports minister; former French captain Walter Spanghero was Toulouse's police chief; recently retired former stars Christian Califano and Fabien Pelous are now making their first steps on the political stage. In fact it takes a brave politician down here to dismiss rugby. One did – the recently elected mayor of Toulouse, Pierre Cohen.

Born in Tunisia, Cohen said he preferred football and was warned he would never get elected. He was – just – but now makes sure he goes to each Saturday Stade Toulousain game, and like his predecessors, he ensures he's the first in the changing room after the game, congratulating the players.

The people who run French rugby in Paris admit they have a problem. They have spent years trying to work out how to get rugby to take root anywhere outside the Southwest. Think of the unknown undiscovered potential out there, they say. France hosted the rugby World Cup in 2007. That was supposed to be the moment rugby would take off as the country rallied around its team. Except things didn't go that way. They lost their first game to Argentina. They somehow staggered into the semis and were knocked out by England again. The rugby revolution didn't happen – a missed opportunity.

But if you go to Vincent's bar in Toulouse this weekend, you will find plenty of people who will say that's ok – they don't need Parisians to tell them how to run the game.

Mohed Altrad – The Billionaire Syrian Rugby Club Owner

During my frequent trips to Montpellier to see various players there including the gruff Georgian captain Mamuka Gorgodze and the former scrum half Fabien Galthié, I got wind that there was a mysterious new owner of the club – he was from Syria, knew nothing about the game and was extremely wealthy but also very shy.

The more I heard about this, the more intrigued I was. His name is Mohed Altrad and he's one of the wealthiest entrepreneurs in France. His background and success are extraordinary. I ended up persuading *Total Rugby* to send me down to see him with my long time cameraman Patrice Chavaudra. It was a great outing, people like him you don't meet too often.

Shortly after my TV report, I did a separate one for *From Our Own Correspondent* for BBC Radio 4.

Mohed Altrad Profile
BBC Radio 4
October 2014

I had never met a billionaire before. I had assumed the self-made ones in particular would be, as a rule of thumb, pugnacious, outspoken, domineering and blunt, reminding you that you were using up extremely valuable minutes of their day and it wasn't entirely appreciated. So I was a little surprised when Mohed Altrad's press officer gave me Altrad's own mobile phone number and said to call him if there was anything I needed to know before we met. I was even more stunned when Altrad did indeed answer the phone and didn't seem in the slightest put out.

Don't get me wrong, Mr Altrad has all the trappings of a very wealthy man, from his English style mansion – quaintly called 'Le Cottage'- surrounded by huge walled gardens in the centre of Montpellier, to the amazing swimming pool and Lamborghini parked in the front.

His office, opposite, is a converted small manor with busy employees, but nothing that indicates this is corporate headquarters for a company with 8000 employees in 100 countries.

Mr Altrad himself speaks very softly in precise French with a strong Middle Eastern accent but is very shy and must be a great poker player because it's hard to imagine him as the tough guy negotiator he is in his hard ball field – the construction industry.

Mohed Altrad was born in a Bedouin tent close to Raqqa in Syria. He knows neither the day nor the year of his birth. In a poke at French bureaucrats who wouldn't give him a French passport without declaring his date of birth, or accept the explanation he gave as to why he didn't have one, he has given three different dates for the three passports he has held.

His mother died soon after his birth and he was passed around the desert tribe throughout his childhood. But in a stroke of luck, promising pupils in each region of Syria were given a chance to study abroad.

He took his and came to France in 1970 and has only been back to Syria once since. Through hard work and willpower, he built the biggest scaffolding company in the world.

Despite his success, Mohed Altrad had a very low profile, but in the world of French professional rugby, the local club Montpellier saw him as a potential saviour. The city of Montpellier already had a first division football team, a highly successful handball club as well as the rugby team. The town simply didn't seem big enough for three high level sports teams and the rugby club was teetering on the edge of bankruptcy.

So when the club went to the billionaire, cap in hand with a request for €3 million in emergency funding, you could consider the deed audacious, especially as Altrad had never seen a rugby game in his life, let alone know the rules. But it was a gamble that paid off. He gave a big cash injection and has dedicated himself to the club as President with the same determination he has applied to the other businesses he has created or bought on his way up.

He goes to all the home games, has done his sports homework and scrutinised the accounts. The club is now close to breaking even, and in Monsieur Altrad's own words, he wants the club to win titles, something it has never done in the past. He doesn't know when it will happen, but it means hiring new talent.

As manager, the club already has a former world class French rugby captain Fabien Galthié, who played in the key position of scrum half when 'French flair' meant something. The former Australian captain Ben Mowen has just joined and it was Mohed Altrad who scouted him and asked him to move to France.

But don't think Altrad is doing this out of charity. He says it's down to a simple fact: when he arrived in Montpellier he was given a second chance and this is his way of saying thank you. In his words he's 'sending the lift back down for others'.

Mohed Altrad has already received the Legion d'Honneur (the equivalent to a knighthood) from a former French Prime Minister, but there is clearly more to his linking up with the French rugby community than trying to help the local team.

He told me that whenever he is introduced to anyone in the French establishment, he is always 'the businessman from Syria' and never seen as a French citizen in his own right. He says that has always bothered him and he knows it won't change – it's part of the French mindset. By linking up with the cosy, traditional world of French rugby, he is clearly trying to find another way of fitting in.

In fact he hasn't returned to Syria since 1972 and where he

grew up is now a stronghold of Islamic extremists from ISIS (or the 'Islamic State of Iraq and Syria') and he says he feels helpless in exile. One doesn't think of tycoons being sentimental but Mohed Altrad is atypical in this rarefied billionaires' club. He keeps a small jar of Syrian sand in his home and in his spare time writes novels which feature individuals living young and wretched lives in the desert and then tortured new beginnings in faraway exile. In other words, his own story. In real life, his painful upbringing and outsider status are unlikely to ever completely heal but if Montpellier ever win the French rugby championship, it will certainly be one more hurdle he has overcome.

About six months after that report went out, I turned my phone on when I got back to my car after going out jogging and saw I had received a text from Mohed asking me to look at a Youtube video and then to get back to him.

The video was a very slick short biographical story about one of his players – his identity growing up in southern France with ties to west Africa and the opportunities rugby had given him.

I studied it and then got back to Mohed. He said he had liked what I had done on him and with my own background torn between different cultures, he wanted me to do a video portrait of him too, that he could use for a seminar and offer to the media when they were looking for pictures of him.

He gave me carte blanche to do this. So I studied a novel he had written which was pretty much a disguised look back at his own earlier years. I bought archive video (that cost a small fortune) of the region in Syria where he grew up and got him to charter the jet that he uses to travel between games and his business so we could film him pensive on the aircraft, and I had him do various things in Montpellier with us.

The bottom line is that money was never an object, how I filmed it and the angle for the story were undisputed and I was paid without even having to show receipts etc.

My friend Gordon Ray, a British cameraman turned director for a public broadcasting station in Atlanta said to me afterwards that I'd never ever find a customer like that again. Well, what he actually said was this: "Anyone else who wants a portrait done of them will be a white trash tight-fisted loser who will want you to film him getting his torso rubbed down by his bikini-clad girlfriend and at the same time rubbing her breasts with his hand gun. And on top of that he will want it cheap and won't ever pay you."

Well that hasn't happened yet, but the economy is not going well and there are few opportunities for ex-journalists in their 50s, so who knows what assignment I will get offered next and of course accept with obsequious gratitude…

But anyway, I have stayed in touch with Mohed and I am not entirely sure about the ethics, but I have done another profile of him for the BBC programme Sports Hour, it was of course positive but I don't think it went too overboard. He came close to his dream of having Montpellier win the TOP 14 in 2016 for the first time. In the process, he had hired a South African coach – Jake White who had won the World Cup with South Africa. He's brought in lots of South African players (some even have French sounding names) but unfortunately it's another example of French rugby following top level English club football with lots of stars but few slots for local French players, and the national side is suffering as a result.[2]

***

---

2   Jack White left at the end of 2017 – Mohed was under pressure from the rest of the club to find a replacement who would focus on nurturing local talent. He chose Vern Cotter another foreigner, this time a Kiwi.

Rugby, a Cure for Cancer?

I admit I tend to choke up easily – at the end of a film in a packed cinema I try to conceal the tears as the lights go up (which is pointless everyone knows what you are up to).

In fact, I get sentimental about a lot of things. I mention this because when I heard about a really positive initiative between the world of rugby and the Canceropole – a centre which brings together thousands of research and medical staff in Toulouse, all more or less under one roof – it was a genuine tear jerker for me.[3] Also, a previous girlfriend, Sylvie, who has one of the healthiest lifestyles I know, got breast cancer. Thankfully she made a full recovery after all that harsh treatment.

Interestingly the women who were cancer survivors and participating in this venture were all bubbly and seemed pretty upbeat, it was me who was holding back tears when I interviewed them.

Anyway here is the story that I did. If you cry, I understand.

Sports Hour
BBC World Service
February 2017

On a particularly cold night for Toulouse in southern France, young rugby teams train. They are clearly very good at the game. Opposite them is an astroturf pitch and a small group is playing there too. It's made up of women mostly in their 40s and 50s. They are playing

---

3   Now don't get me wrong, I haven't been totally brainwashed by the rugby world, of course this kind of initiative could work I guess with any group sports activity, but it seems the rugby professionals had the idea first, down here at least.

touch rugby. It's not pretty to watch but their presence here is an extraordinary act of defiance.

They are receiving treatment for cancer. For some, it's breast cancer, others uterine or colon cancer. For many of them, a year ago walking would have been difficult enough, and now they are running and barging into each other one hour a week. The atmosphere is lighthearted.

Sylvie Denot is one of the sports instructors looking after the group. She told me: "We have seen a lot of changes, first of all physical ones. The women run more and more, they have a lot more endurance and do more and more on the pitch. There are also psychological changes which is really important. They want to spend time together, they are in a good mood, always smiling. That's the big evolution and it's great."

Why and how did they get here? A year ago, France's governing rugby board, the FFR, invited the country's leading cancer specialists to their headquarters in Marcoussis outside Paris where the French national team train.

They said they were convinced physical sport could play a key role in helping cancer patients recover. And in the last year much of the medical profession has been won over.

Canceropole, just outside the city of Toulouse, is one of the biggest research centres in Europe in the fight against the disease. Under one roof there's a hospital, researchers and pharmaceutical labs, pooling together the resources of several thousand staff. One of them is a surgeon, Dr Stéphanie Motton. Just back from the cancer ward, she told me there is increasing evidence that in around 20% of cancers, physical sport is just as effective as some drug treatments:

"There is no study assessing team sport compared to individual exercise but we see all day in our practices that patients engaged in team sports feel better. We know that exercise – and particularly supervised exercise – improves quality of life and physical function in patients with cancer. Moreover, several clinical trials have shown an improving prognosis and decrease in cancer recurrence."

Several hospitals across France have now set up cancer sport units to see if the results are as positive there too. Back on the icy cold rugby pitch, the French Rugby Federation is paying for initiatives like this one – providing the coaches, the grounds and the equipment. But in the long term they could be refunded by the state if there is tangible evidence that cancer patients' physical and mental health improve thanks to group sport.

Guillaume Bonmaison spends most of his time training upcoming rugby players before they turn pro – and one hour a week here.

"What is interesting and positive about this is that unlike some individual activity, these patients are all here together and the doctors tell us their patients forget their illnesses while they are all here playing together. For them, it's a moment of escape where they can forget their cancer situation, even if it's only briefly. It's a moment of freedom for them."

Women like Germaine who has breast cancer, are won over. She said before she started playing the sport she couldn't run and could barely walk. Now her health is better and she gets amazing pleasure out of this once weekly activity. Another survivor, Veronique, said rugby eases the stress the illness creates and she can sleep better afterwards now.

When these women first started playing rugby, they needed to take a break every 6 minutes, now they run around for up to 20 minutes before pausing and there are other positive signs of their self-confidence coming back. Some have lost all their hair from chemotherapy and wear wigs all the time in public. Recently and for the first time, two chose to take them off in front of their team-mates to play.

Philippe Douste-Blazy
The Chancer

---

hilippe Douste-Blazy is the kind of politician that journalists need, but not necessarily the kind the country needs. He will always take your call, and there is no subject he is afraid to comment on, no matter how little he knows about it. On top of that, far from being scared of making a fool of himself, he's totally shameless – no matter how much he may be humiliated by columnists or politicians (often on his own side) he just gets back on his feet, dusts himself off and goes straight for the next challenge in the limelight.

Slippery, fawning with his superiors, utterly dismissive of underlings unless very attractive models/assistants (and he had many of those), constantly on a charm offensive with the media, he first came to my notice when he was mayor of Lourdes and a rising star on the centre-right, holding several junior ministerial posts.

With his medical background as a heart specialist, a family with local roots, his clean-cut image and soft southern accent, Douste (as he is known) was hugely admired in Lourdes, not surprising as it's the number one Catholic pilgrimage site in the country. (Lourdes by the way, has more hotel rooms than anywhere else in France except Paris – good for your pub quiz).

Most of the visitors are Catholics who come to soak up the atmosphere at the *Grotte* where the Virgin Mary is once said to have appeared, others fill up on local spring water – sometimes referred to as 'miracle water'- as numerous miraculous healings of the very sick are said to have occurred here. In fact, many of the pilgrims are frail or desperately sick and brought on stretchers to drink the local water and pray and hope to be cured. The town also attracted an Albanian schizophrenic who planted a knife in Douste's back, claiming the mayor was the devil himself wandering amongst the Catholic faithful in Lourdes.

Douste was lucky to survive – the knife narrowly missed piercing his lungs. As he was Minister of Culture at the time[4], there was general surprise that even after the life-threatening incident, unlike most of the political class, he chose to wander around without a large entourage of police to protect him. His refusal to have a large escort was both brave and rare in France.

Philippe Douste-Blazy was a very popular mayor of Lourdes, until the day he switched. An opening came up for Mayor of Toulouse and he jumped at it. Of course most politicians don't go from mayor of one town to another. They will become MP, or head of regional government. He chose a bigger city instead and that went down badly in both Lourdes and Toulouse, but remarkably he managed to win the elections in the Ville Rose ('the Pink City' as Toulouse is fondly known throughout France).

The opportunistic switch was characteristic of Douste's way

---

4   He was mayor and minister at the same time – a very French exception whereby you could hold several political posts simultaneously. Since then, the government have realised the French were getting a little sick of this accumulated power and have voted to reduce the number of positions politicians can hold at the same time.

of thinking – he merged his centrist party UDF with the Centre right RPR when Jacques Chirac dangled real political power in front of his nose; and later, when he was 'exiled' in the political wilderness by Nicolas Sarkozy, he tried to jump back to his old allies in the centre.

I was in the press office at Toulouse town hall the day I first met him. I had come to cover the visit of the Israeli ambassador to France (on a regular basis, the Israeli ambassador tours the country, meeting the local political elite, and this was one of those occasions). I was introduced to Douste by his press secretary as 'the BBC's man in the region', and his first response was to say he would be available for an interview straight after the meeting with the ambassador. I hadn't actually asked for anything but as I learnt afterwards, that was pretty much standard behaviour, as he never shirked a media opportunity. As it was, I sat in the background as Douste talked to the Ambassador with a couple of aides and I remember him saying: "Tell me Ambassador, what can Toulouse do for the peace process?" It was pure Douste – brazen and meaningless.

But the good thing (for me if no-one else) was that he kept getting promoted by Chirac. He became deputy chief of the UMP, the newly created party merging the centre and centre-right factions. And suddenly with that hat, he was able to respond to all sorts of questions within his remit, even if it's fair to say he was usually clueless.

Sometimes, when a policy dreamt up by the opposition seemed to make sense and he didn't know what the party line to take was, he would reply: "If someone says they like the sun to shine in the summer, that doesn't mean I should say I prefer it when it rains." Who needs Voltaire? For me it was great.

He was convinced his star was on the rise, and rumours began to circulate in the press that he was in the starting blocks as a potential new prime minister. At a drinks party at the town hall I asked him if – in the event the rumours turned out to be true and he was chosen as the next prime minister, I could have his first foreign interview? His reply: 'yes of course'. No attempt was made to bat away or dodge the rumour, so supreme was his confidence.

That job offer never materialised and when other, more lowly ministerial offers did pop up, he declined, saying he could not abandon the Toulousains in their moment of need.

He became mayor just a few months before the worst industrial accident in France since the Second World War struck, at the AZF fertiliser plant, just outside the city, in September 2001. Thirty people were killed, thousands injured and repairing the infrastructure and buildings damaged took years. Many thousands of local residents still suffer from trauma and jump nervously at the sound of any innocuous bang.

He had another rather corny but good line when the Toulouse born jazz singer and artist Claude Nougaro died. When the mayor heard the news, he was caught on the hop in Paris, but knowing a media opportunity when he saw it, he flew down immediately from the capital, telling the local media to meet him at the airport where on arrival he announced solemnly to the microphones: "We Toulousains are today orphans."

Voters were nevertheless not entirely convinced of their mayor's desire and pledge to stay close to the city and put them ahead of a ministerial posting in Paris. And sure enough, when the job of Health Minister came up, he couldn't resist.

Naturally he said he was simply responding to the call of duty. With his medical background, he insisted, he was needed in the field he knew best. His most prominent action as health minister, as far as anyone can remember, had nothing to do with legislation but rather with the emergency treatment of a fellow MP who had a heart attack during a session of parliament.

Dr Douste went to the rescue and tried to give him CPR. Alas the MP died a few days later and some wondered if the doctor – who hadn't actually practised medicine in years – had really followed the right medical procedures[5].

One day, Jacques Chirac announced a cabinet reshuffle. It wasn't the kind of thing I paid close attention to, but the next morning as I read the local paper, it suddenly hit me – Douste-Blazy had just been appointed Foreign Minister. Douste had never expressed any real curiosity in anything happening outside of France's borders, spoke no foreign languages (not even Spanish which is not uncommon here in the Southwest, with Spain just over the border, as kids here are taught it at school). His appointment to one of the top posts was a total stitch up. Chirac felt he owed Douste for his political support bringing over the rump of centrist MPs to his party, and his Prime Minister, Dominique de Villepin who saw himself as a glamorous world statesman, definitely didn't want an independent minded foreign minister under his command, so Douste was their compromise yes man.

Douste on the other hand saw it as a great opportunity to make his mark, with a goal to tame the world and make it a better place… and I offered to be his global witness.

One thing about being Foreign Minister in France is that you get your own Airbus to fly around the world. I am not sure the French taxpayer would approve, but on my first trip with

5   One place he didn't hang about in as Health Minister was a psychiatric ward in the town of Pau. Back in December 2004 in a horrific crime straight out of something in the film "Halloween", a nurse arriving for the morning shift discovered the severed head of one of her colleagues who'd been working overnight, posed on a TV set; another nurse bludgeoned, a few metres away. Needless to say, the hospital staff were traumatised and terrorised. The day the ward re-opened, Douste arrived by helicopter to comfort the staff and then with his police escort headed off fast saying good luck and he was thinking of them. Imagine the fear for the nurses turning up for the night shift, especially as no-one had been caught. Of course they had police around to protect them but I still have this image of Douste hopping onto his chopper to get out of there as fast as possible. The killer, a former patient, was caught 2 months later – he had a grudge against women in white uniforms.

him to Uganda and Burundi, Douste was in Toulouse on the Friday that the diplomatic mission was setting off, so the plane flew from Paris with his cabinet staff and several journalists and landed in Toulouse to pick us up.

The plane had around 50 seats in all, it was pretty much like being in business class throughout except Douste also got his own bedroom and shower and an intelligence officer in a small room near the back to send and receive faxes and secret documents in the air. Of course, several armed police were also on board.

When I got on, I mentioned to one of the cabin crew staff that I don't eat meat but I do eat fish and she replied: "That's fortunate then because today we are serving lobster".

Being on a diplomatic mission is very much like being in a vacuum, where normal rules do not apply. People smoked on the plane; no-one paid attention to any of the standard regulations that you are normally forced to adhere too; 70s style overt flirtation with the crew was part and parcel of the package…

I remember flying through a sandstorm on take-off from Burundi and going through extreme turbulence. Everyone was wandering about, seeing if they could stand up (apart from me, who's scared of flying at the best of times. But since most of my fellow passengers had spent weeks on end in places like Baghdad, there was a vaguely macho swagger aboard that meant I had to hide my fear. I'm not sure I did that very well).

Of course being on a mission with the Foreign Minister means you have the French police with you at all times to protect you with wailing sirens in whatever country is hosting you. You are part of the VIP 'diplomatic pouch', with gun-toting local soldiers at the front and end of your convoy, soldiers surrounding your hotel and others to shadow and protect you if you step out of the bubble to explore – You can't help feeling untouchable and fleetingly part of that select group that rules the world.

In those circumstances you begin to understand how it all

goes to the heads of the powerful and how they can lose touch with reality pretty fast.

We went to Uganda to see the refugee camps in the north of the country that had been set up to protect the victims of the *Lord's Resistance Army*.

It was a pretty depressing experience, but the idea was to single out Uganda for not doing enough to protect the refugees and to get a peace process moving in the region.

Then we would travel to Burundi which was considered a positive story, as a civil war had ended and child soldiers were being rehabilitated and getting a second chance to get on with their lives.

(Sadly, a few years on it seems Burundi is going back to its old ways again).I think it's safe to say no major policy initiative came from these trips, but what I did learn is that there is an unwritten rule amongst former colonial rivals that you don't tread through each other's former colonies for political reasons. In fact, seeing the pictures of Douste in Uganda broadcast in my news reports of the trip on the BBC annoyed the British Foreign Office in London enough for them to dispatch their Consul General in Bordeaux, Tom Kennedy[6], to my flat to find out from me what the hell Douste was doing on their turf!

---

6   Tom Kennedy went on to bigger things including becoming ambassador to Costa Rica, but I remember once he called me up saying the Deputy Ambassador in Paris, Giles Paxman (yes brother of Jeremy and future ambassador to Spain) was heading down on a fact-finding mission and he didn't want to be stuck on his own with him – would I join them at a top class restaurant and in return tell the deputy ambassador a little about Toulouse. I was sold. And then a couple of hours before lunch I was told they were running very late and lunch would now be at a self-service cafeteria. I mention this because I got my revenge when over lunch they expressed disappointment that they had not been able to meet the Prefect in Toulouse as he had suddenly been fired on Douste's orders. You should have seen the look of shock and speechless envy on their faces when I said they shouldn't feel too sorry for him – firing him had meant finding him a post where he could cause no harm nor be of use – he'd been made France's ambassador to Kenya…

Coming back to my diplomatic mission with Douste, we had planned to arrive back Monday evening but since you don't have to adhere to anyone's schedule or landing slot, we arrived a lot later in Paris than originally scheduled. I had planned to stay at my journalist friend Anthony Jeffers's home for the night but when I called all I got was his voicemail.

Suddenly, as we were dropped off at the gates of the Foreign Ministry in the centre of Paris, the diplomatic envelope unwrapped – the police vanished or followed the minister, the aides and journalists wandered off to their central Paris flats… I was suddenly stranded on my own, late at night with a TV camera and equipment and my luggage. It was midnight and I had obviously missed the last flight back to Toulouse so I decided to head to the train station at Montparnasse to wait for the first train home at 6am.

I arrived in a grim, cold, dirty, slightly menacing train station, a little confused – after all I had just flown in from central Africa where I'd been treated as part of the Foreign Minister's entourage… I bought a ticket and tried to go to sleep in a waiting room with bright neon lights overhead and drunks and others down on their luck as neighbours.

At around 3am I found myself woken up by a ticket inspector flanked by a couple of policemen and two overnight subcontracted security guards (with *Les Miserables* written all over their faces) with German shepherd dogs at their side. Nothing out of the ordinary it turned out – they chase out anyone who shouldn't be in the station overnight. I showed my ticket and was about to explain how my diplomatic plane had arrived late and then thought, no don't – then they will really take me for a crazy like all the others huddled around the station at night time.

Instead I opted to simply say I had missed my last flight. The situation was so surreal – the two worlds that I had crossed in the space of a couple of hours. It was all very strange and extremely funny (well, I saw the funny side later) and I was very relieved they let me stay in the waiting room until my train left.

There were many more attempts to save the world and with me as witness. On diplomatic excursions, Douste had a tendency to start speeches or background briefings to the travelling journalists with the phrase: "I am the only one who is prepared to tackle this problem/this issue/this crisis/this situation…" or: "I am here on the direct orders of the President of the Republic of France to sort out this situation/resolve this flashpoint, etc." You get the idea.

On the aircraft, he usually invited the travelling journalists to come up to the front in groups of 2 or 3 for off-the-record briefings on what he planned to do during this trip – just how important the mission was and how he would be sticking his neck out like no other predecessor or civil servant diplomat had dared to in the past.

I was one of that small group when a call came through to his cabinet chief asking if Douste could be the main guest on France Inter's morning phone-in programme when he returned to France (something similar to the Today programme's 8:10am interview slot). He said sure no problem. Then a few minutes later he asked his cabinet chief, by the way, what do they want to talk about? Like I said, he was a dream for frazzled researchers/bookers who have to find guests at the last minute.

During his presidency, Jacques Chirac came up with a plan to try to resolve the humanitarian situation in Darfur and the Khartoum-backed civil war there. Douste was the messenger boy as we headed there with stops beforehand in Cairo and the Sudanese capital.

We were leaving on a Friday and when we were handed a programme schedule it said we would be returning to France on the Tuesday. But something just did not add up. At that particular moment the European aeroplane manufacturer Airbus was in real trouble. Its double-decker super jumbo A380 aircraft was going through major industrial production problems, it was years behind schedule and costing the company billions of dollars. There was management turmoil, jobs in their thousands had to be cut to save money. Before we had even left for Cairo, the then Prime Minister Dominique de Villepin had announced he would be coming to Toulouse on the Monday to see for himself what the problem at Airbus was and to establish the facts on the ground[7].

There is no way I could imagine Douste not being in his own city as mayor while the Prime Minister trampled through town trying to show compassion for the Airbus workers and promising to come to their rescue, surrounded by cameras and microphones.

Douste's travelling press officers[8] were adamant we were to be there for however many days it would take for Douste to come up with a breakthrough in the Darfur situation. And in meetings with the Egyptian President and his foreign minster in Cairo, and with the Sudanese President and his head of intelligence in an office in Khartoum that no doubt housed torture cells below, Douste said he would not give up.

In Darfur itself, the situation was extremely dangerous – armed rebels on pickup trucks patrolled the towns, while UN troops, just as well-armed, protected strategic offices and food warehouses along the dusty roads. Traumatised refugees in their thousands were housed in camps all over the region.

While the minister's protection team were very nervous, Douste himself was calm and showed genuine bravery (or maybe was unaware of how tense the situation was).He seemed sincerely angry when the Sudanese authorities showed little sign of negotiating and said he would not let the Sudanese people down and would continue to bang heads together.

But then news began to filter through that Douste had urgent business to get down to in France and suddenly we had

---

7   My friend Anthony Jeffers wisely pointed out later that if Douste was able to receive faxes in the air tens of thousands of metres above Africa then Prime Minister Villepin surely could find out what was happening at Airbus HQ by just picking up the phone in his office in Paris.

8   For the record, all women and beautiful, but not experts in world affairs, they had simply transferred from the Health Ministry to Foreign Affairs with their boss.

to be back for Monday at the latest. No explanation was given for this urgent change to our schedule and what this meant for the French peace plan for Sudan and the Foreign Minister's earlier determination to stay as long as it took, but guess what, Monday afternoon, the French Prime Minister was in Toulouse speaking to the Airbus workforce and reassuring them that the government wouldn't let them down – and Douste was next to him. Darfur would have to wait.

Douste was to make a couple of major political miscalculations that wrecked his high-flying domestic political career. One when de Villepin looked set to be the front-runner of the right after Chirac decided not to seek re-election for a third term as President: Douste put his support behind de Villepin, and was never forgiven by Sarkozy... Political wilderness beckoned[9].

Secondly, he miscalculated his return to local politics. Ostracised by Sarkozy, he couldn't even fall back on his power base in Toulouse, because as so often in politics, he had taken too much for granted. His assumption that his loyal right hand man, Jean-Luc Moudenc, would look after the town for him while he was on the national stage and then hand the job back when Douste decided to return turned out to be ill-founded – the handing back never happened.

While Douste had been travelling the world, Moudenc had decided to stay mayor and cleverly plotted his former mentor's removal from local politics. Douste wouldn't go quietly however and Sarkozy's team apparently realised that if Douste chose to fight

9   The night Sarkozy won the presidency, he celebrated at the flashy Paris restaurant *Fouquet's* – a bad move that was to haunt him throughout his time in office as it painted him as a flash, slightly trashy figure, obsessed with bling. But for Douste the evening was a body blow. He turned up at the restaurant with his official ministerial car and body guards – he was Foreign Minister after all – but he wasn't allowed in by the bouncers. Apparently Sarkozy's team had made sure he was not on the invite list and he had to turn around and leave.

his corner and create a divided right leadership race, they stood to lose Toulouse in the next local elections. So they offered him a way out: Sarkozy used his clout to get him a job as Deputy Secretary General of the UN, in return for his swift departure from the city.

It worked. Douste got his job and his revenge because Moudenc lost Toulouse (replaced by the socialist Pierre Cohen, before making a comeback later).

I still bump into Douste from time to time. He still harbours a hope of returning to the big time – but what politician doesn't. He backed Macron (once it became clear Francois Fillon was out of the running, bogged down in a corruption scandal) and he launched a campaign to become the head of the UN body the World Heath Organisation, but that didn't go far.

Whatever Douste's flaws, he gave Toulouse some international stature that it has since lost. And for me, getting a chance to be a witness to the inner workings of international diplomacy, no matter how briefly, was an eye opener, a very lucky break and one I probably won't get again[10].

---

10 There was one funny story that Le Monde revealed (and for which it was subsequently heavily criticised by more traditional readers claiming it was acting no better than a curtain-twitching concierge). One New Year's Eve, Douste was staying at the grandest hotel in Morocco, El Mamounia – a must for all of France's elite – with his wife. But the New Year's celebrations didn't go to plan. The couple had a massive row in their room over his alleged continuing infidelity, and his wife threw an ashtray at him which he managed to avoid. Except it smashed into an expensive painting. And other things flew too, forcing the French Foreign Minister to seek refuge, in his underwear, on the interior balcony outside the room in front of startled and no doubt amused French revellers who may have thought they had drunk too much. He then went to his bodyguards' room and stayed with them (but who went back next door to get his clothes?) and he left in the morning for France on the first flight he could find. The hotel claimed thousands of euros of damage had been done to the room, like rock star bands of old, and sent the Foreign Office the bill. His chief of staff said it was extortion – for that amount of damage the Foreign Minister and his wife would have had to used a jack hammer. According to Le Monde, the King of Morocco decided to pay the bill.

More Frivolous Opportunities

Lunch with the Queen *(it didn't happen)*

Apparently my table manners are pretty appalling. I remember my ex, Isabelle, trying to get me to change my ways, saying 'imagine if you're invited one day to have lunch with the Queen thanks to your friend Douste'... Well that actually just about happened.

The Entente Cordiale celebrations in 2004 marking one hundred years of friendship between Britain and France provided the real breakthrough for me in terms of my visibility as a media presence here in south-west France.

Queen Elizabeth and her husband, Prince Philip, were coming to Paris to mark the event and they also had to do an excursion outside the capital – Toulouse was chosen, mainly because it has a high British expat population (I always say it's the highest in France outside Paris, but I'm not sure I have genuine facts to back that up!). Also, with the links between France and the UK in the aerospace industry stretching back to when the two countries shared in the development of Concorde, the city was a good place to mark the *Entente Cordiale.*

And then came the dilemma I never envisaged I would face – the BBC asked me to fix the southern France stage of the Royal visit, in other words sort out guests, deal with passes, where to go live with a satellite van, book hotels and brief the presenters. They were sending down a team of around 10 including Nicolas Witchell and Peter Hunt, the Royal correspondents[11]. I accepted. And then Tom Kennedy who was the Consul General in Bordeaux offered me the invitation… Would I like to have lunch with the Queen and yes, Douste would be hosting as it would be held in the splendid Salle des Illustres in the Town Hall. Of course if I accepted, then I couldn't really be with the BBC…

So my chance to show my improved table manners never materialised!

A couple of things about the royal visit. First of all, for Royal correspondents it's probably the easiest job in the business. They don't have to worry about getting soundbites from the Royals – none of the Royal Household staff will talk – and they even pretty much avoid getting interviews from people in the street. They provide flowery scripts with the odd clip from the Royals' speeches (which they see in advance) and then end with a piece to camera with a lovely backdrop. Of course their producers – who are never seen on air but have to do all the leg work – are put through the grinder and treated appallingly, especially by presenters like Nicholas Witchell.

He was actually quite nice to me though and Alan Little was there too. Rarely will you work with a gem like him, sadly they're a dying species in the business. He was pleasant throughout despite being a Scottish Republican who couldn't stand being

---

11 In hindsight, considering what was at stake, it was kind of risky of the BBC to pass this responsibility onto me as they didn't know whether I was really competent or not. Maybe I was just cheap and that's what counted. I raised my prices later.

there especially as he had to speak gibberish about the Queen to the rolling news channel in deferential tones. It probably goes down as one of his worst assignments.As for me, the assignment put me firmly on the BBC map, and what's more, also finally gave me much-needed credibility with the French authorities[12].

Until then, at the Prefecture for example, the Prefect and his chef de cabinet – having done background checks to make sure I wasn't a spook no doubt – thought of me as an oddity who wouldn't be sticking around much longer anyway, after all who could become a viable foreign correspondent here, in the sticks? Well, once they had received direct instructions from the British Foreign Office on my role during the Queen's visit, their attitude towards me changed entirely.

A couple of amusing things occurred during the visit. The Millau viaduct (more on that later) which was partly designed by the British architect Norman Foster, was on the Royal itinerary. The Duke of Edinburgh wanted to visit it and the British Embassy called me asking me to try to get coverage of him there. So I called up my chain of command in Brussels and London who said sure, if the embassy paid for the TV camera crew and the truck to beam the pictures back. The Duke never got on air.

The other memorable incident happened when the Queen was at the Airbus factory. It just so happened that Virgin was scheduled to take delivery of a brand new plane the very same day that the Queen was visiting. Richard Branson never misses a trick and lo and behold, the powers that be decided that the

---

12   When I set up in Toulouse as a registered press agency, the British Embassy in Paris sent me a note wishing me luck in my new venture but also their words seemed to be tinged with a foreboding 'this is doomed to failure' tone. Nevertheless they actually sent me lots of work down the years. One year though I was irate when a senior UK minister came down and I wasn't informed in advance. I sent a sharp message to the press team headlined 'the Foreign Office isn't working'. I got a pretty witty return from the then head of press at the embassy Richard Morgan: 'The Foreign Office isn't working for Chris Bockman'. Nice, I couldn't argue with that one.

visit would be the ideal occasion for Her Majesty to bestow a knighthood on the businessman in front of Airbus staff and the media. British Airways was absolutely livid.

A diplomatic showdown was only prevented when the Queen's household agreed to BA's demand that to make up for the slight on the national flag carrier, she return home from Toulouse on a British Airways aircraft sent down especially for her and that the shot of her going up the steps to the waiting British Airways plane be made available to the TV camera crews.

Just a side note: a couple of years later, Airbus called me up saying Prince Andrew was coming down to check out the brand new A380 super jumbo and he wanted coverage – could I provide?

At a loss at what to do, I called up the then BBC Europe bureau chief Andrew Roy (who since then has moved up to become Foreign Editor at the BBC) and explained the situation. His reply more or less went like this: "Well you call up Prince Andrew and give him a quick history lesson – A few centuries ago, there was a civil war in England, the king was executed, and since then Britain has kind of moved on. The BBC is not some kind of plaything for bored royals! Britain is now a parliamentary democracy. Chris, could you pass that on to Prince Andrew for me?"[13]

***

---

13 Some time after the Queen's visit, which was deemed in higher circles to have gone well, the British Consul General Tom Kennedy took me out somewhere decent with the long time Honorary Consul in Toulouse Roger Virnuls and asked me if I would like to replace Roger. At the time, I said no, thinking it would compromise my journalistic independence, would be a sell-out, and gosh what a pain it would be dealing with Brits either on the lam or drunk and in trouble, dealing with lost passports etc. I wasn't even sure the BBC would have accepted it. Anyway, I declined. In hindsight I'm not sure about that decision. And years later when I raised it again with the embassy, they said there was no point as they were closing down the honorary position in Toulouse.

The Millau Viaduct

As I mentioned the Duke of Edinburgh and the bridge – or as it's officially known: the *Viaduc de Millau* – earlier, this is a good place to talk about it in its own right. I must have done close to a dozen stories on this for the BBC, France 24, Reuters, CNBC.... but it still bowls me over every time I see it. You really don't have to be a transport bore or a bridge geek to be fascinated by this remarkable feat of engineering.

I first stumbled across the bridge by accident one Sunday, out in my car visiting the Aveyron region. I saw these incredible pylons and cranes in the gorge above me. I had no idea what it was about but even then, when the bridge was far from taking shape, the sheer scale of the project was phenomenal.

The bridge was built to link Paris quickly to the Mediterranean via the A75 autoroute – apparently until it was built, one of the great stress factors for holiday makers heading south was how long would they be stuck in the provincial town of Millau[14]. Since you had no choice but to descend the steep gorge and drive through the relatively small town, crossing the river in Millau, you could be snarled there for hours.

The bridge did away with the traffic jams and in fact there were great fears amongst retailers and restaurant owners in the town that it would become deserted as tourists no longer would stop there but zoom across the bridge towards the south.

But they couldn't have been more wrong – the bridge is so remarkable to look at from so many angles that in fact it turns out that people go out of their way to see it. Maybe a little less

---

14   Millau was made famous later when the Che Guevara of the Aveyron, José Bové dismantled part of the roof of a McDonald's there in protest against globalisation.

than when it was first built when it had real novelty value, but nevertheless, it has become a sightseeing location in its own right. If the Golden Gate bridge in San Francisco is spectacular in the fog, so is this one in the mist. It's also impressive at night when lit up. It's meant to have a feel of sails floating in the skies and does it work!

I did stories on the bridge from all angles for numerous broadcasters, from visiting with the British architect Sir (now Lord) Norman Foster before its completion, to the tourism boom it triggered once opened, to the economic windfall it provided to the region in the long term and the huge security surrounding the bridge. I was even taken inside the bowels of the bridge with the roaring traffic above me and the river below. Here is one report I filed back in 2005.

BBC World News
August 2005

Last December, the world's tallest bridge was opened near the town of Millau on the southern edge of France's mountainous region, the Massif Central. Since then 400,000 people have headed there, not so much to cross it as to simply gaze at it. If you drive very slowly along the Millau bridge using the hard shoulder as the BBC did, not only are you breaking the law, you can be sure dozens of security cameras above you and sensors built into the road are monitoring every inch of your progress.

It's not just the world's tallest bridge, it's probably the most monitored two and half kilometres you will ever cover in a car. Frederic Dune is Director of the Bridge: "It is after all the highest bridge in the world and the newest bridge built, so it is obvious that we have to put in as many security measures as possible to ensure that crossing this bridge occurs as safely as possible."

In many different ways this bridge exceeds expectations. Firstly and remarkably, it was ready three weeks ahead of schedule, on budget. It will also make a lot more money for its owners than forecast thanks to far higher traffic than expected.

Officially the bridge is 2,460 meters long, but we were given a view inside its belly as traffic roared above and its steel innards are actually built to expand by two metres during the summer heat.

Travel times between northern Europe and the Mediterranean have now been cut by more than an hour. What the planners hadn't expected was that thousands of motorists would come here turning the bridge into a major tourist destination.

Like columns of ants, drivers are pulling off the motorway to take in the view and marvel at what they see. This is what a couple of them said to me:

"I am very impressed. It's incredible how they built it. You can't imagine how many hours and how many days and months it's taken to build it. It's supposed to save time on the trip and for most people it's probably adding time to the trip because they are stopping to see the bridge."

At a time when France is going through a lot of soul-searching over high unemployment and its reduced influence in the world, the bridge has become a rare modern symbol that the country is still capable of bold, dramatic gestures (even though the bridge's architect is the British Norman Foster).

Jacques Godfrain, the mayor of Millau and a former government minister, is basking in the glory too. He explained to me that he had five different projects to choose from – he picked the British design. He told me: "It was the most attractive proposal. It didn't damage or obscure the landscape, it made it look different. In fact what is extraordinary about this bridge is that it has made the valley even more attractive than before."

In the past, Millau was synonymous with mammoth traffic jams as motorists heading south prayed they'd be able to get through the town in less than two hours. Now they want to stop.

Just like the Guggenheim museum brought hundreds of thousands of tourists to the rundown city of Bilbao in northern Spain, Millau's bridge has turned its town into a tourist destination.

***

Speeding UK Motorists

Sticking with the car theme, even those who are furious that their compatriots voted for Brexit can take some comfort in the fact that now there is even less chance of losing points on your British driving license for offences in France than there was before… It seems any joined-up thinking between the British and French authorities on car offences has now been ruled out just about for good.

It's no surprise that rich city types hold cannonball run races across continental Europe. Unless they are physically stopped, the fines and bans will never catch up with them for a simple reason: the British government doesn't trade information on speeding violations or most other driving related law, breaking yet again with its European counterparts.

So the only way the cannonball racers can be held to account is if the French police catch them in the act and frog march them to the nearest cash machine or confiscate the car keys. It was the perfect summer story as I spent the day out with the traffic cops.

For tens of thousands of tourists, the A64 autoroute outside of Toulouse marks the final stretch before reaching their holiday destinations. Most are heading either to the Pyrenees Mountain range that follows along the motorway or to coastal resorts like Biarritz or St Jean de Luz in the French Basque Country.

And often they are in a hurry to get there, especially after hours coming down from northern France. In fact the French police say foreign drivers make up a large proportion of motorists breaking the speed limit, because they know there is little chance of being fined.

EU figures show that foreign drivers make up 5% of road traffic but account for 15% of speeding offences.

Under new EU legislation that has come into force this year, member countries can now exchange motoring offences data across borders. In concrete terms, if a Spanish motorist is caught speeding by a speed camera in France, that fine can now be sent to the driver in Spain and he or she will have to pay.

However the United Kingdom has opted not to share that information and that means the only way British motorists can be sanctioned on French roads is if they are caught in the act by the police and made to pay on-the-spot fines.

A 32-strong special division of the French military police (the 'gendarmerie') based just outside Toulouse are doing just that – trying to tackle the problem of foreign drivers getting away with speeding as they know there is little chance of being caught.

After an early morning briefing, the team head out on motorbikes and cars and take up positions just after the A64 toll booth under a scorching sun. Another gendarme with special binoculars that can calculate speeds is discreetly based about a kilometre before the toll booth (the 'péage'). On that section of the highway, the speed limit is 110 km/hr and only increases to 130 km/hr after drivers go through the toll booth.

He then alerts the team whenever someone is going too fast and the driver is quickly waved to the side by the waiting police once they have passed the toll booth. French motorists are given a fine that they can pay at a later date but foreign drivers are in for a surprise – they have to pay cash upfront. Lieutenant Benjamin Dupain runs the Gendarmerie operation. He says:

"They have to pay on the spot. If they don't have any money on them and they are on their own, they will be driven to the nearest cash point machine. If they really have no money at all, then an on-duty judge will be called to decide what to do. But that can mean waiting around for up to 3 days and the car will not be allowed to move."

If British drivers think they will be able to get out of the fine by pretending not to speak French they are in for a surprise. The police I followed had a more than adequate level of English. One had spent a year training with the British army and another had once even been an au pair in Buckinghamshire.

British police sometimes even join their French counterparts on missions in northern France though they do not have the authority to issue fines on French territory. The police stressed that British drivers are not the worst offenders and said some of the fastest drivers on French motorways are Dutch and Swiss motorists.

The UK Ministry of Transport says the UK chose not to share driving offences information with other EU countries because they have different penalties and fine levels. The UK only has an agreement with the Irish Republic and that only covers drivers who have been banned from driving. This refusal to share information with its neighbours means that foreign drivers on British soil are also unlikely to be sanctioned if they break the highway code, unless British police catch them on the spot too.

***

Lourdes – *The Day the Bishop met the Devil (me)*

People who live in the Southwest tend to be divided into two camps when it comes to opinions about this town. For some, it brings back memories of when it had an extraordinary rugby club and legendary players – but that was a long time ago and they are a dying breed. For others it's a particularly sad destination and comes across as nothing less than the Catholic Church's own rather cheesy theme park, with its own shakedown industry to boot.

Dozens of stores outside the gates of the 'Sanctuary of Lourdes' as its called, sell tacky photos, mainly of Pope John Paul II ('Pope Saint John Paul II since 2014, when he was canonised), or glittery crosses. Each week the one-way road system that tourist buses take changes direction so that all the stores can profit from the business opportunities. Of course most of the pilgrims who come from around the world don't see it that way. For them the town represents something else entirely, something far more profound… and there are lots of them – Lourdes boasts it has more hotels than any other town or city outside Paris and 5 million people visit each year.

The story goes that back in 1858, Bernadette Soubirous, a poor peasant woman saw an apparition of the Virgin Mary in a cave – the *'Grotte'* – near the river. Ever since, the town and the river running through it, the *Gave de Pau*, have been associated with miracles.

Lourdes has become a major pilgrimage destination for Catholics from around the world and many of them are extremely ill and literally brought there in wheelchairs and stretchers to be blessed in the 'miracle water'. Many are just days from dying. I understand how a visit to Lourdes can provide some comfort and reassurance – if I was terribly ill, a believer and had little other hope, I might head to Lourdes seeking a miracle too.

I have been to Lourdes numerous times (first of all because you have to travel through Lourdes to reach some of the most stunning mountain resorts and hiking trails behind it) and some of the stories I covered included a wake when Pope John Paul II was on his death bed and then of course I returned for the services when his death was announced; then not long after that, I went back to witness the preparations for the arrival of his successor, Benedict XVI, who was coming to celebrate the Jubilee in 2008 – 150 years since the Virgin Mary's apparition. I once visited with a Chicago priest filming a documentary – more on that later – but I used to go quite regularly, especially for the stories on the numerous miracles that are said to have occurred there.

Officially, there have been 69 miraculous recoveries, often from life-threatening illnesses. The most recent involved an Italian woman who visited Lourdes in 1989 with severe blood problems. So that means official miracles have been few and far between in recent decades. One reason is that in the medical world, doctors now tend to find explanations for most health recoveries. So in 2006, the authorities in the Church decided to change the way they treat the issue. Now they refer to "inexplicable healings". There is even an official at the Sanctuary of Lourdes administrative offices who heads a committee of 300 experts across the world to analyse each 'inexplicable healing'.

The Bishop of Lourdes at the time was Monseigneur Jacques Perrier. He would talk to the media but he was also extremely touchy. When I suggested, as others in the media already had, that the decision to move from "miracle" to "inexplicable healing" was a publicity stunt to ensure that pilgrims continued to come to Lourdes because without the faint hope of a miracle, visits would dry up (a bit like if the Loch Ness monster mystery was scientifically explained to be an optical illusion), he was not a happy man.

At the mere question – which I thought the Bishop would be prepared to handle without problem as I wasn't the first to raise it – he suddenly gasped for air like something in a scene from *The Omen* and seemed to blow up in size. He turned crimson in the face, pointed his trembling finger at me and then began to shout. In fact the only thing he did not do was take his cross from around his neck and try and brand it on my forehead while reciting Hail Mary. I believe that day he genuinely thought the devil had finally made its way into his sanctuary. As you can imagine, our encounter ended a little awkwardly. I think my report broadcast was more than fair, here it is. I didn't mention the Lucifer moment but I admit I was kind of glad when the Bishop retired as, like I said, I had to go back to Lourdes often.

BBC World News
November 2006

Lourdes, a remote town nestled in the French Pyrenees Mountain range, is not easy to get to, but six million people do just that each year.

Many are very sick and come here on a pilgrimage hoping to get better.

That tradition started after the Virgin Mary is said to have appeared at a cave entrance here almost 150 years ago. Since then, the Catholic Church claims around 70 people have made miraculous recoveries from severe illnesses while here.

The last recorded miracle here occurred 20 years ago, and since doctors in general believe there is a rational explanation for why people get better, the Catholic Church has decided to change the rules and now refers to "inexplicable healings".

The word 'miracle' has now been scrubbed because doctors have an answer for everything. But Church officials say that does not mean they are always right. Mgr Jacques Perrier is Bishop of Lourdes: "These days doctors can only explain their patients' illnesses once the patient has recovered, but imagine their reasoning is wrong and maybe something else can explain why they got better... But doctors won't consider that possibility once a person is cured."

The Church's decision to come up with new guidelines has caused a stir. Some commentators have referred to the new terminology as 'miracle-lite'. But the Church strongly denies it's all a publicity stunt to continue attracting pilgrims and tourists.

It's the job of Patrick Theillier to determine whether someone has recovered because of a visit to the Sanctuary in Lourdes. He heads a team of 300 who check out each claim of sudden cure. He denies his team have watered down the criteria for a miracle to occur:

"The word miracle has become sensationalised when in reality there are tiny miracles here. It's clear people are being healed here all the time, more than we imagine, everyday. In Lourdes people are constantly being cured from physical, psychological and internal illnesses."

It's clear from the people we spoke to in Lourdes that they agree with him: "Yes miracles happen and there are lots of ill people here so they clearly believe it too."

"You know there are miracles everyday, some you will see, others happen that you don't even know about."

Later this month the Lourdes healing committee won't be using the word 'miracle' but it's expected to announce that more than a dozen people have made 'inexplicable recoveries' from illness here in the past year.

***

Pique-assiettes (plate nickers)

This is a great French expression that refers to people who turn up at events like art gallery openings with the sole aim of eating and drinking for free, or to journalists who do the same at press conferences. It's not something I do – but there is an exception: I sometimes go to see Toulouse Football Club play.

Most ends of season they are one game away from relegation but survive in the first division with a half empty stadium (except of course when PSG come down). But in recent times, Toulouse Football Club has started winning a lot thanks to a new turnaround coach named Pascal Dupraz. They don't play attractive football but it makes a change to see a local team win, especially as across the river the Stade Toulousain rugby club are not the winning force they once were.

But what really attracts me to TFC (and what similarly draws my friend Justin Dubon who works on the Airbus press team and strangely was at Reuters television in London at the same time I was) is the tantalising possibility of decent food and champagne free at the match.

Let me explain. The press and the businesses that pay for corporate hospitality use the same entrance. I use my press pass to get through the first controls, which is entirely normal as that's what the pass is for (Justin uses his Reuters lunch card from 1997, that's a little odder, I think you will agree). Then we pick up our sports ticket seats from the Union of Sports Journalists desk and turn to two usually gorgeous girls working for a hospitality agency who hand out our special bracelets giving us access to the warm bar area inside the stadium, where local cheese and meat suppliers provide trays of food and wine producers an endless flow of local reds, then at the end of the game, there's

Champagne. In fact you quickly forget who is playing and what the score was. Naturally, all this corporate hospitality is paid for by business owners who then invite clients and friends along too. No-one has ever asked me what I was doing there.

None of my journalist colleagues try it on but I guess I don't feel the same peer pressure as they do as they work together day in day out… or maybe they have a more aloof 'we are journalists with integrity' working attitude, or maybe they are just more professional than me and I haven't quite entirely got over my freeloader days as a student…

What is more outrageous and would probably spark a new revolution if the fans knew the truth, is that the real working class die-hard fans in the cheap seats at the end of the ground pay for their tickets and then drink their tepid beer and wolf down the sandwiches that they had to pay for at half time, in their seats in the stands… They come to every home game regardless of the weather, for often shocking football. They are the real supporters, the ones behind their team and yet they get none of the treatment that we 'pique-assiettes' do.

***

Freebies

Now I take pride in being able to persuade big businesses, NGO type organisations, government departments etc. to pay up for me to fly to far-off destinations in return for doing a report on location. And I can honestly say that I have never taken one of these rides without being sure I would be able do a report of some sort when I got back, so in that sense my conscience is clear.

There are general guidelines on the financing of these trips, but of course print and broadcast outlets are so stretched these days that they take what is offered most of the time. Even the BBC, which is supposed to always say no to freebies, bends the rules all the time. I remember I got an invitation to fly to China with a bunch of French aerospace suppliers as they were being encouraged by Airbus to set up there to get costs down. Everything was paid for and so that was a no-no from the BBC business department. I remember the editor at the time, Peter Eustace, saying he was refusing because 'it was a freebie'. So I got back to him and said no it wasn't, I was paying for the Toulouse-Paris leg. Ah! That's ok then, he said, go ahead and provide us with a package.

When I travelled with the French Foreign Minister, it was the same thing – I said I was paying for one of the nights in a hotel and that got me over that hurdle. Anyway, what I'm trying to say is that I am a bit of a pro at this and yes, that does in effect mean I'm selling my soul, but as my friend Wolfgang Spindler (a culture producer at the station Euronews who is no amateur himself at getting festivals to pay for his trips in exchange for coverage) says, I could sell snow to eskimos. I kind of agree but less so now than in the past – I haven't got the same energy, sadly.

Now why did I ramble off like this? Well because I met my match – Father Robert Barron. At the time Father Robert was a priest in the Catholic Diocese of Chicago but these days he is a Bishop in Los Angeles.

The NBC producer in Paris got in touch with me and said she wouldn't be available and would I mind being a fixer when Father Barron came down through Toulouse to see some churches there, and go with his entourage to Lourdes, and make sure they got on a plane in time for the next leg of their trip (to Portugal I think). They had already done Italy and England for the documentary.

Father Barron has written several books and presents religious programmes on the theme 'The Word on Fire'. He also managed to convince his faithful, mainly in the Chicago area, to finance this trip to Europe and the Middle East for a '*Word on Fire*' documentary. And he didn't slum it either.

In his entourage, there was a personal assistant, a PR manager, a cameraman who freelances for NBC in Chicago, as well as a reporter/producer who does the same thing, and a fellow priest.

In fact there was a 10 strong delegation for this documentary and they didn't skimp and save, staying in decent hotels everywhere, driving around in a minibus with a driver (when they weren't flying). They paid me in cash, I was happy, so was the sound man they asked me to provide for the Toulouse and Lourdes leg of the doc, and everyone was very friendly.

When they returned to Chicago I ended up on a mailing list asking for new financing so he could continue the TV series elsewhere in the world. I unsubscribed!

The New Poor

When I first settled in France I was taken back by the countless beautiful medieval villages and the vibrant city centres and the healthy looking population that seemed to get the work/personal life balance right.

I was surprised at the number of restaurant owners that chose not to work on weekends, if they made enough during the week, why slog it out for the rest? So different from England where you were used to several different sitting services per night for your table, the best tables in the same restaurant costing more, and meals cheaper if you ate early – price gouging to the max. There seemed to be less obsession with 'what you do for a living' but more interest in how you actually spend your life.

But gradually that's changed. Any other outsider like myself who has spent time here will say the same thing.

If France has often been disparagingly described as the last genuine socialist country in Europe, where the State runs and decides everything, it's because others were jealous that things seemed to work here.

But since I moved to France in 1998 I've never known the country without mass unemployment, always yo-yoing around the 10% mark and much higher if you include the overseas territories in places like Guadeloupe and the subsidised job schemes for young people at the post office or train stations where they learn little apart from turning up on time and wearing a garish uniform.

The State with its massive budget deficits and crippling bureaucracy has neither the money nor the energy anymore to provide for everyone. And for the French themselves, breastfed on centralised government, it's all highly destabilising.

And so much that I admired and took for granted in the French system has disappeared.

Just a simple example – I marvelled at the number of fishmongers, charcuteries, butchers and cheese shops in city neighbourhoods and small towns. They are vanishing from the landscape, people simply don't fork out as much for quality food as they used to. And there is no doubt in my mind that it comes down to reduced purchasing power. Whole towns with populations between 10,000 and 25,000 residents in southern France have seen the life sucked out of their centres – restaurants replaced by kebab vendors, specialist stores by discounters. The big cities from Toulouse to Bordeaux or Lyon have managed to hold onto their well-to-do middle class in the centres but even they have seen a US style 'white flight' to the suburbs and near countryside[15].

Some of that is understandable, as companies set up on the outskirts, but the vacuum has been filled by the poor with their housing paid for by local councils, and students in flats divided into small 'studio appartments'.

And it seems little has been done to stop the rot, with the proliferation of shopping centres in the suburbs, especially in small towns where out-of-town shopping is a guaranteed death sentence for town centres.

---

15   Though even in the US in recent years there has been a reverse as middle class families return to city centres, of course regenerating them, so there is still hope.

You could ask why don't elected officials do something to stop that trend... I wonder if they are not hostage to the big stores almost blackmailing them. The supermarket chains agree to government demands to provide a guaranteed minimum price to farmers and growers, but in return they are given a blank cheque to build where they want.

The 'new poor' as I referred to them in my reporting are not the homeless you see on the streets – often street dwellers come from Eastern Europe these days. No, the new division is between those with full-time jobs in big CAC 40 companies with all the job security and perks that come with it, and those who are on the periphery, working on short term contracts or for small employers without the labour law protection of their counterparts or with little idea of what their rights are.

I am always astonished at how the French media expresses outrage and provides extensive coverage when a big company like Michelin, EDF or Peugeot announces layoffs or voluntary redundancy, yet totally ignores the highly advantageous terms the affected work force will receive in terms of unemployment benefits, training and alternative job placements elsewhere. When a small private company cuts jobs, the workers affected there are invisible and the hardship is immediate.

Even the famous French civil service with its massive army of 'functionaries' has created a class of nearly impoverished employees. My ex-girlfriend works for the INRA, the state-run French agricultural research centre employing thousands up and down the country and it pays huge swathes of its staff salaries of around €1,500 to €1,600 a month despite decades of service. It didn't use to be like that. Or at least one salary used to be enough for a family to live on. Here is one story I did for BBC Radio 4's *From Our Own Correspondent*, though I did many stories on this theme over the years.

Recently one of the most active French charities, the "Secours Populaire" which runs soup kitchens across the country, warned that over half of all French citizens they questioned admitted being close to the breadline or knew someone on or below it. The charity said poverty was now impacting people of all classes and ages.

Poverty is often hidden but in one famous street market in the southern city of Toulouse, it's very much out in the open now.

The 'Cristal' market in the centre of Toulouse is the biggest open-air daily fruit and vegetable market in France. It's been around for more than 50 years and is named after a bar called the Cristal that closed down years ago. Every day thousands of shoppers head here to buy locally grown produce or fruit and vegetables imported from over the border in Spain or from Morocco, further south.

Television crews turn up nearly every day to record the outraged views of punters on the latest national news story. Big city politicians on the campaign trail rarely miss a chance to shake hands during a stopover at this market. I've seen the French Foreign Minister Laurent Fabius hand out leaflets, while former French rugby captain Fabien Pelous campaigned on behalf of the centre-right here.

Traditionally markets like this one were patronised predominately by affluent middle class city centre dwellers keen on fresh food and dismissive of supermarkets. But that has changed – more and more middle class families are leaving city centres for calmer, leafier suburbs. They are increasingly being replaced by students in once grand apartments cut up into tiny studios, single elderly residents and others living in subsidised housing.

Jean-Jacques Bolzan is an elected councillor at City Hall in charge of the open-air markets and small businesses. He says the city is getting poorer – a pattern that started 15 years ago across the country – and gives me an example: the national electricity supplier EDF cuts off the electricity because of unpaid bills to more households in the city centre than anywhere else in the area.

And the Cristal market reflects that trend. Just after 12 noon, stall owners start packing up. If they are not gone by 1.15pm they face a big fine as the rubbish collectors have to move in and clean up.

They chuck out crates of fruit and vegetables either close to rotten or bruised. And that's when the urban poor begin their shopping. As the regular shoppers head off, they move in. They seem to appear from nowhere, huddled over the piles of discarded food. You can see them with big plastic bags or wooden crates, sifting through the produce. When I was there, one picked up several kilos of red peppers, many already mouldy. Another had a bunch of over-ripe bananas.

Most are on their own, elderly, hunched over and badly dressed. They are surprised that anyone should show interest in them and few are willing to talk to me. One lady, Carmen, in her 60s, said she comes here because she receives a pension of just €400 a month, her husband €600. She said ever since being laid off from her factory job she had never found another job but still had to pay her mortgage.

Of course there have always been people on the margins of society searching for free food, but the situation has got far worse according to those who would know – the market vendors themselves.

Alain Truffert has been a stall owner at the market for more than 20 years and he's the official market delegate when negotiating with the City. He says the scavengers are known colloquially as the 'Collectors' and the problem has been getting worse over the past decade. He told me even traditional paying customers are feeling the squeeze. He can see it every day. They want to make cheap long lasting soups, so they buy a few carrots, onions, leeks, and potatoes. Alain makes half the money he made a decade ago and his colleagues say the same thing.

But it's not just the elderly rummaging for still edible free food. Many are younger, in their 20s and 30s. Some are students making a militant statement, others are simply desperately hard up. Many of the young filling up the crates to take home are foreigners.

One 23 year old Spanish girl told me that with her part-time job, she simply couldn't both pay her rent and buy food. I came across a couple in their 30s, Pacome and his Italian girlfriend: she is doing a doctorate while he is getting work experience in the alternative energy sector. They are both here because neither has an income. They said they had met other couples here doing the same thing and they often all shared food or meals together.

The Cristal Market is open six days a week – Tuesday to Sunday. Stall owners say Saturday is their best day because it's considered the bourgeois outing. It's when the city centre's remaining well-off do their shopping. They scrutinise the vegetables with as much attention as the poor and pay extra for their courgettes, tomatoes or chasselas grapes if they are locally grown. But as Alain Truffert points out: they are now a distinct minority[16].

***

Municipal Showers

When I heard that there is a legal requirement for cities and towns with populations over 50,000 to have washing facilities for anyone to use, I knew right away this was an interesting story. I called up homeless shelters and charities as well as government

---

16 I've noticed that whenever British broadcasters want to interview the huddled masses, they speak to people in shell-suits at the entrances to shopping malls, while in France it's always at outdoor food markets (and they're rarely in shell-suits).

offices across the UK to see if something similar existed in Britain. Not only were they amazed that something that seemed to hark back to George Orwell days was still up and running, but I got a feeling from charities in particular that they didn't like the idea at all, after all it would kind of be encroaching onto their raison d'être. Anyway this is a story I filed on one municipal showers facility very close to where I lived in Bonnefoy, just outside the city centre in Toulouse.

From Our Own Correspondent
BBC Radio 4
January 2014

I have come to take a shower. The address is the "Douches Publiques", showers open to all and run by the city council. There used to be five in this city but there is just one left. It is in the suburb of Bonnefoy and it has been here since 1929.

The entrance is simple and low-key, in a nondescript street in a drab neighbourhood, literally on the other side of the tracks from the prosperous and attractive city centre.

From the outside, the building looks a bit grubby, but inside I am pleasantly surprised. Out on the street, it might be unseasonably cold for this time of year but the clunky metal radiators within are working overtime.

The walls are bright, it is all freshly repainted. The look is simple but, most importantly it seems clean. I have brought my own shampoo and towel but need not have. The attendant hands me a clean towel and some shower gel. There are nine cubicles to choose from and there is a sign up saying I have got 20 minutes.

The water is warm, 40°C and there is a hair dryer and mirror outside in the hallway. A long bench by the entrance allows users to stay warm next to the radiators after the shower rather than head straight out into the winter cold. It costs €1 if you pay at the door, but you can bring the cost right down by buying vouchers at the main railway station. In fact, unlike most things in life, the cost of this facility is lower than it used to be, providing a little dignity for people in distress.

Many of those who come to use these municipal showers are what you might call traditional long-time drifters, people who shuffle from city to city and who prefer to clean up here rather than in a homeless shelter which might have a less wholesome atmosphere.

The attendant is a former boxer called Joël Prat. He sits in a tiny office which has a window hatch like the ticket office at a station. He makes sure his customers play by the rules. Alcohol and drugs are not allowed on the premises. Pets are not permitted either – you will sometimes see dogs tied up outside.

He does admit that one customer managed to smuggle his poodle in under his trench coat. All was revealed, though, when the dog started yapping in the shower. Joel has been in the job for nine years and says it has given him real insight into who is hardest hit in French society.

While down-and-outs are not new, he says he has noticed the emergence of a new working poor among his clients. Men and women who have jobs but are finding it nearly impossible to make ends meet. They cannot afford the rent, so to get by they live in their cars or vans on quiet streets and come here to wash. Most live alone in their vehicles, but there are some with young children and they come in together to get clean.

Businessmen who have fallen on hard times also pass through – everything was going well until they lost their jobs. Perhaps it was coupled with a costly divorce and suddenly their car is their only possession.

Then there are students or low-income families who can't afford to install a bathroom or use their hot water, as heating bills keep rising. And young squatters who live in abandoned or empty offices where there is no running water.

Stéphane Cazaux from Toulouse social services says the

municipal showers are not just about hygiene these days. He says they play an increasingly important role in a society that is more and more individualist and made up of people who may be more isolated and cut off from each other. That's why, for some, it is less money problems than a need for human contact that brings them here, especially the elderly.

Rene, who is 82, is one of these. This former painter and decorator comes three days a week for his morning wash. He does have a shower at home but lives alone and admits he is here mainly for the company. It is the one moment in the day when he can have a conversation with other people, whether it is about politics or the latest rugby results.

But Joël says not all of the reasons for using the facilities are sad ones. He runs a public service, he insists, telling me about the day one of the tallest, most beautiful blondes he had ever set eyes on appeared, in a panic, desperate to have a shower.

It seems she had a romantic rendez-vous and her boiler had just exploded.

Crime and Brits

I would hate to be a full-time court reporter but from a freelancer's point of view, it does have its advantages. Defendants don't turn up on time, or lawyers have the wrong paperwork, or are missing crucial documents, translators are required when no-one had taken into account the fact that the victims or accused aren't French, jury members are sick or did something they shouldn't have, requiring a new trial... All those things happened when I was court reporting, and of course since I was already 'there' I had to be paid and a new day in court beckoned. On top of that, defendants often appeal their verdicts, so the whole thing starts all over again.

When I was considering whether to apply for the British Consul job (having declined it the first time it was offered), I was warned I would be spending a lot of time visiting French jails. Brits on the run would head down here and either through lack of money or loneliness would turn themselves in to the local police. Of course the French were not going to pay to send them back home, so the Consul would have to negotiate with the Brit on the lam and usually ask their family back home to send the money or pay for a one way ticket themselves to send the offender home to the waiting authorities.

Strangely, most of my crime stories involved Welshmen and I ended up working extensively for ITV Wales as well as the BBC and various independent radio stations in the Cardiff area.

The first Welsh story involved a fugitive, Trevor Master, who was arrested near Pau accused of rape. He had a court-appointed lawyer, Claude Garcia, who said these cases made more money for him than those Basque separatists. No money in that, he told me. And he appreciated the fact that representing British criminals got him media attention so didn't hesitate to help me out or call me whenever a Brit was in trouble with the law and he had the case.

For example, it was thanks to his lawyer that I managed to get word to Trevor Masters that I would be filming behind the courthouse when he was led out in handcuffs with the police, and that he should shout at me that he was innocent, he'd been framed and who by. That got the top story in ITV Wales that evening.

There were always British drug smugglers arrested near the border with Spain and that usually required a visit to one of their court appearances. Of course the big advantage in France is that the judge often allows a camera into the first 10 minutes of any proceeding – which always left newsrooms back home ecstatic.

My long relationship with Claude Garcia was sealed with the arrest of several members of Bridgend rugby club who, after losing a European rugby game in Pau, had got drunk in a pub and started behaving badly – or as they said in their defence, behaving just as they would in the same circumstances back home. Except a local handball team were also celebrating there. The outcome: the Bridgend 4 were accused of lewd behaviour in public and sexual aggression against the girlfriend of one of the handball players.

In itself it's not a huge story (well maybe for Welsh TV as they have been known, in moments of giddily excitement about similar stories to call up their graphics department and demand an international map with France on it). No, what made 'rugby players behaving badly' a story was that one of the accused was Gareth Thomas. At the time he was not yet captain of Wales but he was getting a name for himself, and this did his reputation no good at all. As he was about to join the Stade Toulousain too, the last thing he needed was a criminal record and being put on a sex offender list in France. And of course we didn't know then – not publicly at least – that he was gay and that the last thing on his mind was probably touching up French girls.

In the end, he came back several times for the trial but not his colleagues who were found guilty in absentia – if they ever return to France they could be arrested and jailed. Gareth Thomas got off with the equivalent to a warning.

The creepiest thing about the whole affair for me was this sinister sounding tabloid reporter for the Welsh Daily Mirror who kept calling me up and introducing himself with "How are you doing my good friend…" and then asking for the latest lurid details on the misbehaving players. When it was all over, I was glad to have no more dealings with him.

But that (like many of the cases I covered) was basically a small story. I remember one much bigger, genuinely tragic story I had to do in 2004 for both ITV and BBC Wales about a chap called Aaron Powell. Having first suffered a personal family tragedy, Powell, through a series of terrible circumstances, had found himself in the wrong place at the wrong time and ended up murdered.

Aaron Powell was a mechanic from Cardiff. His daughter had been killed in a hit-and-run accident at home and 18 months later, to help him get over it, he had decided to go on holiday to Spain with a friend. They chose to drive down.

They had a car accident on the way, just outside the city of Orléans and decided to take the train down from there. Their train was leaving very late and Aaron had a few drinks at the station. He then went on a scout for somewhere to eat. On his way between the station and a shopping centre next door, he bumped into 20 year old local delinquent Elias Laguedani, a young man of Moroccan origin who lived on one of the town's far flung rough housing estates.

What happened next will never be clear but it seems Laguedani approached Powell and spoke to him in an aggressive manner, Aaron who had been drinking and didn't understand French didn't reply or was possibly irritable and said something back. In the altercation that followed the young thug stabbed him with a big kitchen knife he was carrying.

Aaron's family had to come down to Orléans twice – once for the trial, then again for the retrial in which his killer was given a reduced sentence on the grounds the killing wasn't pre-mediated. Both times the atmosphere was electric when the verdict was read out and both times, the victim's family all had to be escorted from the court with a massive police presence and were urged to leave the city as quickly as possible – Aaron Powell's young killer came from a well known local criminal family and they had managed to pack the court with all their heavies to put pressure on everyone.

A tragic story but sadly also a fairly mundane day in a court with France's urban immigrant underclass.

***

The Lady in the Lake

There are plenty of stories that I did on the number of Brits who move to France looking for a new way of life, often bowled over while on holiday here during the summer. They see the wonderful street markets with great local produce, and the same festive casual ambiance with night markets, the huge friendly crowds and feeling of nonchalance and a growing comfortable feeling that life is clearly better down here. Of course, I've also heard that numerous times on holiday on Greek Islands or in Tuscany.

Anyway some couples decide to move here. And things go great at first, they are embraced by locals and the local mayor will sometimes even host a reception for them. Of course they might not understand what the mayor is saying to everyone chuckling with glasses in hand as they don't speak French and also another niggling detail in the back of their minds is that they don't have a job lined up yet. But that's down the road, don't ruin things yet, they say to themselves. They may have sold up or rented out their property back home so they have savings for now, they say.

September turns to November and the big crowds at the markets have dwindled, some of the things that seemed so quaint at first are turning out to actually be quite difficult, especially when dealing with local bureaucracy, and of course after mid-November (which isn't a bad run, it has to be said), the weather suddenly turns, and you begin realising it actually gets colder here than say, back in London.

And those other friendly Brits you drank rosé with at outdoor tables who said they had moved here years ago and hadn't regretted it, had neglected to say they still have a business of sorts running back home and were in fact over there most of the time between November and June, popping over to France just occasionally to make sure an antiquated pipe hadn't leaked in their absence.

Those small shops that seemed to do a roaring trade over the summer, crammed with sweaty tourists seem to have closed – in some cases you discover for good, as you learn they hadn't properly figured out their business plan to stay open all year around.

If the home with a massive garden and extraordinary view and the quiet came at such a low cost, well there's a reason for that – quite simply, much of the French countryside is divine, beautiful and unbearable if you spend too much time there in one go[17].

Of course estate agents or others like the local councillors who have a vested interest in persuading you to come over (i.e., the primary school is lacking pupils and facing closure) don't tell you that.

Anyway, as I've said, I have a house in the country and love it – but for limited periods at a time. It gets cold, lonely and too far away from anywhere where anything is happening. Those sophisticated French you share a drink with at the end of the summer market seem to disappear – often those left behind out of season are drunks, the unemployed, misfits and locals who have always lived there and will never adopt you and neither will you ever have anything in common to share with them.

On top of that, without speaking French, finding a job is next to impossible, and if you do the wages will be shockingly far below your expectations as you compare them to what you were earning back home. Couples who thought their relationships were strong discover they are now having rows over money. Daily bouts of boredom loom, flings break the monotony, some hit the bottle and in the end, divorce is seen as a solution. In one tragic situation I know of personally, Tim, father to three kids, got divorced, became a full-blown alcoholic then took his own life.

Others cut their losses and just head home. Thankfully there are also lots of positive stories, but the one involving Robert Lund and his wife Evelyn – known in the French media as the 'Lady in the Lake' – isn't one of them.

The Lunds had moved to an isolated farm house north of stunningly beautiful UNESCO world heritage listed Albi, from

---

17 I love my country home in the achingly beautiful village of Penne but rented and then bought a flat in the centre of Toulouse very rapidly.

Lancashire, in search of a better way of life, back in 1997. Except they didn't move to Albi itself but about 40 kilometers away, which was a big difference. Things turned sour pretty rapidly. They lived in rural isolation. Neither had much money, the house belonged to Evelyn. She had turned to alcohol and their rows were violent. In 2000 Robert reported his wife missing, saying she had disappeared after a heavy night of drinking. He said she had simply staggered off during the night and he wasn't sure where she was headed, maybe to England or to see other friends in France. Despite a major police search, she wasn't found.

Two years later during a long drought, the water level in a lake near to the couple's home went down spectacularly and a car roof emerged. Evelyn's body was strapped inside. Robert Lund at one point became technically the longest serving defendant in a French jail. I say 'technically' because although he was found guilty of killing his wife and rolling her car into the lake to claim the life insurance and the house, he appealed – which made him in effect innocent again in the eyes of the law – but he remained in custody. In the end, Robert Lund was found guilty three separate times of killing his wife Evelyn.

I covered the final court appeal in 2011 for BBC Manchester. It was pretty low cost – I even had to film my pieces to camera to myself. It took place in the town of Montauban and lasted a week. Lund spoke little and very quietly and denied murdering his wife again and again. Police from Manchester provided evidence against him as did Evelyn's family. They said it was down to money, without hers he would have been homeless and she was threatening to return to the UK. Once all his options had run out, Lund was jailed for 12 years for killing his wife. The relatively short sentence suggested that the jury weren't clear whether it was pre-meditated or simply a drunken violent dispute that went too far.

Experts throughout the trial gave different accounts as to how Evelyn Lund's car had ended up in a remote hard-to-find lake. One said it was clearly an accident, another said someone had put the gear stick into neutral and rolled the car into the water. Her eyeglasses were found at her home suggesting she must have returned home after seeing friends that night, exposing flaws in Lund's argument that she had set off by car and didn't return. On top of that, the friends who had seen her the night she disappeared told the court she had been wearing her glasses then.

Whatever the accusations, Lund constantly said he was innocent and his defence lawyers, who deal with a lot of criminals in the region, seem convinced of his innocence to this day…It's odd that when the Lunds originally chose to move to the south-west of France, they chose a particularly bleak spot, a rundown farmhouse with no neighbours, and particularly cold surroundings both in terms of the actual weather and of the social atmosphere – or lack of it. It struck me as a strange way of looking for somewhere where the grass was greener, but like I said earlier, some property down here is cheap and there is often a reason why.

Of course throughout the trial I got used to seeing Lund with police escorts, in handcuffs. In archive footage of him in custody he's also always surrounded by police and solemn looking investigating judges while being taken to the lake etc. So my next encounter with him was strange to say the least.

Lund had been sentenced to a 12 year jail term just before Christmas in 2011. By then, he had already been in custody for seven years and that time of course counted as part of his sentence, so he was due for release in 2016. When in 2014 I came across a picture of him in the local paper, La Dépêche, stripped to the waist at his home, and saw he'd been interviewed just recently, I was somewhat surprised.

So I thought why not pay him a visit. I am sure Jim Clarke, the News Editor at BBC Manchester, broke all the health and safety guidelines when he immediately said yes go… yes, go and see this murderer, on your own because there's no budget for a cameraman...

To my surprise, Lund's landline was still listed and was even connected and he picked up the phone. On my way to a remote farmhouse to see a convicted killer who had no doubt heard about my reports for the BBC about his case...hmmm, I must admit I was a bit apprehensive.

Wearing a Manchester United shirt he welcomed me with a smile into his dilapidated farmhouse and served me coffee. Robert Lund was softly spoken but incredibly calm and coherent – it was a strange experience. Even more so when I got him to cut bread with a very big knife in his kitchen for the general shots I needed for the report. Not the best idea I've ever had, I said to myself... what if he suddenly flips? And not the best image he really wanted to show of himself on TV either I reckon. But I guess he hadn't done much media training over the years.

He explained all over again that he was innocent but also that he'd learnt all the tricks of the world of crime from his cell mates during his days locked up. He said his was a tragic miscarriage of justice.

I have no idea of course, but what struck me was that his life looked pretty bleak: no money, no transport apart from a bicycle in a very hilly area, and he was supposed to go to the unemployment centre about 30 kilometres away on a regular basis to prove to them that he was looking for work.

At the same time, his late wife's family had begun proceedings to have him evicted from the house in order to sell it. I suppose I could have followed up in the coming months to see what happened to him. I should have but didn't, and that is one of the great criticisms of spot news journalism: you intrude, leave and usually forget.

***

The British Exodus

This tale's not really in the crime section but I'll tell it here since it follows the woes of those who come to France looking for a better way of life. One story that I did ended up generating wide scale publicity at the time – it was on how the Brits were turning their back on France and returning to the UK.

Rewind a second. When I bought my house in the beautiful Cathare village of Penne back in 1995, I was still living in London and prices then were remarkably cheap for homes in the southern French countryside. Mine cost the equivalent of €20,000 (though of course I put another €50,000 into fixing it up and it still looks unfinished and I still have to fork out large amounts each year whether it's to redo the shutters or the drain pipes, change the septic tank because of new sanitary regulations or something else).

And then in the early 2000s prices soared. Those locals who inherited property and sold it, or second home owners who had bought cheap and got out at the time, did very well.

I remember about 6 years ago going to the highly attractive nearby town of St-Antonin-Noble-Val which is besieged by foreigners, especially Brits but also Dutch and Belgians. A couple of local French rural types were shaking their heads in disgust at house prices in the local estate agent's window. I asked why, they said these homes weren't worth anything like what was being asked for them. I said maybe they were wrong, supply and demand, etc. No sir, one replied sharply, it's completely ridiculous, these properties have never been worth that much money.

And you know what, from about 2009 onwards prices plunged in the countryside just about everywhere. In my region they fell by between 40 and 60%. Economic woes back in the UK and a yo-yoing sterling frightened off buyers, while others who had second homes in France cut their loses and sold up. Low cost airlines cut back on routes, even reducing services to summer schedules only, making it difficult to come out cheaply or all year round. Petrol prices rose significantly at one point making it more expensive to go away on weekends to distant country retreats. The government did its part too, hiking stealth taxes on second homes.

When I looked into the pattern, the British exodus wasn't huge – around 5% returning – but it meant the end of more than a decade of rising British ownership of the French countryside (Le Monde newspaper recently did a study that showed Brits physically own 2% of the French countryside). In the end, I don't think Brits beating a retreat was all down to economic reasons. I think maybe the widescale riots in cities and provincial towns across France in 2005 – well before contemporary Islamic terrorism came to the forefront – got some Brits realising that France faced some of the same problems they had at home. The stories I did on the exodus aired in a lot of places and this is one of the stories I did for France 24

France 24
March 2008

For the first time in decades, British expatriates who have made France their home are now turning back and returning to the UK. The reason: the credit crunch means Brits can no longer afford to live in France and are having to head home. Most of them settled in the south-west of France. Jeannie and her husband are among them, packing up and heading back to Norfolk in eastern England.

The Kilburns have spent more than five years in the stunning village of Najac in the south-west of France. Giving up their home

'Château de Pic' with dramatic views of the local town is a wrenching decision but they have decided it's time.

Jeannie Kilburn says: "We have been very enriched by the experience but we really do have large families at home and that really is the good reason for going back. We could have left it longer but if we get too 'wobbly' we won't manage a move like this which has been absolutely huge to organise."

And they are not alone in making that decision. The British embassy believes around 5 to 8% of British families are now leaving and the current economic woes are key. The pound has plunged against the euro in the last year, making it very hard for those dependent on funds from UK banks.

Roger Virnuls the British Consul in the southern French city of Toulouse explains: "Pensioners who are living here on their pensions or income from the UK have effectively lost 20% of their purchasing power in the past 12 months. That is a big issue when you also have inflation in France making life difficult for them."

The evidence of the British retreat is everywhere. Many Brits live part time in the UK and France, with homes in both countries. With house prices sinking back home, their property in France is now a luxury they can no longer afford.

One British estate agent, Charles Smallwood, has been selling homes for foreigners in this part of France for two decades. He says sellers have to be realistic: "They have either brought their prices down substantially or will do. Those who don't want to – or can't – cut their selling price will just have to wait and hope this recession ends and prices go back up."

Until recently low cost airlines flew into tiny airports all year around, making it easy to commute between rural France and the UK. But because of recession and high fuel prices, those airlines have slashed routes or only fly to some destinations during the summer.

And many Brits who moved to France to open gîtes or bed and breakfast accommodation have seen the flow of customers dry up due to oversupply or tourists looking for cheaper holidays at home.

At the BiBNT, a group of France-based British small business owners who meet once a month for lunch, they say too many Brits have moved over in recent years to buy much bigger homes, thinking a good job would come along. That's a big mistake according to one of the members Heather Hughes:

"I think it depends on what you want to do and where you want to be. To buy your dream home in the middle of the countryside and get a job, that's not going to work."

Nevertheless there are some diehards in the countryside who have no intention of leaving. One is Lorraine Walker. She says emphatically: "No, we are not moving back. No, never I don't think."

In fact it's not hard to spot the long term Brits in France – they are the only ones who don't think twice about sitting outside drinking beer on a chilly winter night.

Blair Job

The Day I Lent Tony Blair a Tie

There is nothing funny about the Omagh bombing – the last mass killing by a splinter group of the IRA, in August 1998. But one spin-off from that tragic event was that every year, Tony Blair would have to spend a small part of his summer holiday with me. I don't think he found that amusing either[18].

Tony Blair's "New Labour" had only recently been elected into office and the Prime Minister himself was the fresh new young face on the European scene. The European Union had high hopes for him – he had spent time as a young adult living and working in France, he even spoke French and he was making encouraging noises about joining the euro and embracing EU legislation promoting workers rights.

Blair was a genuine francophile which couldn't be said for his predecessors John Major and Margaret Thatcher. And the proof: he chose to spend his holidays in France. I spoke to the

---

18   A friend of mine, Wolfgang Spindler, who is a TV producer in Lyon with Euronews, referred to these annual summer assignments with much smirking innuendo as my "Bl*air* job"

Paris bureau of Reuters television and said it would be a good idea to cover the beginning of his holiday in France. It was after all summer – what else was going on – and of course just a couple of comments from him on anything from why he chose France to his reaction to whatever was the 'big' news event of the moment back in the UK, would get a lot of pick up from broadcasters. Well, that was my pitch anyway.

For the holiday proper, the Blairs were staying in a small château in the small village of Saint Martin d'Oydes in the foothills of the Pyrenees about an hour and half from Toulouse. However on the day of their arrival, the children and all the suitcases went to the château while Tony and Cherie headed to another village, Miradoux in the Gers, where some personal friends of theirs have a home.

I went along with a cameraman and of course when the Prime Minister arrived with his discreet police protection unit, he gave a few waffle phrases in English and French about why he liked spending the summer in France – food, relaxation, sunshine, etc., and end of story as he went into the house. We headed back to Toulouse to send the video[19].

It was while we were on the motorway back to Toulouse that we heard that a bomb had gone off in Northern Ireland and there were many casualties. At this point in time, the peace process in

---

19   In those days – and it wasn't so long ago – you had to find the nearest what is called in the business, 'feed point' to send video, in other words a TV station or video relay point with a machine that could play broadcast standard video tape. Of course you had to find the TV station and often it was closed or you were 'welcomed' by a surly engineer grumbling that he had to stay an extra hour to wait for you. They always charged a fortune and things usually went wrong with the satellite connection, or they didn't have the right cables, or someone hadn't booked the time slot etc. etc. Now of course you just send video from your computer wherever you have a wifi connection, including your hotel room, but that creates a whole set of other problems because now the news desk knows how easy it is to do and can ask you for more video or to go and shoot something else and send it back or 'Could you just change a couple of shots and redo it and send that back?'

Northern Ireland was well underway and with it, the release of hundreds of inmates with blood on their hands. So of course we rushed back to Miradoux as we were the only international broadcaster in the vicinity and were told to come straight in by the UK police. Before the interview Tony Blair was on the phone with his media master Alastair Campbell and then it turned to a three way conversation – where to do the interview somewhere that would give as little clue as possible that the Prime Minister was on holiday in southern France. So we chose a row of books in the background, taking out any that might have a holiday feel that you would get in any second home – cook books, travel guides etc. and we kept the lights off to make the atmosphere gloomy, even though of course August in the south of France is anything but. But there was a problem – remember Tony Blair's luggage had been sent to their holiday château several hours away... So the next crisis was finding a jacket and tie – a quick call to the local mayor's office produced a vintage jacket, but no tie. In observance of a long-held journalistic tradition (that I have myself since abandoned) I had a tie with me for precisely this kind of emergency – except it wasn't me who wore it but the Prime Minister.

Over the next couple of days I became the 'pool' producer, acting as a go-between for the Blairs, the media and his own media operation in London.

Obviously for me it was a great coup and the ensuing goodwill from the PM meant that while he was in office, every summer holiday after that, I was invited to cover at least one or two days of the Blairs' holiday in France[20].

Another year, a Russian navy submarine, the Kursk, exploded, sending it to a shallow ocean grave. A British rescue team was sent to help try and save the crew of 118. But it was too late. Again this occurred in August, while the Blairs were on holiday in France so I tried to speak to the Prime Minister. This time however, the direct national importance wasn't there and he said he was on holiday and didn't want to be hassled.

On another French holiday, after a period when he had been getting roughed up in the press at home, he went to church in the local village with his family and new-born baby Leo. It received a lot of media attention, including video by me for Reuters.

I remember as the first photographs were sent around the world as well as our video, we received a number of irate phone calls from the media department at Downing Street asking us to back off and stop "farming out the video". To the Reuters news editor's credit, they refused. And the next day when all the tabloids had pictures of Blair in his summer holiday outfit holding baby Leo in his arms outside the church, the Blairs were delighted. When I spoke to Downing Street the attitude had changed significantly too. And after that, an unwritten yearly deal was struck: it was OK to film the Blair family trip to the church but after that they were to be left alone. It gave me real insight into how the Blair media machine worked.

---

20 A few days after the Omagh bombing and my weekend with the Blairs, I received several phone calls from the Daily Express. They were very keen to know more about the Blairs' hosts in the village – what they did, how they knew the Blairs, etc. I found it a little distasteful and told them to do their own homework. I was in no mood to turn on the Blairs especially as they had been pretty helpful to me. The Express called me several times and in the end, rather than risk being even vaguely associated with whatever hatchet job the paper was planning, I called Lance Price, one of Blair's key spokesmen at the time, to tell them to be careful about the upcoming story. He said he would deal with it. It's not something I had done before or have done since but at the time I thought the Express were being was intrusive and nasty considering what was unfolding in Omagh.

Just about every summer the BBC Foreign News gathering desk would call me urgently as some politician, judge or big personality had done or said something controversial and now they were on holiday somewhere in my patch and needless to say had no desire to speak to the media but would I mind awfully knocking on their holiday home door.

The number of remote holiday homes that I have filmed from the outside over the years as a backdrop to a story is countless as understandably, nobody inside was ever willing to play ball. Sometimes I did stories where I knew there was not a chance of the VIP being there. One was Nick Clegg, UK Deputy Prime Minister at the time. His family on his father's side have a huge property between Bordeaux and Angoulême and I managed to convince the English service of France 24 to send me there to find out more about the tiny village that hosted one of the most powerful men in British politics (debatable, but that was the story pitch I went with!).

Apart from the mailbox with Clegg written on it outside the large fortified farmhouse, there was nothing to see, and the mayor wasn't even sure he had ever met the Deputy Prime Minister, but he did say the home had been burgled recently. Somehow I managed to turn around a 2 minute 30 report.

All that fruitless door-knocking is one of the reasons I am grateful to people like Nigel Lawson. He bought a large home in the département of the Gers and more or less commutes to the House of Lords: Monday to Thursday in London, Friday to Sunday back in France.

If he had come to this region to get away from it all, he made the silly mistake of agreeing to talk to me once. Blame it on BBC politics producer Simon Coates – he put us in touch. But once in my contacts book, you are never free. Actually, I don't think Lord Lawson ever declined an interview opportunity as I trekked down to see him.

The first time I saw him I was asked to do what the BBC calls a *simul-rec* which is where you record in digital quality an interview being given to a journalist down an ordinary phone line because the broadcaster wants to use the better sound quality version later.

It was for a programme on Radio 4 about the role of the Star Chamber, and while Lawson spoke to Andrew Rawnsley on the phone, I recorded it with my MP3 player. So he immediately got the idea I was some sort of techie wizard and for a while bombarded me with emails asking if I knew how to fix his faulty satellite dish so he could watch the cricket matches without the picture dropping out (I never did as I'm not actually a techie wizard).

Since then I have been to see him a great many times. Once, it was to get his views on the euro, (I – rather cleverly I thought – did the interview at the *Café de La Bourse* which can be translated as *the Stock Market café*). Of course he said then that it was about time for the UK to pull out of the EU and called the euro a slow motion trainwreck – a great soundbite but what does that actually mean?

Then I saw him twice in one week when Lady Thatcher died, once for the BBC and a second time for France 24. He winked at me and said: "Well, her death has been good for someone's business at least."

At one point, I said I was going to refer to him as 'the ex-Chancellor, now living part time in France' – he winced and said he would prefer not to be called a part time resident in France as he didn't want the French tax authorities to get too interested in his financial affairs.

And just one footnote: he gives hope to us all as we get older – over the years that I have gone down to see him at his rather big bolthole, I have noticed that he is often not alone but with attractive women, considerably younger than himself.

Fugitives and Terrorists

Ira Einhorn

I f south-west France is one of the most popular holiday home destinations for middle class Brits, Dutch and Belgians, for a while at least it also seemed to be the place to go for fugitives.

Back in the pre 9/11 days, before terrorists dominated the 'top 10 most wanted' lists on police websites worldwide (especially the FBI's), one name on those lists stood out: Ira Einhorn.

An American, a self proclaimed charismatic environmental leader and visionary, often referred to as a hippie and counterculture guru in the 1960s and 70s, he used his charisma and gift of the gab to appeal to and seduce young females on the university campus in Philadelphia.

It was there that he was arrested and charged with murdering his attractive young girlfriend, Holly Maddux, in 1979. Her festering body was found in a trunk in his flat – neighbours had complained about a foul stench and a brown substance leaking from their ceiling. Einhorn claimed he was framed by the US government because he knew troubling state intelligence secrets.

Strangely his lawyer Arlen Specter, who went on to become a hardline Republican US senator, managed to get Einhorn released on bail ahead of his trial. You can guess the rest – he skipped bail and disappeared for 18 years. Thanks to a mixture of charm and who knows what else (because he was no matinee idol), he succeeded in both seducing and convincing a large number of wealthy women to support him financially as he wandered around Europe under different identities. He was of course spotted from time to time but the authorities had moved on and his case was not exactly a priority except for the Public Prosecutor's office in Pennsylvania that tried him in absentia. The verdict: life imprisonment, but maybe a death sentence if he was ever arrested and retried.

I guess he got sloppy because in 1997 he was living with a well-off Swedish woman in the small town of Champagne-Mouton, north of Bordeaux. He had been living under the name of Eugene Mallon but had figured a long time had passed so when he needed a driving licence, he applied under his original name. That was a major blunder and despite the appalling bureaucracy and antiquated French computer systems back then, the records immediately showed that he was wanted by the US authorities.

The US networks rushed over and broadcast stories that he was living a life of luxury in a château (it wasn't actually, it was more a partly restored claustrophobic mill with damp mouldy walls due to a lack of natural light and a river running past... It was far from luxurious and in a middle of a nowhere region of France). The local US media demanded justice, as did the district attorney's office in Philadelphia. In fact he became their obsession.

But France wouldn't extradite him because he had managed to convince the French authorities that he would face the death penalty if he was sent back. So he continued very much as before, and apart from having to check in with the local police on a regular basis, he carried on living the life of a happy expat but now also holding court, titillating the local expat and hippie communities with his newly obtained 'heroic jail bait anti-American establishment' credentials.

However, he rarely talked to the media, especially the Americans, as he – rightly – figured their agenda was that he should be hung or otherwise executed immediately. And they did indeed pointedly accuse the French authorities of thwarting justice and of showing blatant anti-Americanism by turning a blind eye to murder.

Over a period of months I managed to charm him on the phone and by email and he finally invited me up to do a radio interview for a US broadcaster called Pacifica, a legacy of the community radio network in the 70s and far less establishment than National Public Radio (NPR). Of course my plan was to persuade him to give me a TV interview down the road, as NBC in particular were offering me a few thousand dollars for just such a thing.

It took hours to get there and when I arrived, I found his home under 24 hour police surveillance – the American pressure on the French had finally paid off and they were taking the case a little more seriously. But like the man himself, the police presence wasn't quite what it seemed – as Einhorn told me later, it was all a façade; all he had to do was walk out the backdoor and he was free to roam the rolling countryside, his house standing between him and the gaze of the gendarmes.

There is no doubt Einhorn was highly charismatic, but he was also very weird looking. His Swedish girlfriend was meek and sporting a big black eye, apparently from bumping into something… Who knows whether Einhorn was violent or not but it certainly was in the back of my mind, especially when he got more and more annoyed as I scrambled under a table looking for a socket extension for my radio recorder. We went for a Chinese meal accompanied by a police escort and Einhorn and I got along just fine, we even talked about doing a TV interview sometime in the future. But it never happened. After I left Einhorn's château / mouldy millhouse, I gave the interview to Pacifica Radio of course but also to a couple of European broadcasters. He sent me a message saying I had betrayed him.

That was ok, time was quickly running out for Einhorn. The Philadelphia DA's department agreed to waiver the death penalty if he was extradited and the socialist Prime Minister Lionel Jospin signed an order to send him back.

As his arrest and extradition appeared imminent, the US camera crews flocked to his mill again. And they certainly got some remarkable footage: in one final dramatic act on the eve of his extradition, Einhorn appeared in front of the lenses with a large knife and cried: "Mr Jospin, we are part of the same generation, how can you do this to me?!" and then slashed himself just below the neck. There was lots of blood but experts say that was the purpose – maximum impact but little real risk. After he was stitched up by a medical team, he was sent back to the US with CNN providing breaking news of his arrival back on US soil.

He is now rotting in jail on a life sentence with no possibility of parole.

***

Terrorists

When I arrived in the Southwest, violent Basque separatism was a big issue. There were attacks on the Spanish security services, national politicians and even local Basque councillors who did not follow the hardline of ETA. Business owners had to pay protection rackets. On the French side, the situation had historically been less toxic as the French authorities took a very alternative approach – don't cause trouble here and we won't crackdown on you.

For a while, that seemed to work: ETA cells operated in the Southwest and kept their weapons in caches in remote farm houses and nondescript flats in towns.

But the French approach changed in the 1990s. There were hundreds of violent French-born ETA members too and they also began to target French police, judges and businesses that they considered enemies, especially estate agents in the Basque Country. That, combined with new pressure from the French police's Spanish counterparts, triggered a crackdown on ETA cells operating on French soil and nearly all of its senior leaders hiding in France were taken into custody. Shadowy armed groups with some sort of state backing in Madrid were also carrying out their own shoot-to-kill operations in France on the grounds the French weren't doing the work themselves.

I spent a lot of time in courts as ETA members were put on trial or sent back to Spain. I interviewed their spokesmen who had grungy offices in the otherwise beautiful town of Bayonne. Often they had been in and out of jail themselves on charges of supporting terrorism.

They actually made very poor media spokesmen, breastfed on Marxist Leninist theory, they were very bad at getting their message across clearly and never said anything that really made sense. Just trying to get them to explain the conditions for a peace process led to long-winded, confused and incomprehensible monologues. The tide had clearly turned against extremism and many of the new generation of ETA supporters seemed to be nothing more than disenfranchised kids with bleak job prospects who saw separatism as a way of existing and getting some respect in their closed-off communities. That lack of real ideology or raison d'être played a large part in their group's self destruction and the decision to call an end to the violence – they simply didn't have the skilled operators and depth of feeling necessary to keep the fight going. Often their supporters in the courtrooms seemed to be urban hippies with a mean streak. The latest recruits were young and very amateur – one was arrested in France after going to a launderette and leaving his backpack and gun behind. When he came back to pick it up, he was arrested. As is often the case, the separatists had a very ambiguous relationship with the established media. They accused it of being the propaganda voice of the French and Spanish governments and treated it with huge scorn and suspicion and at the same time accused it of deliberately ignoring them. Maybe because I wasn't working for either the French or Spanish media I had a little more access and a slightly warmer reception. But otherwise I had nothing in common with them and agreed with nothing they had to say about their contemporary struggle which struck me as entirely archaic.

However, after several years of covering ETA's arrests, demands and off-and-on ceasefires, I met one former senior member of the terrorist organisation that I got along with very well – I'd even say that maybe if I was a little less conservative, I wouldn't have a problem going out for a drink with him or seeing a rugby game. He was passionate about French club rugby. He himself suggested we go out and see a game, though I think it had more to do with him having a crush on Catherine, my girlfriend at the time. His name was Daniel Derguy. He spent more than 13 years in jail for a number of offences including sending booby trapped bombs in the post and extortion. When he was freed he was banned from living in the French Basque Country and ended up getting the chance to run a furniture store on a bleak industrial estate outside of Cahors in the Lot département.

He told me that when he when first arrived in Cahors and checked in with the job centre to sign on and get benefits, he was treated with disdain and told he was eligible for nothing as he hadn't been looking for a job up to then. When he showed his court papers saying he had just been released after more than a decade inside for terrorism, staff at the job centre suddenly became very pro-active.

Anyway he had popped up on my radar when he was arrested in Cahors by a group of heavily armed masked gunmen in the middle of the night. He said he was terrified and initially thought it was a group of right wing extremists from Spain who had come to get him. In fact it was anti-terrorist police acting on a new extradition request from Spain.

Needless to say he was in and of court for a year trying to avoid extradition. That's when I got to know him a little. When the French judges rejected the Spanish request claiming it was a politically motivated, Daniel went back to running his furniture store.

Of course as a permanent peace process began to take shape, Daniel Derguy became my go-to guy for official comment on all the latest twists and turns. He'd always give me a quote or do an interview, but looking back on it, I'm not sure his cooperation with me was really a good thing for him – he was after all trying to run a business and he knew very well that his militancy had wrecked his chances of becoming a more conventional figure (or even a father – his girlfriend who ran a bar in the Basque Country had stood by him for years, before giving up on him, bitter that she had spent so much time supporting him while the chance of their having a family waned).

One my scariest 'ETA moments' was when I took the wrong road at the wrong time of night. I was travelling with my cameraman Michel Cross. A native of Toulouse, Michel liked rugby, good food and talking about the idea of illicit affairs with women (he had been happily married a long time and never went beyond the talking) so you could say he was a chatty, fun travelling companion who was easy to get along with.

We were heading over the Spanish border to Zaragoza to do some filming in the very dry region of Aragon (an almost desert-like landscape) that was about to become even drier if Madrid had its way – the government was planning to divert water to the coast and its second homes and golf course communities, etc. Anyway, since it was a long drive, Michel suggested we stop overnight at his cousin's home in the foothills of the Pyrenees to break up the trip. It was a great idea and we dropped off our bags and equipment with the cousin before heading along a quiet road towards the nearby ski resort, St Lary, to get some dinner. Of course this was November – it was dark, the ski season hadn't started and autumnal tourism was well over. In other words, there was hardly anyone on that road at that time of year.

At a roundabout a few kilometres from St Lary, we suddenly saw dark shadows ahead of us and big vans blocking the road. These dark shadows were in fact as I soon discovered, a unit from a special anti-terrorist gendarme brigade based in Bordeaux and they had shotguns aimed at my car.

I don't think it would have taken much for them to shoot at us – it was that close. For a start, I kind of look Basque, well dark anyway; in those days I had crap old cars, (in other words nothing that suggested glamorous foreign correspondent) and why would two people be driving around at 11pm there at that time of year anyway?

While two of the officers had shotguns pointed at the car, others inspected it. Michel Cross was silent the whole time, I think he was trembling. And of course I didn't have any documents as I had dropped everything at his cousin's place. Thankfully though I did have the tripod in the car and crucially, my French allocated press card – both a considerable help as I tried to explain what we were doing there.

It was the press card that saved us, because to get one of those you have to be vetted by the police anyway and they ran it through their system and gave us the all clear. It was then they told me about a tip off that an ETA cell was heading through…

By then it was way too late to find anything to eat in St Lary. So two words of wisdom: never look for anything to eat in a ski resort out of season and for journalism students, always have your press card with you – it can provide more than free food at corporate hospitality sports events – it can in fact save your life if you come face to face with nervous anti-terrorist police.

***

The Red Brigades

Unlike ETA, 'reformed' members of the Italian extreme left terrorist organisation the Red Brigades had been allowed unofficially to settle in France under Francois Mitterrand as long as they lay low and kept out of trouble.

Many chose relative anonymity in Paris and I met some of them there. In a strange twist, some have gone back to Italy in recent years while other wealthy Italians are now amongst the biggest foreign buyers of property in the French capital. Sergio Tornaghi is not one of them. He chooses to live in a farmhouse outside Bordeaux. Cocky, handsome, with an attractive wife and stunning daughters, he fled Italy more than 30 years ago as he was facing charges of killing a factory boss.

He has never been able to leave France since, as the extradition warrant against him still stands for any other country. He gets by doing computer repair work. He is always very coy about his exact role during the Italian 'troubles' but there is a newspaper photo from the period which seems to show him with a gun in his hand in some urban skirmish.

Every once in a while the police would turn up, arrest him and keep in him in custody, as the Italian government (especially under Silvio Berlusconi) tried to divert attention from other issues and focused on the exiled Red Brigades, demanding they be sent back to Italy. Each time, the courts dismissed the extradition requests and Tornaghi says the statute of limitations on his alleged crimes has now passed and he can no longer be charged with offences dating back to that period in Italy's troubled relatively recent history. He has always told me he is prepared to go back and explain his role as long as the Italian state examines its own conscience about that particularly sensitive period in the late 70s and early 80s.

However, since other ex-Red Brigades are still on the run including several in South America, the issue pops up from time to time and Sergio still gets my occasional visits.

***

Pre-Charlie Hebdo Islamist extremism

Even before the Merah shootings (more on that later) and the Charlie Hebdo newsroom massacre in January 2015, there had been a rapidly rising awareness that Islamic extremism on French soil was spreading and was to be found not just in the heavily immigrant populated housing projects on city outskirts or 'banlieues' as they are called here, but even in provincial towns with plenty of idle youth with bleak prospects.

But when I read a story about a group known as the 'Chechen connection', I found it to be something entirely different, almost surreal – their current situation would be comical, farcical even, if it weren't so downright dangerous.

Basically, they're a bunch of extremists of Algerian origin who had fought in the Caucasus region and then headed to France with plans to blow up the Eiffel tower and the American Embassy. Their plans were thwarted, they were sentenced and did their time but couldn't be sent back to Algeria as their safety couldn't be guaranteed. So France was forced to house them in rundown hotels across the country at great expense to the taxpayer. I did several stories on them, this one for the BBC maybe sums it up best.

The Tour de France of Crummy
Hotels for Islamist Radicals
From Our Own Correspondent
BBC Radio 4
September, 2011

You have to make a real effort to find the small town of Aiguebelle, surrounded by stunning countryside in the foothills of the French Alps. It has a population of just over one thousand and one hotel on the main street that to be honest has seen better days. In fact when I visited, there was just one guest staying there. Merouane BenAhmed arrived on the 16th June and for the time being has no scheduled checkout date. In fact to paraphrase the famous song 'Hotel California' by the Eagles, he can try to checkout but he may never leave. And that is because Merouane Benahmed was and may still be considered one of the most dangerous Islamic radicals on French soil.

He has just spent 10 years in jail accused of being part of the so called Chechen connection – a group of Islamic militants mainly from Algeria that fought alongside Chechen rebels against the Russians. When they were evicted from Georgia they returned to Paris where they were charged and sentenced to long jail terms for planning terrorist attacks on the Russian and American Embassies and the Eiffel Tower in the French capital.

Around ten of the group have now been released but the courts won't allow the French government to send them back to Algeria because their safety cannot be guaranteed. As Merouane BenAhmed told me in a dingy, poorly lit hotel room where he cooks, eats and sleeps, a death sentence hangs over his head in Algiers because he took part in the civil war there too, fighting against the military backed government. And for many of the other members of the Chechen connection it's the same story.

So the French State is stuck – it can't send them home and nobody else wants them and yet they have served their sentences. So until a solution emerges they are being housed separately in cheap out of the way hotels in small villages and towns across France. The bill for the hotels, food and pocket money is being picked up by the French taxpayer and this could go on for years. The proof: another of the group who was released three years ago has been living in hotels since then. He gets moved on from region to region after hotel owners and their unwilling guest get sick of each other. You could say they're on their own respective Tours de France.

Merouane Benahmed's average day is punctuated by four daily visits to the local police or Gendarmerie where he has to check in at 9am, 1, 3 and 6pm without fail. If he doesn't, he could go back to jail. At the same time he is confined to the village. His authorised area is 750m in length and 250m in width which means he will never get a chance to visit the beautiful national park just outside the village limits.

He told me that he has been released from one jail and simply put in another one, far from his family and friends and with nothing to do. One obligation he also has is to show evidence each month that he is actively looking for a country that is prepared to take him in. Needless to say with his CV and background, takers are scarce. Sitting together at his new local café within the inclusion zone, he asked me if I could think of any country that might be willing to give him a second chance to resume a normal life. My geopolitical knowledge failed me – I admit I was lost for words.

Another member of the Chechen connection is Menad

Benchellali. He was nicknamed 'the Chemist' by the French media when he was sentenced because in court prosecutors alleged he tried to create chemical explosives in his flat. He spent 9 years in jail too but unlike the rest of the group has greater freedom of movement because he has French as well as Algerian citizenship. But there is no question his movements are closely monitored by the French police. He spends his time visiting the rest of the group isolated in their village hotel rooms, trying to keep their morale up.

He said the situation is ludicrous: they have served their time – give them a chance to rebuild their lives in France since nobody else wants them.

They are unlikely to receive much compassion from the French state or a groundswell of popular support, so their French lawyer, Bérenger Tourne, is using a different approach – he's pointing to wasteful state spending.

With the French government (like most of its neighbours) desperately looking for ways of cutting the budget, he points out that the French taxpayer is coughing up around €600,000 a year to look after his clients – surely it would be cheaper to relax the restrictions over them and let them work and even pay taxes. On the surface it doesn't seem like the strongest of arguments but it doesn't seem like either the French State or the long term hotel residents have a lot of other options available...

That was in 2012 and since then Merouane BenAhmed has been back in the news again. He kept getting moved on and of course each time the latest town chosen to 'host' him discovered his past there was local outcry. What the French State really wanted was for him to do a runner and that is exactly what happened – some Middle-Eastern looking men picked him up at his latest hotel residence in western France in September 2016 and he disappeared. He was later traced to Switzerland. It remains to be seen whether France will make a passionate effort to have him extradited...

The Silly Season

Pig Squealing

From June to September, France has a lot of festivals and while I haven't done a scientific study, I am sure there is a far greater concentration of absurd 'cultural' events in southern France than elsewhere in the country. Naturally with news slow on the ground during those months, they made ripe pickings for me and were particularly lapped up by Reuters TV and the BBC.

Take the Pig Squealing championship...

From Our Own Correspondent
BBC Radio 4
August 2010

Finding the village of Trie-sur-Baïse is not easy. But the journey through an extraordinary part of rural south-western France is well worth it. Once you leave behind the gleaming modern factories of aeroplane manufacturer Airbus on the western outskirts of Toulouse, you quickly drive through hectares of sunflower fields and smooth rolling hills. Signs along the road make it clear you are in foie gras and Armagnac country. Soon the Pyrenees Mountains with all year round snow on their peaks loom ahead and then finally, after criss-crossing a lot of villages along winding roads, you find signs indicating the village of Trie-sur-Baïse.

At this time of year, there are hundreds of festivals across France but the one in Trie has to be one of the weirdest (and hardest to reach). The French Pig Squealing Championship attracts hundreds of tourists each year. The village more than doubles in size. With temperatures hovering around 30°C, spectators roast under a long canvas tent in the former farmers' market as competitors take to the stage to mimic the sounds of a pig.

A powerful sound-speaker system blasts out the squeals – even now my eardrums are trembling. But the five judges, all local VIPs, don't settle for the simple sounds of oinks.

With marks out of 50, competitors have to recite the various stages of a pig's life from birth to sexual reproduction right up to slaughter for the inevitable local cassoulet stew. That means the pig squealers – dressed up as pigs, naturally – are actors more than anything.

Either as solo acts or working in pairs they have to convey what pigs sound and look like when mating, just in case you had ever wondered. And it all ends in tragedy as the pigs squeal in terror and agony as their throats are cut. The sounds are horrific but apparently very realistic.

The winners this year are a pair of truck drivers – Noël and Bruno from Normandy in the north-west of France. Bruno had an advantage – inside knowledge. He was surrounded by hog sounds as a child brought up on a pig farm. The judges said the winners had interpreted with extraordinary accuracy the sounds a pig makes at various stages of its usually short life. They take home a trophy, €800 and yes, they get their 15 minutes of fame as they appear *in the local press and on the radio. They even received international coverage thanks to a team of 4 from South Korean TV who were also in Trie to witness and broadcast this cultural event on the Korean Peninsular.*

The French Pig Squealing Championship is now in its 35th year. Foreign tourists, mainly from northern Europe, and local holiday makers from the Southwest make up the majority of the audience. Most said it was extremely amusing and really really odd.

Championship Director Jean-Claude Duzer told me if you are looking for intellectual stimulation this is not the place or time for it. He says life is heavy enough as it is, wouldn't it be miserable without some absurdity. But when this championship was first created it was actually a cry for help.

The south-west of France may now be the world's foie gras capital but it was once a major pig breeding region – not for nothing is the local cassoulet stew or Toulouse sausage known worldwide.

Trie-sur-Baïse used to have the biggest pig farmers' market in France. Every Tuesday, 8000 pigs would be sold here. But business began to drift north to large scale farms in Brittany. Small pig farmers and butchers in Trie got together to launch the pig squealing championship to promote their business.

If that was the aim, they failed – the market closed down for good in the 1980s. Most small pig farmers went out of business or retired, no-one took over the farms. The Championship organiser Jean-Claude Desbats told me this festival is part nostalgia – remembering an artisan industry that no longer exists.

The population of Trie and surrounding villages was around 10,000 thirty years ago – now it's down to 3,500. The younger generation abandoned the countryside; wealthier second home owners moved in. But small scale pig breeding in the area is now trying to make a comeback, counting on a population more aware of how meat is produced and turned off by large scale food production.

The local black pig known as the 'Noir de Bigorre' was almost extinct 30 years ago. Foodies rave about the incredible taste of the pork but probably talk a lot less about the cost of this meat...

With the black pigs roaming free and fed on acorns, they have become a symbol of a more environmentally friendly form of breeding and a taste to die for. The regional council is now pouring money into trying to resuscitate the black pig industry. But it's still in the early stages and for the time being, the performers on stage were unable to tell me if the mating sounds of a black pig differ from a traditional hog. But they all vowed to return next year and try to claim what in this region at least, is considered a much sought after prize.

Since that story, the pig squealing championship has ceased to exist. It's difficult to know why. Some in the village found it too weird, others say it came down to simple economics – it was costing way too much – others say they simply couldn't find enough contestants each year prepared to perform on stage[21].

***

---

21 The editor of Reuters television in Paris, Yann '*How much*' Tessier at the time, put a headline on my video script: "The French act like pigs" and almost got lynched. Apparently outraged French journalists at the agency complained and it took him a very long time to explain the headline, story and well yes you saw it coming, to save his bacon. I called Yann "How much" because that was usually the first thing he said to me when I pitched an idea to him – it usually meant he liked it but didn't like how much I would charge him for it. In return he said I was a little like a drug peddler, hinting at a decent story for him, allowing him to sniff the bag but then retracting it and saying well do you like it, kids?

Snail Racing

The international snail racing competition in the small village of Lagardère in the Gers was another favourite. Even the organisers couldn't understand why I was there as it takes nearly 3 hours to drive there from Toulouse and occurs on the 15th August which is a Catholic public holiday and usually the last long weekend for the French before the return to reality and work in September. You almost got the feeling that they felt their sporting festival was so ridiculous that they would rather the outside world didn't know too much about it.

The competition amounts to a bunch of tables painted like target boards and wiped down with liquid to get the snails to move faster. Each participant places a snail in the middle of the table and hopes his or her racer gets to the edge faster than the others. Each snail has its shell painted in special colours and a number to distinguish it from the others. A master of ceremonies dressed in drag provides live commentary. At the end of the day, everyone sits down to eat snails that have stewed in massive metal tubs all day. The village itself has no particular historical connection to snails, the locals simply decided one day to launch an idea for the summer and the competition has now been happening every summer for over four decades. The 'international' element by the way, comes down to the odd UK family with a second home there that gets their kids to take part.

But thanks to my coverage, the village has got GLOBAL recognition. After the London Olympics I managed to pitch the story on the lines: 'the Games are over – but the sport continues...' Thanks to Reuters syndication, even the Chicago Tribune (how slow a news day was it over there?!) went for it with the headline "Ready steady Slow". CBS News affiliates didn't have much to run that day either, it seemed. They took my story, chopped it around a little and came up with this.

LAGARDÈRE, France (CBS) – As Usain Bolt was hanging up his running shoes after the 2012 Olympic Games on Sunday, the world's fastest snails were descending on the small French village of Lagardère for the next big event in the global sporting calendar.

"Welcome to Lagardere for the 49th World Snail Racing Championship. We are not in London but the sport continues" said Master of Ceremonies Jeff as he officially opened the contest.

Spectators described Lagardère as a lively village that has played host to the unusual event for more than 30 years, with tourists and locals alike flocking to the village in the Gers every August.

The rules are simple: the snails are placed in small red circles in the middle of round tables with the first to slime its way to the edge crowned the winner. But these competitors are not just fighting for a gold medal, they are fighting for their lives. The competition is followed by a feast served up to the spectators with snails cooked with ham, garlic, and tomatoes – the day's special. "We usually eat them and now before eating them we make them run. It's that simple!" Master of Ceremonies Jeff said. Despite these threats, the snails took the contest at a leisurely pace – it takes place over two hours with playoffs, semi-finals and a nail-biting grand finale.

According to organisers, this year's event was slower than usual with the 30°C heat making both the snails and their owners more sluggish than normal. "It's rather warm. I don't know if it helps the snails at all but it certainly helps people enjoy the rest of the celebrations!" said British tourist Julie.

Around 80 competitors take part who are invited either to bring their own snails or to hire them from the race committee. Spectators who had worked up an appetite during the afternoon tucked into the unlucky contestants in the evening in the traditional post-race meal. But Lagardère's mayor Patrick Dubos explained how one lucky individual *was spared:"We eat 375 pounds of snails tonight except the one that wins the race. It's given an amnesty just like in a bullfight," he said.*

No anthems were sung or medals awarded to the owner of this year's championship snail, a seven year old called Sebastian, but he was given the prestigious Snail Racing Trophy in recognition of his achievement.

***

Drinks with the Queen of Denmark

I had heard on the grapevine that the Queen of Denmark Margrethe II spent her summers at her château in the département of the Lot and while she avoided the media back in her kingdom, she would traditionally invite the Danish media down for a press conference at the start of her holiday which would then be followed by a drinks party with the Royal Household.

The odd locally based journalist would be invited too. I won't go as far as to say I gate crashed but I got myself onto the invitation list as I thought there could be a great story there, it's not like Queen Elizabeth would ever do something like this.

So sure enough, as Catherine and I were on holiday at our own home in the country about an hour and half from the Queen's, on one hot July morning, we went along with camera in hand to cover the royal press conference. This is the story I did that day for the international TV channel France 24.

France 24
August 2011

At this time of year many heads of state and leading politicians head to the south of France for their summer holidays. They are usually hidden behind high walled residences and the locals often have no idea they have VIPs in their own backyard. The Danes on the other hand, with a well-earned reputation for openness, do things differently. Queen Margrethe II invites the press to her home in the Lot region for a press conference and even for drinks. Her home is known as the Château de Caix.

The Queen and her French-born husband Prince Henrik have been coming here for decades. This year the royal couple's own security has been stepped up substantially in the wake of Muslim outrage against Denmark after cartoonists there drew caricatures of the Prophet Muhammad.

The Queen made clear she backed free speech at home. She said:"I think most Danes would agree that freedom of expression is very important and I think that is where the matter rests. I think in general as time goes by it will blow over as these things do."

Moving to a more positive note, the French government has also made clear lately that the Danish economic model is the one its most keen on copying, with its low unemployment and generous social security system.

The Queen said: "In many ways for someone of my age it's quite a surprise to find countries looking to Denmark for that kind of thing, because in Denmark we used to have quite a lot of unemployment. And suddenly people are looking to us which is really quite flattering."

The large media presence clearly left the royal pets unamused. The dogs are known for wandering out into the vineyards and getting lost – this time they have been equipped with GPS collars.

While the Queen says she will spend a lot of time buying fresh produce at the local market, her husband produces his own local wine – he says that will keep him busy over the summer. Prince Henrik admitted:"I am not a fortune teller so I don't know how my wine will turn out this year but it has a good reputation and I expect *this year it will turn out good too." His wine is naturally for sale at the château.*

In fact the royal presence is good for the local economy. The Danish go out of their way to visit the château too and buy royal merchandise spinoffs. It could be called 'voyeurism tourism'.

The locals aren't unhappy about the situation. The local mayor of the town of Luzech, Jean-Claude Baldy said: "It's true the economic benefits are there as tourists are here. They come to Luzech on purpose, and wouldn't otherwise be passing through. That allows them to discover the region which, I might add, is exceptional."

Not many royal heads of state invite the press to stick around and have a drink with them, but cameras were ordered to be switched off. Even among the Danes there is a limit to openness.

***

Truffles

Now normally you would associate the 'Silly Season' with the summer but of course off-beat stories happened all year around.

Anything to do with truffles is a case in point and one that my friend BBC World Service producer Eddie Horton, constantly referred to in mock dismay as 'that hairy chestnut' every time he saw one of my truffle stories on some bulletin or foreign correspondents running order.

Now south-west France produces truffles, but far fewer than say the Drôme region below Lyon or northern Italy, but somehow it manages to punch above its weight in terms of publicity and generates the impression that it's the only region in Europe that grows what is essentially a tree root fungus, although a rather expensive one.

The first story I did on truffles took me to a small village near the town of Lalbenque in the Lot département, where I had heard that an elderly peasant woman managed to make a lot of money with her own 'truffle safari'.

She would plant truffles in the woods near her house and then get her pet pig to look for them. Meanwhile a coachload of tourists would be dropped off to watch this 'authentic everyday peasant routine' take place. Replace the pig with a lion in the bush and you get the idea: dozens of tourists taking photos from a safe distance and this old peasant woman, seemingly on her own in the woods with a pig on a leash, scavenging.

Of course it also played up ideally to a certain British idea of what rural France was really like, and naturally it triggered a whole series of reports on the truffle industry whether it be business news, rural life in southern France or even criminality! Criminality you ask? Well, let me give you a clue: think how the lucrative trade encourages theft. Here is a story I did on that for BBC Radio 4.

From Our Own Correspondent
BBC Radio 4
February 2013

It's early Tuesday afternoon in the medieval village of Lalbenque. Like so many villages in this part of south-west France it's very attractive and well preserved and you would expect it to also be eerily quiet. But it's anything but. The main entrances are closed off. Wandering through the main street are elderly men and women with wary eyes and firm grips on small baskets.

Their desire to keep their baskets' contents safe from preying eyes is understandable because they contain truffles or 'black diamonds' as they are known down here.

Truffles can sell for up to €1000 a kilo and once a week farmers sell them in the local market. In this part of France, black truffles – which can grow to the size of your average potato – are found in shallow soil on the roots of oak trees. Thanks to the local earth and weather conditions they thrive in this part of the country.

Hundreds of cooking enthusiasts flock to the market to buy a truffle or two to put into omelettes.

Brokers buy up truffles for restaurants around France. Some chefs prefer to come and smell the merchandise themselves like the dapper, trilby hat wearing local dandy and Michelin star restaurant owner Alexis Pelissou.

Down here he is treated like a rock star and comes each week with a large canvas bag to snag several kilos. He told me his black diamonds will be shaved and sprinkled over foie gras or an omelette.

A whistle is blown at 2.30pm to announce the start of trading and there is little time for haggling.

Tourists who have to come to photograph this slice of rural French life have to fight for space and take their photos fast. Within 20 minutes everyone has sold their 'diamonds' as the buyers have smelt and negotiated their purchases discreetly, ahead of the whistle. Like at the close of day on the US commodity markets, the local radio and newspapers are on hand to get the latest on truffle prices — are they up or down, how many kilos sold and the quality compared to the week before.

And this year when it comes to quality and quantity, both figures are definitely down. Guy Dehler is a local truffle hunter. His beagle, Matrix, can sniff them out amongst the oaks next to his home. But this year there are not many around. He told me that there is a real shortage because there was very little rain over the summer followed by a deep frost in late December. He says many farmers in the area are struggling to get by and truffles are their own sort of annual bonus, helping boost their incomes especially as trading tends to be cash in hand.

And shortages have triggered a new problem – thefts. Poaching has always existed but it took an ugly turn over Christmas in another region of southern France, La Drôme. A farmer shot dead a man he claims was hunting for truffles on his land. He says he was acting in self-defence and dozens of truffle farmers demonstrated outside the police station where he was being held, in a show of support for their colleague. Around Lalbenque nothing so dramatic has occurred but the local police or 'Gendarmerie' are stepping up their patrols. That means getting out of their vans and using mountain bikes to cover the vast and hilly woodland. They also keep a highly visible watch on the Tuesday market, looking out for anything suspicious.

Captain Gérard Catala explained to me that truffle hunting requires a certain expertise as well as local knowledge, so often it turns out the criminals are truffle farmers stealing from each other. Gangs have been known to steal dogs with a reputation for a good nose to put them to work.

Alain Ambialet runs the local truffle farmers union — yes, there is one. He says most of the thefts occur during the day either when there is heavy mist, or when there is a funeral service, leaving poachers several hours free to roam while the church is packed. But if the weather and thieves weren't enough to give truffle farmers the winter blues, another formidable foe is here to stay – globalisation. Even truffle farmers in deepest France can't avoid it. It's come in the form of Chinese truffles at a tenth of the price.

It's no great surprise to hear that farmers here say the Chinese version is flavourless, and that in a clear act of protectionism they want the government to introduce a law requiring all Chinese truffles used in restaurants to be labeled as such. And if that doesn't work, they want a law limiting how many tonnes of the Chinese version can be imported. That hasn't stopped the odd French truffle seller from putting a Chinese one in the basket and trying to sell it at the market.

Local authorities now check the baskets before the market starts to make sure they are the genuine local article. They say the French truffle is far darker in colour than its Asian counterpart. Meanwhile, it's not just the farmers feeling down. The sniffer dogs like Matrix are feeling the hard times too. They don't like the taste *of truffles but each time they find one they get a treat to encourage them on to the next one. And with so few around, the rewards come far less frequently too.*

***

The Oyster Police

Another silly season story with a criminal theme that comes around each year is oysters. France is the third biggest consumer of the shellfish after the United States and Japan. And being a big fan myself, there is something I find warm and positive in seeing shoppers in France dashing around just before Christmas or New Year's searching for oysters for their various celebrations. It seems so much more civilised, sophisticated and fun to see people enjoying food like that and making it part of their annual festivities, rather than dutifully buying groaning supermarket trolley-loads of mass-marketed processed stuff to be eaten just as dutifully.

There's a statistic I have heard several times – unfortunately nobody official in the medical world has ever been able to back it up, but I like it so I will repeat it here: apparently the most common reason for emergency visits to casualty wards over the Christmas period in France is people slitting their wrists by accident trying to open oysters. And I have in fact injured myself several times doing just that.

Just before Christmas each year, the French media do their story on the oyster thieves lurking in the foggy inlets of Brittany and the Bay of Arcachon. So naturally I had to go out with police to hunt down these criminals.

French military police are out in the Bay of Arcachon near Bordeaux. But they are not looking for international terrorists, drug dealers or illegal immigrants. No, what they are looking for are oyster thieves.

This bay contains some of the most famous oyster beds in the world and they are being plundered by professionals and re-sold elsewhere. Captain Eric Delain is with the Arcachon military police. Out on the water he tells me: "Oysters thieves steal one or two tonnes with each raid and have special boats and knowledge of the bay in order to know where to find the oyster beds and steal them discreetly and quickly."

Far out in the bay the police come across oyster farm workers in freezing fog. A quick check reveals this is their patch and they are urged to be careful. Their oyster beds are so far from the shoreline and out of sight, they are particularly vulnerable. Mamadoud is an oyster farmer with thick, raw hands. He says: "It's a big problem – if people steal our oysters it means we don't have enough to sell and we lose money especially as this is the most important time of the year for us to do business."

This is traditionally the busiest time of the year for oyster traders – the French are the biggest oyster eaters in Europe and 70 percent are consumed over Christmas and New Year. And that's why thefts are so high at this time of year. But according to the police it also turns out the thieves are none other than oyster farmers down on their luck stealing from each other. Why? Because of the poor weather conditions here, many oysters didn't develop properly and they are relatively scarce this year. Many professional oyster farmers are stealing from each other to make up for the lost revenue.

Some farmers have had around 10 percent of their production stolen. Oyster farmers have formed their own 'neighbourhood watch' scheme, keeping their eyes open for any suspicious activity in an *industry where workers say little and keep to themselves. And yes the oyster farmers have their own union. Marc Druart runs it: "We all have flat aluminium style boats. In the past, farmers had different coloured boats which were easy to identify but these days at night or at dusk its difficult to see who is out on the bay in a fast moving oyster boat especially as all the vessels look the same – so it's difficult to catch anyone."*

The thieves may be professionals but most of the oyster openers are amateurs. People cutting their wrists accidentally while trying to open oysters make up a significant number of injuries in French hospital casualty wards over Christmas

***

Baywatch

Over the summers I would invariably be called by news desks to chase down a politician, a magistrate, celebrity, journalist, etc. who was in the news back home and of course was on holiday in the south of France. Often the call from the BBC Foreign Desk was to go and knock on someone's door in Nice, as I was in the south after all. When I pointed out it was a 5 hour drive away the response was usually: "Oh, I didn't realise... Well can you still go?"

The number of beach stories I did I can no longer keep tabs on. When I first started I had a reasonably small sony camera – a PD150 it was called – and it was an amazing piece of equipment at the time. Except it had some unexpected disadvantages. I once did a story in the resort La Grande Motte near Montpellier. It's famous for its 60s pyramid style landmark buildings on the waterfront. It was all intended for the higher end tourism market but things didn't turn out that way. The beach resorts there are the nearest southern France has to Benidorm. So, in an effort to clean up the town's reputation, the local mayor decided to enforce a ban on women wandering through the town in bikinis and men shirtless.

I went out with the municipal police as they tracked down offenders, all rather good fun of course. But my cameraman Michel Bousquet almost got lynched. At one point I went to a café for a drink while he went to the beach to film topless bathers, etc. A couple of suspicious boyfriends threatened to knock his teeth out for filming like some dirty pervert. When he reassured them he was doing a report for the BBC, it didn't quite seem convincing with the very compact, handheld camera he had... Nevertheless, when I eventually traded that Sony in, it was like saying a final farewell to a long time family pet.

Another frequent story involved the riot police or *CRS* on 'Baywatch duty'. The CRS are usually deployed for days on end in cities, waiting for a riot to take place in a rough neighbourhood, or a street demonstration to turn ugly – they don't have the best reputation.

One of the annual perks of the job is to become lifeguards on the beach during the summer where they still maintain order and arrest troublemakers but get to dress in shorts and t-shirts with 'CRS' printed on them. It's a lot more fun than dealing with burning cars and dodging stones thrown from high rises. And for the younger ones, kicking off after work on the beach usually means a chance to pick up lots of scantily dressed beach-goers.

So who can blame them for expressing outrage and holding their own demonstrations each time the Ministry of the Interior back in Paris questions whether it's really a good use of taxpayers' money, sending CRS to be lifeguards for two months a year. Despite years of threats and attempts to stop the tradition, they still get that summer job opportunity by lobbying, alongside beach town mayors. Together, each summer they preach the same foreboding message: without the CRS presence on the beaches, these resorts would descend into summer anarchy.

Of course after the Bastille day lorry attacks in Nice in 2016, the CRS made a big return to the beaches. Not only are they more numerous now, but their beachwear discreetly hides handguns, as the great summer fear of an Islamic beach massacre similar to that in Tunisia in 2015 is now one of the key preoccupations of the authorities over the summer months.

I had plenty of other summer stories to do over the years. While my regular beat was the Southwest, unsurprisingly at that time of the year I had to make quite a few trips along the coast between Marseille and Nice.

One such story concerned Mediterranean yacht thieves. What?! you ask... There was a spree of gangs (mainly from Eastern Europe) prowling along the Côte d'Azur, stealing boats – some of them very big ones – and selling them on to buyers who didn't ask too many questions, in places like Tunisia, or Ukraine. It was often a very sensitive issue for the French authorities, especially when one yacht ended up being found in a harbour in North Africa, owned by a half-brother of then Tunisian President Ben Ali.

The Toulon naval police had a special surveillance unit in the harbour and I got a chance to visit. A few men wearing large headphones listened in on conversations on boats across the Med, hoping to catch one of the gangs at work and then of course give the order to their colleagues out on the water to intercept suspects.

When I went out on the Gendarmerie's heavily armed boat on a scorching summer day, the authorities seemed more interested in pulling over and boarding massive millionaire-owned boats with lots of tanned, bikini-clad women than hunting down say Kosovar gangs. One of the police officers told me a few days earlier they had even managed to get onto Jennifer Lopez and her rap friends' hired yacht.

With no thieves in sight, the gunboat pulled into various ports along the coast and invited the local mayors to join them for the ride, a valuable PR exercise to keep the locally elected officials happy. The entertainment included lots of wine, and like I said it was extremely hot. By the time we arrived back in Toulon everyone was quite irritable from too much drinking and too much heat.

I myself have to admit my four hour trip back home from Toulon was neither easy nor particularly responsible.

***

The Jelly Fish Police

One of my favourite 'pointless' stories was out on jellyfish patrol. Cannes had been hit hard by a jellyfish invasion. When I say hard, I don't mean anyone had actually died or suffered severe injuries and the tourism industry hadn't collapsed. But nevertheless, one hot summer, swarms of jellyfish – which are unpleasant – had reached the coast around Cannes.

In fact they are pretty common most years, but that year, the hot weather and higher than normal pollution levels scaring off jellyfish-eating fish, had seen their numbers grow. They didn't come to Cannes on purpose, rather than say neighbouring Antibes or Nice but the town had decided to take action: which meant putting up lines of floats to protect bathers and prevent the jellyfish from actually reaching the sealed-off shallow areas.

Nowhere outside those protected zones was actually off limits since the actual risk was no more than a sting and a nasty red mark to spoil the victim's revealing evening outfit look. But the mayor nevertheless set up a jellyfish patrol unit with his local police force.

I went out with them for the BBC travel program *Fast Track*. I am not really sure what the police were supposed to do, apart from tell bathers to beware of the jellyfish and where they could go to have lotion put on them afterwards at the nearest lifeguard hut. Sometimes they went out in small boats to see if a swarm of *Pelagia Nocticula* as they are officially known, were heading en masse to the coast and then decide to close the beaches down. Good luck with that in July.

When I went to the town hall to meet the mayor, Bernard Brochand, in his vast top floor office with an amazing view of the harbour and its super sized yachts owned or hired by the world's 1% community, he was actually fully engaged in watching the Tour de France on a big screen.

Turning to me, he said with a chuckle, why is the BBC interested in jellyfish? He just couldn't get over that... fair point it has to be said.

Apart from being paid for that story, I had a friend of a friend living near Cannes, Claire Hanna, a gorgeous blonde who sadly was not single, but who had two other beautiful friends with her too, and going out for cocktails with them in that beautiful setting was pretty good for the ego.

Soon after my jellyfish story the mayor had other things to worry about, all of a sudden, he was no longer mayor and under investigation for kickbacks and an undeclared Swiss bank account.

***

The Village that Banned Dying

There was a 'golden' period when any oddball story from rural France would be snapped up by the news organisation that I called first, including the BBC. Especially the BBC. As Eddie Horton, a one-time commissioning producer pointed out, the BBC's audience is largely made up of middle class people who daydream of living in south-west France throughout their working day, so any offbeat story from there lulls them to sleep at their desks.

So when I heard that a mayor in a small, bland, flat village, alongside the Biarritz-Toulouse autoroute had officially banned his residents from dying due to a lack of space in the graveyard, I knew it was a winner. I gave this story to Reuters TV and the BBC. Here it is.

The mayor of a small village in south-west France has issued a local decree banning his residents from dying within the village limits. He says if they break the law and die they will be severely sanctioned. He hasn't said what the sanction is, but they will find out when it happens.

The Mayor of Sarpourenx Gérard Lalanne has taken the drastic action because a French court in the nearby town of Pau has refused to give him planning permission to build an extension to the graveyard. He says he has a plot of land available to build a graveyard but his application was turned down by local officials. He says his order banning residents from dying is necessary and no joke because the current graveyard is full and there is absolutely no space left.

The village of Sarpourenx has less than 300 residents and none have died since the new ruling came into force. But the mayor said even though his residents are in good health, anyone can get sick and die suddenly. He hopes his publicity stunt will encourage the court to take another look at his planning project before it's too late.

This story even got lots of air time on BBC World News, so it must have been a very slow news period. A few months after I did that report, I read in the local paper *Sud-Ouest*, that after the town council got its way and was able to expand the cemetery, the mayor died unexpectedly... and was duly buried in his village.

***

The Vegetarian Foie Gras Correspondent

A few years go there was a vegetarian agriculture minister in Wales and she didn't get a very warm welcome from farmers.

In my case, reporting on the single biggest industry in the département of the Gers as a vegetarian was a little uncomfortable for everyone, including myself. Now strictly speaking I am not a vegetarian as I can eat lobsters and oysters washed down with a glass of dry Blanquette de Limoux any time you ask, but as for actual meat, no thanks, and it's been that way since childhood.

The camera crews I worked with were always delighted to get rich lunches and take home jars of freebies. I tried to reassure the farmers that if I was vegetarian it was because eating meat gave me allergies, and that I would cover their work fairly, but it was always awkward. I had more luck dealing with Roquefort cheese makers near Millau. I love the blue cheese and when tariffs were hiked on imports to the US as part of a trade war, I often went up that way to see how the farmers were getting on during the international squabble (and to stock up on free cheese).

Roquefort was considered a luxury item and singled out because the Europeans wouldn't import US cattle injected with hormones.

But the thing is, foie gras proved to be a 'rich' source of material from so many angles: countries banning the French export on grounds of cruelty; stories about animal rights activists promoting a vegetable pâté alternative. There were even the hippie farmers in the Dordogne that I met who use the excess fatty oil from their organic, corn-fed birds to run their diesel tractors on homemade biofuel.

It was a BBC producer, Gordon Harcourt, who hit the nail on the head when he referred to foie gras as French peanut butter.

I can't count the number of times I was sent out as the industry was facing yet another wipe-out because of a bird flu epidemic. Even as recently as February 2017, I returned to the Gers to see farmers told to destroy their ducks in a government ordered mass culling. From a business angle there were lots of possibilities too. Like I said, in the département of the Gers, something like 30,000 people are employed in one way or another in the making and distribution of foie gras. In the small Tarn town of Gaillac there is a Muslim halal foie gras producer (his wife is Catholic and this way both could celebrate in the Christmas spirit and at the same time seize a huge market opportunity).

Then there was the 'Will the French continue to buy foie gras – a luxury food – over the Christmas and New Year holiday period despite the economic crisis?' I did that story several years running until the Reuters bureau chief in Paris, Yann 'How much' Tessier called me out saying: "I think that foie gras shopper made her mind up on that a few years ago, don't you?"

A line I have heard many times from foie gras farmers is

how force-feeding their ducks and geese is natural – after all, in the wild they have to fill up with food before heading off on their long migratory trips south... So in fact it's their instinct that drives them towards the farmer to receive a tube rammed down their throat to stuff them with more corn.

And yet although it's not a pretty sight to see ducks held by their necks and barely able to waddle, it's never made me angry to the same extent as say some slaughter houses and the barbaric cruelty they show. Maybe it's because the foie gras farmers I met and were willing to have me there, observing, were more humane in their approach compared to big agribusiness. Also, the ducks often weren't in cages but out in the open when not being fed, and their life spans are very short anyway as they will be killed within a few months – unlike some animals on factory farms, reared in cages for years.

And I have another confession to make – a couple of times I have been at receptions drinking champagne and picked up a petit four or some finger food thinking it was a chocolate eclair, only to discover there was in fact foie gras inside... My initial reaction is always 'that's not so bad', swiftly followed by psychological revulsion.

One evening, I joined friends at a bar in Toulouse after a day trekking through a duck farm. A sparkly cute English girl over visiting said: "I've heard about you, you're the foie gras correspondent aren't you?"

Football

Fabien Barthez

Of course silly season stories didn't have to occur in summer and sometimes they didn't even have to be true. The small town of Lavelanet is in the foothills of the Pyrenees in the Ariège département. It's considered locally as a natural contender for the Gallic version of hillbilly country in the Appalachian Mountains, USA.

The town used to be industrious and busy thanks to the textile industry. But like so many other towns dependant on shoe, glove, hat and clothing manufacturing, it hit hard times from the 70s onwards due to cheap imports first from North Africa and then from Asia. With the factory closures, it didn't have a lot going for it until 1998 and the World Cup. The link you see, is Fabien Barthez – he comes from the town and his family still live there – his sister is the local tobacconist.

After France's `98 World Cup victory, the local café (called *Le Rap*) naturally became a living shrine to the French goalkeeper and there was no shortage of local people who ran the local football club ready to take credit for spotting Barthez's talent in goal, including the elderly gentleman Aimé Goudou who said that at the time, Barthez wanted to play up front and it was he, Aimé, who explained to the young player where his natural position clearly was…

Anyway, after World Cup glory, of course he was a national hero and when he went to play for Manchester United it was assumed he would conquer hearts and minds there too. Except he didn't and the British tabloids at times referred to him as a clown (of course players have been called far worse by the red tops). Anyway, spotting an opportunity, I approached the mayor of Lavelanet and said their favourite son was being treated as a circus act on the other side of the Channel and surely they should express outrage and come to the rescue, and naturally the BBC was the place to make those feelings clear. It didn't take long to get them stewing and ready to come out vocally, so I called up the BBC and said Fabien Barthez's hometown folk were outraged at the treatment their star had been receiving and they wanted to defend his honour.

Needless to say, BBC Sports jumped at the opportunity. So off I went to explain how the local football club was demanding respect for Barthez from the English, and how the mayor and several members of the town council had drawn up a statement defending the reputation of their favourite goalkeeper.

Interestingly the only ones who wouldn't play ball so to speak were members of Barthez's family.

The story that I filmed didn't just air on BBC Sports, I also spoke to the Times correspondent in Paris, Adam Sage, telling him that the small town of Lavelanet was up in arms over the treatment Barthez was getting, and of course he ran the story too, with my quotes.

It all gets me thinking this is probably how a lot of wars get started.

***

Luzenac FC – *The Mouse that Roared and then got Stepped on*

I didn't have any more dealings with Fabien Barthez for the next decade. While he continued to live in Toulouse, he had focused on motor car racing and he had a reputation for being prickly – wary of the media and lashing out at them whenever journalists came knocking, especially when they came for comment on the ever sinking French side after that 4 year period of glory up to 2000 when they also won the European Championship.

So it wasn't until 2014 that I came across him again. As I said, Barthez came from the Ariège département; where, he had become an unofficial partner of a local football club in the small village of Luzenac which is off the main road between Foix and Andorra.

It's not the kind of place you are likely to visit deliberately. Most people use that main road to go skiing, or for duty-free shopping in Andorra, but stopping in Luzenac is not part of their itinerary. However the village is also home to a big talc quarry. Money generated from that industry helped fund the local football club, Luzenac FC. Through some extraordinary hard work, a little bit of luck and some amazing signings, the club kept rising and rising and unbelievably it found itself in the 3rd division called the *Nationale*. But as if that was not enough, on 18th April 2014 they won 1-0 against a team from northern France, and direct promotion into the second division – with five games in hand.

I was there. Here is the story I did at the time for the BBC World Service Radio programme *World Football*, but be warned, this one does not have a fairy tale ending.

Dreams can come true, according to the saying. And for one small football club in southern France they really have and will inspire thousands of small Saturday morning sides around the world.

Luzenac FC – village population of 650 – was in the regional league 10 years ago – next season it will be just one league below PSG and Marseille. The sound of thunder is in fact that of the supporters of Luzenac football club. It had just been promoted to the French League 2, the equivalent to the Championship division in English football and with 5 games to spare... This was the reaction of one player, Cameroon born Donna Indou: "We are very happy to create history in this small village, we are just like a family ... we just play our luck and it happened like that..."

In fact this tiny village club is full of surprises. Its goalkeeper Quentin Westberg with joint US and French citizenship had even played against the likes of Messi and Fabregas with the US Under-20 team.

"It's a great feeling, 'mission accomplished' – tiny club and great adventure, great group of guys. Hopefully it's only getting started. I am building my career and writing a new page of my career, five games before the end we got promoted so we obviously got something right – great chemistry, great group of guys."

Just 10 years ago, Luzenac resembled most other football clubs from villages with a population of 650. Except this village, in a valley in the French Pyrenees, next to a major road used by skiers on their way to the slopes, had two major factors working in its favour.

One was the wealthy local entrepreneurs who helped provide financial backing that improved the clubs facilities. Another was a neighbour – Fabien Barthez. The bald, quirky French World Cup Champion goalkeeper from the incredible '98 generation who played alongside Zidane and Didier Deschamps comes from the region and decided to take the club under his wing and share his experience.

Nicolas Marky the club director explains: "Fabien is a great professional and when he came he talked to the players and he has done a very good recruitment and takes good players and talks to the players every week and sometimes he takes the training for the goalkeepers and he built the medical structure of the club. Last year we had lots of injuries and this year none and we had all the players all the time."

As the club continued to get promoted, the village football pitch was no longer adequate as the number of supporters rose from 200 to 1500. Once in the third division, the club expanded its recruitment significantly, hiring from all across France.

The sudden rise means the club now has to find a new home – its current stadium in the town of Foix is not up to French League 2 standards. But that shouldn't be problem – promotion means with TV revenue, the club's budget has jumped overnight from €2 million to €6 million for next season.

Fabien Barthez told me where he got his club management inspiration from: "It's a fabulous story but it's just the start I hope, and I learnt everything in the French national team and working alongside Alex Ferguson and Manchester. It's the feeling of family and that's what I've tried to create at Luzenac. I have the same vision of football as Ferguson, Aimé Jacquet and Jean Tigana and I used the same values as them: solidarity, respect and humility, and that is what I found at Manchester which was one of the richest clubs in the world and also had simple but genuine values."

The squad are living on a cloud right now. They have gone from anonymity to overnight fame – all the major French TV channels have headed down to this mountain village to see what the fuss is all about and meet the team.

Already agents are calling the manager wanting to know more, and to get their players pay hikes now that the club is relatively cash rich. Luzenac is definitely on the map now.

I wrote that story in the week after that remarkable night when Luzenac qualified for the 2nd division. Except Luzenac was never to play in the 2nd division. The following season it was actually relegated to the 7th division!

French commentators like to say that France has the strongest second division football league in Europe. I'm not a sports expert but I find that analysis perplexing. How did they figure that out? I asked my expert friend Anthony Jeffers (who is a football commentator for the sports channel Eurosport) about that and he is just as mystified. He says its a good line to use, especially as it's one that simply can't be verified.

But what is clear is that the officials running French professional league football felt they had nothing to gain from having a small hick village team from the Pyrenees playing in their league, especially as Luzenac by now only had one local player. They no doubt felt it would make a mockery of professional football in France, just at a time when it was trying to earn international credibility – PSG was becoming one of the big cats of European football thanks to Qatari investment, and other clubs like Monaco and Lyon had big ambitions too.

And so when Luzenac were officially promoted, league officials told them they had to find a stadium that was up to League 2 standards to play in. Failing that, the club would not be accepted.

A frantic search got underway by the club to find a stadium, but each time they did, the League found a reason why it didn't meet their standards. It even went as far as the courts, and despite intense lobbying by Barthez, a huge media outcry and cries of 'shame!' from all quarters, Luzenac wasn't just denied promotion – it was demoted back to the 7th division. Its players, who had done the hard work, left the club in disgust or had already been signed up in the inter-season by other teams as scouts saw cheap talent. The club who had been counting on a massive windfall from League 2 promotion, had been scouting for new players and had made clear to some of the team who had earned the promotion that they would not be needed in the future. Volunteers who had been working at the club for years had handed in their notice in their real jobs as they looked to work full-time at the club in marketing, PR and generally running a professional club in League 2. As it became clear the club was going back to amateur days, they found themselves without their original jobs to go back to. Fabien Barthez quit the club entirely in disgust after that.

While rugby was the focus of most of my sports coverage, as you can see, football wasn't ignored. There was a brief period when Jean Tigana came back to France to coach Bordeaux and that seemed to have the UK based TV news agencies like SNTV very excited. I went there to see him many times and when he quit suddenly, he didn't realise how much that hurt me financially! But the most fun was had going to meet France's equivalent to 'Big Ron' Atkinson though the French version is far richer.

Louis Nicollin was a hugely overweight wheeler-dealer type who knew no political correctness and became a billionaire in the waste disposal industry. To keep his garbage collectors (but clearly not himself) fit, he set up a football club for them in the 1970s.

Through mergers and investment, it turned professional and made the first division. Montpellier was less associated with football than it was with another sport – handball. The local handball team was highly successful and had its own stars. So Montpellier football club's image was personified by its outspoken boss Nicollin – better known by his nickname Loulou – who brought the club recognition with constant and ever outlandish comments.

These are some of the things he is said to have said at random throughout the years: "I prefer Rolland Courbis to Carlo Ancelotti. Great coaches are the ones that win titles with half good players. Courbis, he won promotion to League 1 with a half mongoloid team." Courbis, with his Marseille sandpaper voice and time in jail for various kickbacks on transfers, seemed a natural partner for Loulou. When he was picked to run the club, Nicollin came out with another gem: "I couldn't care less so long as he gets me into the top division. If he had been selling drugs or raping young girls, I wouldn't accept that. But I don't worry about such silly things." Another time it was: "Well done Bastia! They have bigger balls than us. We have shrivelled olives instead."

Well, you get the idea. He was called 'pagnolesque' which referred to a certain type of southern French character (after the French writer Marcel Pagnol, he of *Jean de Florette* fame).

During the 2011-12 football season, Paris St Germain (PSG) had already been bought by a Qatari Investment fund that had started buying players with big international reputations for sums the like of which French football had never seen before. Montpellier, with the 10th biggest budget in French football, found itself at the top of the table, partly thanks to intelligent transfers like Olivier Giroud… For the first time, I was getting requests to go down there and see what was up with this club, Montpellier.

The first press conference I attended there was also my first encounter with Louis Nicollin. He waddled into the woeful pre-fabricated hut that acted as the press centre for the club. It was packed regardless, as regular media visitors to the club knew he couldn't hold back and would always say something worth reporting.

A lot of questions were asked about the possibility his club could end the season in the top 3 and win a Champions League place for the first time. After a moment he turned to his sultry press officer Katia (who was wearing a very short skirt and high boots) and said:

"Enough with the Champions League nonsense, if you all think we are going to be in the top 3 then fine – Katia and I can just head off to a hotel somewhere, make whoopee and let you get on with the rest of it. What do you think Katia?"

She squirmed a little, no doubt fearing the offer might be more serious than it seemed on the surface. Like I said, he wasn't thin. He was actually obese (and that's what finally killed him)[22].

After a few questions from me, Nicollin realised it wasn't a French journalist asking him questions and asked what the hell I was doing there. When I said Montpellier was making news outside France he said he was flattered and then spent the rest of the time mocking me, chuckling and wondering out loud what the 'Engleesh' was doing here. And then he invited me to see his private museum, on his ranch outside the city.

The farmhouse where he lived was staggering – out on the flat humid plain outside Montpellier, on the edge of the Camargue marshes. It was filled with horses and mosquitoes and it was spectacular. As we drove through the gates of his ranch, it was one of those times when you say to yourself you are lucky to have a job that allows you to have these kind of encounters.

The museum is just extraordinary too and you don't even have to be a sports fan to be dazzled. It's vast – on two floors with 3 full time curators, and you need an electric golf buggy to visit. It's stuffed with football and rugby memorabilia from around the world, including shirts worn by sporting legends. He would send his scouts out across the globe to acquire new objects when they become available.

As Montpellier got closer and closer to the title, my appearances at the club became more and more frequent. I discovered from Loulou that his English was not great and the only kind of words he picked up were things like 'blow job'. No trouble guessing where he discovered or was taught those words on his world travels. One newspaper column commented that when I didn't show up for one of his press conferences, he asked the assembled media where was the Engleesh? He hoped I was ok and nothing bad had happened to me... When Montpellier went on to win the

---

22 Louis Nicollin died in June 2017 from a heart attack while fittingly celebrating his 74th birthday at one of his favourite restaurants. He won't be replaced quickly in the staid world of French top division football ownership.

title and a chance to play Arsenal in the Champions League it was an extraordinary – but alas short lived – success. Giroud had left for Arsenal and their successful manager René Girard had had enough of his club president too and headed to a new club, in Lille, about as far away from Montpellier as you can get in France. Sadly I haven't found an excuse to return since the beginning of the 2012-13 season. As it is, Nicollin took a back seat to his son a few years ago and has since died so it's all a bit less exciting down there these days anyway. But between his semi-retirement and his death, sometimes he couldn't help himself come out with fresh outrageous comments when he found the force to get up and waddle with his cane from his chauffeur driven car to the club house microphones.

***

Corsican Football and the Mob

Ever since I moved here I have heard news stories about the beautiful, incredibly well-preserved, mysterious island of Corsica… which has a proportionally higher mob-related death count than Sicily.

Corsica is tarnished by a violent mix of mobsters, protection rackets and separatism. Shortly after my arrival in France, the island's Prefect, Claude Erignac, was shot dead. His replacement, Bernard Bonnet, was given orders to restore the state's authority on the island. So he told the police to burn a beach restaurant to the ground during the middle of the night and make it look like it was carried out by one of the local trouble-makers against a rival. It was a botched job and one of the police officers was badly burnt in the operation and smuggled secretly out of the island to a hospital in Toulouse for treatment.

The Prefect was sentenced to a prison term, but strangely not the police officers or gendarmes working under his command. They were just following orders – strange that… Didn't we hear that before about senior members of the French civil service during Vichy and the occupation etc. ? And weren't we told it was no longer tolerated?

The mobsters continued to wreak havoc long after that incident – usually killing rival gangs or politicians or decision-makers who had the final say on lucrative state run contracts and who dared organise 'bids to tender' – contracts with at least some honesty – or who handed the business to the wrong rivals. Many of the gangs were named after harbourside bars in Corsica where they tended to gather and collude.

Strangely, the jobs of hit men seemed to be pretty easy in Corsica because their targets appeared to be creatures of habit – during the morning anyway – always taking their coffee at the same café terrace. Usually they were shot dead at that very terrace or on their way to that café. And usually despite the good weather and number of people basking in the sun at the same café terrace, there were no eye-witnesses to these shootings.

One clan name that popped up on a regular basis was the Orsoni family and its patriarch Alain Orsoni. Accused of honour killings and bombings, Alain Orsoni and his extended family and network of friends were the archetypal group mixing separatism and gangsterism with ease. Most of the time Alain Orsoni found himself on the crime pages and one day I was stunned (and it seems a lot of others were too) when it was revealed he had become president of a first division football club – AJA, Ajaccio.

In fact on his return from a long stint in South America (where he had gone to stay alive during a particularly bloody period of tit-for-tat shootings on the island), he had taken over the professional football club that no-one paid attention to, and got it promoted to the first division[23].

Of course being the owner of a club brought a respectability that meant he was able to travel across France for away games and of course host visiting teams in the VIP suites and get to know every grandee in the sport in France. You can imagine the scene in the VIP box at PSG with the elite from the world of showbiz and politics including former President Nicolas Sarkozy, a big PSG fan. For Orsoni it was a position he clearly relished.

In much the same way the one-time New York mobster John Gotti liked to live a very public life in the media gaze, Alain Orsoni adored the media attention, despite frequently being called 'the last Godfather of Corsica'. Of course he had a nice line for that too, he would say to each visiting journalist, including me that he was indeed a godfather – to his godchildren.

I managed to persuade the UK-based TV sports agency SNTV to pay for me to go to the island to interview Orsoni. They went for it – this was back in the day when agencies had budgets for this kind of thing. So I drove to Marseille and took the overnight ferry arriving at 7am at the Corsican dock and there I was, just a couple of kilometres away from the club[24].

It was an impressive achievement getting the club into the French elite. But it sure had its underworld feel – all the managers wore cowboy boots and dark leather jackets; there was lots of hugging and chain smoking. Many of the people associated with

---

23 He resigned as president of Ajaccio football club in 2015 over the club's finances. It was struggling and had been relegated.

24 Sailing out of Marseille and along the coast at night is magical, as you see all the lights of the sprawling city squeezed in between the hills and the sea. The ferry itself was less magical. I had fallen for their marketing which promised luxury cabins and breakfast served there too, etc. There was a special deal at that period of the year but it was actually more of a throwback to Sealink days in the late 70s on boats between Dover and Calais pre-privatisation – the cabin had no windows and it felt like I was in a bunker. A bang on the door was the signal that breakfast had arrived – warmed over, almost stale bread and cheap orange juice served by a sailor with tattoos who grunted I had half an hour to get to my car.

the club's finances have died over the years in the strangest of circumstances. You couldn't make it up.

There's a shooting range on a cliff just above the club's training ground. A few years ago, a hired killer went to the range, turned his aim away from the target to another, below at the club, and shot dead one of the club officials with authority over contracts with local vendors.

Chain smoking Alain Orsoni with his Yves Montand looks was fine with a TV interview on the stands (just below that rifle club) but under no circumstances would he go anywhere outside the club gates nor do any filming in Ajaccio.

He spent most of his time in his village stronghold, Vero, and was driven to his club in a bullet-proof car. Sometimes he spends time in court rooms, usually trying to protect his son against accusations of revenge killings.

There was just a brief moment at the club – when I bumped into Orsoni having drinks in a small room near the main office with his cronies – when I thought maybe I was in for a serious beating. He seemed very annoyed to see me there. All it would have taken was a signal from him to his men. The tense situation didn't last long but it really did feel touch and go.

I ended up doing a report for the BBC on Alain Orsoni. However it had to go to the corporate lawyer's office first and it emerged rather watered-down. Here is what was broadcast.

From Our Own Correspondent
BBC Radio 4
March 2012

If you are big European football fan you probably browse the web for the latest gossip and results on clubs in the French first division too. But good luck if you look up Ajaccio Football Club.

The website is in Corsican – not French – a very political statement from a club where sport and politics definitely do mix.

Ajaccio, with a population of less than 100,000, is the capital of Corsica and its local team has amazingly risen from obscurity to top division football in just a few years – it even has several international players from Algeria and Mexico.

But the rise and rise of the club with the smallest budget in the French first division hasn't just raised interest from football fans but also from the French establishment, along with outright alarm.

To understand why, you have to meet the club's president – Alain Orsoni. With a passing resemblance to the late French actor and singer Yves Montand, the chain-smoking businessman can quickly swap easy charm and a warm, gravely voice with cold hard eyes and sudden silence.

For much of the French media he is nothing other than the last surviving Godfather of Corsica. He strongly refutes the label but his family – or 'clan' to others – is no stranger to the extraordinary political and underworld mafia-style violence that has marred the island for decades.

Alain Orsoni goes to work in a bullet-proof car and rather than sit in an amazing office overlooking the heartbreakingly beautiful Bay of Ajaccio, chooses for his own safety to work in a windowless concrete bunker deep inside the club. And you can't blame him – a gang tried to kill him a few years ago, his brother has been shot dead, his son is in prison in Spain accused of several family revenge killings, Alain Orsoni himself has been in and out of jail all his life accused of racketeering and ordering the killings of business and political rivals.

You could call him 'the teflon president because for the time being, none of the charges have stuck and as he told me with a chuckle, the French Secret Service have certainly done everything they can to try and bring him down. He admits he is no angel but says a myth has been created around his name. He ran a banned shadowy group that demanded independence for Corsica but also didn't hesitate to plant bombs and force businessmen from the French mainland (or 'the Continent' as they call it here) to pay a tax to do business on the island.

At one point he fled to central America for a decade but police have noted that since his return to Corsica to take over Ajaccio's football club, known by the acronym ACA, the island has seen a surge in killings. Last year 22 people were shot dead on the island. Corsica has a population of just 300,000.

Alain Orsoni says that with age he has calmed down. He says football has become his number one preoccupation and he claims that that is what really angers his enemies. Because with top league football status he is now a VIP and rubs shoulders with grandees at other clubs. He tells me he can understand why people are somewhat shocked or appalled at the thought of him running a top division football club.

He has gained a little respectability and with his family background, a slight sense of fear probably helps anyway when it comes to smoke-filled back-room negotiations with greedy players' agents. His club staff – tough-looking men all dressed in standard black leather jackets and jeans, hugging and greeting each other with kisses on the cheek – all adds to the image of a club that is a little different.

The club president told me he has abandoned politics but Ajaccio football club is a vehicle to promote Corsica's cultural identity through different means. Now that the club is in the first division, his ambition is to avoid relegation. And having been rock bottom most of the season it's suddenly gone through a renaissance, with a string of unexpected wins and wide open jaws across the French football world. But almost as a wake-up call, the first political/underworld murder of 2012 in Corsica was that of the former owner of Ajaccio's local football rival, Bastia. In Corsica, football is definitely a dangerous game.

Incidentally for background I had called Orsoni's well known Ajaccio-based lawyer, Antoine Scallaro, to get some more information about his long term client. He himself was shot dead a few months later – another victim of a local conflict that seems to be able to hold its own with Sicily when it comes to mafia violence.

I will probably get sued for referring to Bernard Tapie right after Alain Orsoni but when it comes to football there are a lot of bridges between Olympique Marseille and Corsica. Managers and agents work both sides, the mob has been accused of infiltrating both. The former OM club president Christophe Bouchet told me as much. In fact Olympique Marseille gave me lots of business over the years and would have provided a lot more if I had chosen to live in the city. In 2016 I even interviewed Frank McCourt – an American tycoon and the new owner of the club – for the BBC at his hotel in Paris which he wisely chose as his French headquarters rather than the port city itself.

In terms of attitude, you probably won't get better value for money then spending time at OM. And for expert advice on what is happening at the club, everyone goes to see the handful of fish stall owners on the edge of the Vieux Port.

Bernard Tapie's rise and downfall with OM are well known – including match fixing and subsequent jail time. But what people forget is that incredibly, he was given a second chance to run the club as a shareholder, by the Swiss owner at the time who seemed to be short of ideas. I was at the club the day Tapie returned in 2001. The atmosphere was pretty electric, fans didn't seem to believe it, neither did the players. Only the shaven headed beefy bouncers at the club seemed to think the good times were back.

In any case, that's the only time I have seen Tapie in real life. He was absolutely repellent in the few hours I saw him in the corridors of the club, a classroom bully and obnoxious to boot. His second coming at OM didn't last long – having promised to return the club to its glory days, he was gone within months with barely a beneficial ripple of an effect on the club.

But what I remember most about that 'return of the messiah' style day, was strict orders from Tapie himself that no-one was to film his press conference. Only the club could film it. There were dozens of cameras there and nearly everyone including myself agreed to toe the line. But TF1, the main independent channel which had sent down a small team including a well-known sports reporter was having none of this. They started filming and sure enough in front of me one of the shaven head security bouncers picked up the camera and smashed the lens to pieces against a table. No wonder the security people at OM thought the good times were back with Bernard.

I will never forget the ashen look of the journalist. But no hard feelings – later that evening TFI invited Tapie onto their main newscast in Paris as their exclusive guest, the little incident earlier at the club already forgotten. Things are rather different in France.

**

Zidane – *A Modern day Fairy Tale for One Town*

It was only a few years ago that I discovered that BBC World Service had a great half hour weekly programme – *World Football* and another, *Sports Hour* that would allow me to do the kind of off-beat stories that I did for example for *Business of Sport* for *World Business* on CNBC. The two editors, Richard Padula and Joel Hammer are just about the two most laid-back commissioning editors I've ever pitched to, but then again they also had a very laissez-faire attitude to paying me too!

Yes, it's true, radio pays a lot less but there is actually so much more autonomy and less hassle when you don't have to worry about video, image and all that equipment. People are quite frankly far more open to talk to you when there isn't a camera involved – none more so than Zinedine Zidane.

I got to meet him a couple of times before he became manager of Real Madrid's first team. There is no question he has an aura of mystery, comes across as modest even though he knows the effect he has on people, and basically personifies cool. Rather than going through my first encounter with ZZ here is the story I did for the BBC.

World Football
BBC World Service
April 2013

This story could be called a modern day fairy tale. What you have just heard is the master of ceremonies announce in front of thousands of fans packed into the local arena, the arrival of a new investor in person, his name Zinedine Zidane – one of the best football players of his generation.

The French world cup and champions league winner is now director of football at Real Madrid, the last club he played for professionally. So the question is what is he doing investing his money and time at Rodez Aveyron Football club, a struggling fourth division team in an isolated mountainous region of south-west France?

In typical Mediterranean cultural tradition, it comes down to family connections. Zidane's wife's family come from the town of Rodez and as the club owners realised he was spending time in the area with his in-laws, they plucked up the courage to see the star and ask him to help save the club – and it worked. Zidane explained the next day at the football club:

"I wanted to invest in this club because it needs it. Some people came to see me about their ambitions for Rodez Football Club and it seemed interesting. Things needed to be done and I wanted to help out like others are doing, whether sponsors, shareholders or volunteers. We are talking about the professional players but there is also the junior league and the young kids and all this is important for

the region and I am just one investor. Of course I am better known than most, but our goal is the same – to boost this team."

He says he sees no contradiction between the Spanish club that pays his wages and is hundreds of millions of euros in debt, and trying to save a tiny club that is hundreds of thousands of euros in the red itself.

"I come from the street, a difficult neighbourhood. I have never forgotten my roots. It's not because you work for the biggest club in the world that you forget everything beforehand. It's thanks to my in-laws that I have discovered this club and family. I love this region and spending time here and I feel at home here."

Neither Zidane nor the club will say how much exactly he is bringing in in fresh cash but his very presence triggered a windfall for the club. Zidane spent all weekend at the club, even taking part in an indoor football match with other veteran ex-pros. That brought a smile to the accountants, bringing in €60,000 for a club with an annual budget of €1.1 million.

Like many clubs in the lower leagues across Europe, Rodez has been hit hard by the economic tough times, as businesses and fans have less to spend. Jean François Théfault is president of Rodez Football club. He explained the situation:

"We had serious financial difficulties because we are in a region which is not very well-developed economically, so we have few financial sponsors and local government gives us less and less money with budget cuts, and the club fell from the 3rd to the 4th division. Some of our players were on three year contracts that we were forced to keep, so our club went into debt."

It has to be said that Rodez, with a population of just 50,000, is not used to the star power of someone like Zidane, and a who's who of the local political establishment followed him around all weekend, hoping to bask in the glory and get some rare national and international media coverage.

The football club believes Zidane's pledge to turn up frequently will encourage sponsors to come back, keen to share space with the French legend. But the club is up against one hurdle that few other clubs in Europe face. South-west France is one of the few regions of Europe where young boys want to grow up to become rugby players not football stars. Rugby is king here and sponsors know that. The local rugby team gets far more supporters at its games and wider media coverage than the football club.

Zidane says he will get updates on how the team is doing from his father-in-law. As well as being on the Real Madrid payroll, he is also studying part-time to get a coaching qualification and won't rule out one day even coaching in England.

Rodez once played in the second division and Zidane says he is not investing time and money here for charity. He wants a return on his money and he wants results soon.

"Why not try and get back into the 2nd division one day? So that means everyone has to work hard and put in the resources that are needed. Lots of things are needed but it's up to us, including me now that I am on board, to pull together."

To drive that message home, Zidane saw the local team train and watched their home game against nearby rivals Béziers. When Rodez was in the second division, it usually got between 8,000 and 9,000 fans each home game. These days it's usually closer to 500. But for this match, there were around 2,000 fans. You could call it 'the Zidane impact'. But even Zidane had off moments when he played the game and this time his presence was not enough to prevent Rodez from losing 1-nil.

I mentioned at the beginning, this was a modern fairy tale – and most fairy tales have happy endings… It's way too early to see how this one will finish…[25]

---

25 Since that report the Zidane effect hasn't quite matched the hopes or ambitions the club had. It had more money to spend and even went through a brief surge but didn't get promoted and last season it was extremely fortunate not to be relegated. In fact it should have been, but was saved because another club with dire financial woes went down instead. So you could say ZZ saved the club in one way or another. Not sure he has so much time free these days to keep an eye on Rodez, though he still flies in frequently to see his in-laws.

A marathon on the Millau Viaduct.

The Blairs on holiday near Toulouse.

Airbus A380 convoy through rural France.

Concorde's last flight back to Toulouse.

Philippe Douste-Blazy searching for world peace.

Scenes in Toulouse during three weeks of rioting.

Canfranc - the biggest train station you have never heard of.

Is this a UFO or a bathroom light reflection in the window?

Bugarach - the village and its mountain that may survive the end of the world.

Vintage plane wreckage hunters in the Pyrenees.

Truffle farmers in Lalbenque preparing to do business.

Terrorist Mohammed Merah's funeral.

Notre Dame du Rugby, Mary holding baby Jesus cradling rugby ball.

'Teflon » Corsican Alain Orsoni - loves his football.

World snail racing championship gets underway in the Gers department.

Vietnam-sur-Lot, « temporary » housing for Indochine refugees in Sainte-Livrade.

Football and Politics

Despite their omnipresence nationwide I rarely had anything to do with the National Front. That reflects the fact that firstly I didn't actually cover French politics that much, and secondly that the Front National (or FN) didn't have a big presence in the Southwest. That used to be true, but not anymore. I have done plenty of stories on why people are now voting for the far-right, but physical encounters with key members of the far right have been few and far between.

But I got to see some of the new guard (and they are incredibly young) thanks to a story that I read in a few papers that the FN-run towns up and down the country were cutting back on subsidies for their local football clubs.

The reason behind that decision? Well, because of the heavy concentration of Arab second and third generation immigrant players in the clubs. The far right mayors knew that the Arab community would never vote FN, but that a council decision to stop subsidising sport for them would prove popular with the voters who did put a paper in the ballot box for the far-right.

One such town, Beaucaire near Nîmes, was one of more than a dozen that elected far-right mayors in 2014 in one big sweep in municipal elections. The mayor of Beaucaire, Julien Sanchez wasn't yet 30 years old, had risen fast in the communications team for the FN in Paris and was 'parachuted' into this rundown town that had seen far more prosperous days.

One of his first controversial decisions was to slash the sports subsidy for the local football club and boost the one for the rowers on the wide Rhône River the town is nestled against.

How could I miss an opportunity like this? Here is my report that was broadcast in 2015.

Sports Hour
BBC World Service Radio
August 2015

You can be forgiven for not knowing much about Beaucaire Football Club. It has 400 players from the six year olds to the seniors who play in the French equivalent of the English 7th division. Most of the coaches like Ali and around half of the players are locals from North African immigrant backgrounds, places like Algeria, Morocco and Tunisia. Their parents came here 40 years ago to work in factories, building sites and fruit farms when France's economy was booming.

The town was one of a dozen last year that in a major surprise, elected far right National Front mayors and the one in Beaucaire has just cut the football budget by more than half. The club president Georges Cornillion told me it's down to openly racial politics.

"No-one is going to be able to save this club. When you strip a club of 60% of its budget immediately without warning, a club can't survive. We know that Beaucaire is cosmopolitan – in other words there are lots of North Africans but also lots of Spanish and Italians – we took them all in and we accepted them. Since they are all here, we have to look after them and keep them active, that's the situation and that is where we have our standoff."

Inside the incredibly beautiful 17th century town hall, the young mayor, Julien Sanchez, discusses his agenda with his cabinet team. Barely any are above the age of 30. He says his decision has nothing to do with race or immigration but simple economics and results. The club has not been successful and got too much money while other local sports clubs like the rowing club thrive on the national stage. He says too many local youths are wasting their time playing football, convinced they could be the next Zidane.

"Just like everyone else these kids should be looking for work. Not everyone can become a professional footballer. Just like not everyone can become an actor or singer. I know in today's society we try and convince people they can become singers, actors or star footballers, but the reality is that just a few footballers can make a career out of it. There are lots of jobs to be found locally in agriculture. But many of these youths don't want to roll their sleeves up and work hard. Obviously becoming a footballer is a dream job, especially if you are financed by a country like Qatar and get a great car and a beautiful girlfriend but there are also decent jobs here working on the land or in arts and crafts that aren't bad either."

Wandering through the medieval streets of Beaucaire, you can tell this town of 30,000 was once very rich. But it's fallen on hard times. Aggressive looking youths hang out on narrow streets – some sell drugs openly, some do dangerous wheelies on motorbikes, there are few stores – discount ones, rundown housing and double digit unemployment.

The only big name to emerge from the football club is Johnny Ecker. A decade ago he played for Marseille. He has returned in charge of the youth sides. He says his role is part sports coach part social worker – keeping kids out of trouble.

"It's obvious if they are with us training on Wednesday and Saturday afternoons then it means they are not hanging around on the streets. Too many kids are up to no good on the streets and everyone complains. So we are trying to pass on our football skills to these youths and prevent them from getting into trouble."

Ridiculous, says the mayor. It's not his job to show favouritism to one group over another. He tells me: "So to have calm in this town I have to pay people off?! That's not our way of doing things. We treat everyone fairly and won't do any positive discrimination for anyone. Everyone is treated the same. Other sports clubs didn't understand why the football club got much more money than them."

Later that week I went to the sprawling University of Toulouse campus where Pierre Mignot has spent several years studying the link between sports and politics. He says the far-right mayors are using sports as an undercurrent to focus on immigration. He says: "It's not blackmail, it's social reality – football, rugby and sports help to manage communities, they help to bring all the communities together in a town. It's a mark of integration to be in a local sports club. In fact the National Front don't know anything about local politics. They try to take a subject they know involves immigrant questions and try to use it in subjects like sports, the same with security and economics – they use immigration everywhere."

Back at the football club, it's the only topic of conversation amongst parents watching on the sidelines. They say if the club survives, it will have to cut the number of players by half and increase the membership fee. Many of the parents already struggle to find the €140 annual fee, paying in three instalments.

Stéphane is one father in that situation: "Maybe only one kid will emerge from this club in a once-in-a generation opportunity to become a professional footballer, but that's not the point. It's important to have an activity. Of course there are other sports out there, but football is the most accessible financially for parents like us for the moment."

Beaucaire's case is not an isolated one. Another town with a high immigrant population and its own delinquency issues, Mantes-la-Ville outside Paris, has just seen its football club's budget reduced by 75%. The new National Front mayor there says those who think a highly subsidised multi-cultural football club reduces racial tension and improves community relations are making a big mistake.

**

The sad tale of Jean-Pierre Adams

It was an article Richard Padula had seen in *The Guardian* that sent me heading to a suburb of Nîmes to do this story. It left me thoroughly depressed.

The name Jean-Pierre Adams probably doesn't mean much to you, but his story and that of his wife is worth sharing because it highlights our vulnerability, down to the toughest defender on the pitch, and I guess it should tell us we should make the most of what we have while we can.

World Football
BBC World Service
March 2014

Bernadette speaks softly to her husband, asking whether he's sitting comfortably. It would seem a routine conversation for a couple married for 40 years. But there is nothing ordinary about this relationship. Her husband, Jean-Pierre Adams, is in a coma. And it's been that way for the past 32 years.

He lies in a medicalised bed at their home near Nîmes, his eyes open. He coughs frequently, his tongue protrudes from his mouth, his arms are twisted from lack of use – he is in a vegetative state.

Way back, the Senegalese immigrant had made a name for himself as part of the so called 'Black Guard' alongside Caribbean player Marius Trésor, as the tough solid defence on the French national football side. After 22 caps he was taking a diploma to become a coach.

A niggling knee problem required treatment and he went to hospital for minor surgery. But the medical team were understaffed and overstretched because some of the hospital personnel were on strike. They made a dreadful blunder full of consequences: the anaesthetic injection hadn't been properly measured and it sent him into a coma. That was back in 1982. His wife Bernadette:

"I am still very angry with the hospital. I can never forget. It was a routine simple operation to attach part of his ligament between his thigh and behind his knee and it left him in the state he is now. They didn't care for him like they should have – the hospital was on strike, it wasn't a crucial operation and there weren't enough doctors available. It wasn't essential – they could have said 'we don't have enough staff we are going to put off this operation', I would have understood."

It took twelve years of legal wrangling before his wife was able to obtain damages and compensation to look after her husband at home with around-the-clock supervision. The football clubs Jean Pierre had played for including Nîmes, PSG and Nice all continue to provide financial support for the family. Looking after her husband's daily needs has been Bernadette's full time occupation for more than three decades.

"I felt I did what was my duty because I felt he couldn't be abandoned. His doctors were responsible for how he is and I have to help him. He was a happy and funny individual and I don't regret what I have done at all. We profited before, even if we didn't live together that long."

Bernadette shows me photographs of the young Jean Pierre she knew, who she met at a village dance when she was 24 years old. That's how people often met back then in the French countryside. She said he had a nice face, a happy-go-lucky manner. She had two sons with Jean-Pierre, they both tried to follow in their father's footsteps, with try-outs for various clubs but never made the breakthrough into professional football.

"I will be bitter with the doctors until the day I die – I am angry I did not have the life I wanted, my children didn't have the life they should've been able to share with their father, I will be bitter until my last day."

Patrick Champ has his mobile phone dangling from his ear all day. These days he's in charge of the sports facilities for the town of Nîmes where he and Jean-Pierre played together for Nîmes Olympique. He tells me veterans have made sure Jean-Pierre is not thought about in the past tense.

"We have organised charity matches and raised money that has gone to the Adams family. What happened to Jean-Pierre Adams really brought the football world together. He hasn't been forgotten, even it happened a long time ago, and he is still in our memory. It's as if he is still with us."

Nîmes are now a struggling second division side trying to avoid relegation but when Jean-Pierre played there, it was a striving top division side that saw other extraordinarily talented players emerge like Laurent Blanc and Eric Cantona … The club has just revealed a 26 metre long mural highlighting the club's achievements over the years and a photo of Jean Pierre in his role at the club is there.

When you think of someone in coma, you picture, as I did, someone motionless in a bed, but that is not the case with Jean-Pierre and his wife won't give up. "I speak to him all the day, I try and shake him and stimulate him but sadly nothing changes, he hears things, he jumps if the dog barks or at noise in the house, he hears but I am not saying he understands what is happening. Maybe a miracle will happen one day, but the truth is much of his brain is destroyed."

***

The Search for the Chinese Arsène Wenger

I don't want to end the football section with that depressing story. During my time in this part of the world, I visited the first wine château in Bordeaux to be bought by the Chinese.

When the estate agent who brokered the deal brought my cameraman Sébastien Hondelatte and myself to meet the French château seller, something very odd occurred. The seller rushed out of his grand entrance with a woman in tow, grabbed my hand and started guiding a pendulum over it.

He then fired a number of questions at me, where was I born, my nationality, my origins, who my parents were. Not one for introspection at the best of times, let alone sharing anything public with some odd real-life Professor Calculus out of the *Tintin* comic books, I wasn't very forthcoming. Irritated, he said: "You are not telling me everything".

I more or less pleaded to be left alone, and in disgust he dropped my hand and sulked off. He couldn't have cared less that two journalists had just turned up to ask him about selling his château and vineyard to the Chinese. Sébastien on the other hand was put out, asking why the château owner/medium wasn't in the slightest interested in his own sweaty palms. Strange seller aside, that was one of several stories I've covered pointing to Chinese soft power at work overseas.

More recently, I have looked at the huge influx of Chinese students at Bordeaux universities and business schools, learning about marketing wine and then often hired smartly by French vineyards to help them sell back home in China. I have covered the aviation schools in Toulouse training the next generation of Chinese pilots and airport managers in China, as 20 airports are built each year in China compared to one every 20 years in France.

And so it stands to reason that the Chinese would become interested in football. And it's one area that France has turned into a very lucrative business, teaching their ways of playing the game on and off the pitch to the Chinese Arsène Wengers of the future. I did this story for both France 24 and the BBC.

On a muddy university football field on the outskirts of Toulouse, a group of Chinese PE teachers get a lesson in French football tactics. While some listen to the translator closely, others take notes. This isn't an amateur team on a fun trip to Europe. They are part of a select group picked by the Chinese government to learn from the French how football is taught here.

It's become a priority for Beijing. Just as it is now an industrial superpower, it also wants to be able to dominate in the football sphere one day.

Zhiqiang Dong, a coach with the Beijing Sports Academy is in charge of the group. He says the long term aims from this three month training course are very ambitious: "We are weak in football so we have come here to learn from the French and share their experience and import that back home to see Chinese football improve. In the future we want Chinese football to be even better, not just in Asia but able to compete with the rest of the world."

To get to a European level, these 240 physical education instructors will head back to their primary and secondary schools and their universities across China where they teach, and try to find the next generation of professional players and coaches.

They have paid French universities in Bordeaux, Montpellier and Toulouse €2 million for their know-how. But what has the cash-strapped French universities really licking their lips is the tantalising possibility that 5000 people will have to be trained up somewhere in Europe over the next five years.

Jean-François Sautereau was approached by the French Foreign Ministry to put the programme into place. He says football is a 'soft power' way for the Chinese to project their new status. He tells me: "Football is a game played in the whole world and the results in football are the results of a country. Countries are proud to have results in football – it's very important."

This football training is about far more than say the 4-4-2 formation on the pitch. In the classroom they are taught the psychology of the game, how to treat players with respect and get the best out of them, and the role of positive criticism.

Erwan Robert is one of the classroom trainers: "They want to know how and what we do in France and how we can help them progress. We work with the students to explain how to increase their performance during the match and how the coach should speak to his players. Confidence is important because if players are afraid to play, they don't try or make the right choice between a pass or a shot at goal, so if the coach finds the good words to give the players confidence, they will be perform better."

Incidentally the veteran French manager of Arsenal, Arsène Wenger learnt his football psychology and strategy through the same French university sports programme.

The Chinese group listen politely throughout the class, but they are fascinated and fire off questions when they hear that one French League 1 coach turns off the dressing room lights just before the game to get the players attention and make sure they stay concentrated.

Other classes look at how to draw up contracts, ethics, avoiding corrupt agents or bribes. In light of the corruption investigations at FIFA at the moment, many current top football nations might need to take that course again.

Mysticism in the Provinces

Rennes-Le-Château

The Corbières is a mysterious, beautiful, hilly region attached to the eastern side of the Pyrenees, sloping into the Mediterranean. Much of it is arid, exposed rock and it's sparsely populated. The villages appear to be carved into the reddish soil.

Much of the year it's extremely hot but a wind blows through all year round that can either be very warm or chilly. In both cases the gusts are powerful and the sound harrowing as it streams through the cactus, thistles and vineyards.

While the Cathar region expands far beyond the Corbières, this area has managed to market itself as the real deal and when you look at the near empty landscape when the wind is at its strongest, you soak up the mysterious atmosphere and you can imagine the brutal medieval religious wars that took place here, the scorched soil absorbing the spilt blood.

So you can understand why an area rich in history but poor

economically would have a lot of reasons for actively promoting ancient legends and creating a line in lucrative mystical tourism.

Two villages stand out in particular and are far ahead of the competition in capturing that market – Rennes-le-Château and Bugarach. They are both very attractive, in fantastic settings and no more than 10 kilometres apart. I'd initially heard about Rennes-le-Château because each summer the village seemed to be besieged by treasure hunters with metal detectors from around the world, combing the village and the dry, remote hills around it for hidden treasure. Eventually signs were even posted around the village banning illegal digging.

Experts in the field of archaeology and history would also gather there for seminars to discuss how a local priest, Bérenger Saunière in the 19th century, suddenly became very wealthy. Did he find treasure that had been left behind by crusaders or even earlier by the Visigoths? The fact that the priest spent a lot of money restoring the church and added a tower dedicated to Mary Magdalene added to the conspiracy theories. It was even said that senior officials from the Catholic church came from Vienna to see him and buy his silence after he found evidence of a relationship between Mary Magdalene and Jesus.

When Dan Brown's *Da Vinci Code* also made reference to the priest and the region, it triggered a tourism rush. Some visitors were simply fans of the book, others spiritual and esoteric travellers who just felt there was 'something to it all'.

In any case I went to Rennes-le-Château several times for various BBC programmes and for Reuters, and I don't know if I got caught up or 'contaminated' by the atmosphere – but the place certainly felt magical – black magic that is.

The mayor at the time, Jean-François Lhuilier, was a muscular, often drunk, bullying former paramilitary type who went overboard to profit financially from the new hysteria Dan Brown's book created and hamper anyone else who tried to do the same.

He wanted the tourism revenue but not the journalists who asked too many questions. He harassed anyone in the village who tried to set up a restaurant, bar or hotel and tried to run all mystical-related business ventures himself. His small staff at the village hall resembled a coven and spent their time monitoring our movements and who we were talking to. They had even drawn up a detailed fees table for visiting journalists with a break down of what it cost to film what in the village.

The local residents were divided into two groups – those supporting the mayor and those trying to take him on. One who did, Jean-Luc Robin who wrote a book on the Rennes-le-Château mystery and had even opened a small well-situated restaurant, was constantly harassed by the mayor, who wanted to use his power to strip him of everything he had financially. But that wasn't enough – he also did everything he could to discredit him and everything he had written. The media were encouraged by the mayor to ignore Robin if they wanted his co-operation in Rennes-le-Château. In the strangest of circumstances, Robin died of a heart attack. Shortly before his death, he had sent me an urgent mail asking for support and media backing... I'm not saying he was killed or anything but when I mentioned black magic earlier on, I used those words carefully.

Like I said, I went to Rennes-Le-Château many times and wrote many stories. Here is one.

BBC World News
June 2011

Before the tourists start to arrive, the crickets have the village to themselves. Rennes-le-Château is in one of the most remote parts of France, close to the Spanish border and cooks on an exposed, arid, sunbaked hilltop. Thanks to the mystery of Rennes-

Le-Château and of course the Da Vinci Code book and now film, 120,000 people are expected to visit this place over the next few months. Yet it's very hard to find this village, in fact only 125 people live here all year around and you have to make a real effort to drop by.

The village isn't even mentioned in the Da Vinci Code but tourists heading here are convinced the events in the book are based on a century-old mystery in this village and it all revolves around the local priest, Bérenger Saunière.

Jean-Luc Robin is a local resident who has written his own book on the theories. In a long interview he told me what the enigma comes down to:

"The whole story is that the priest of this village at the turn of the century, from one day to another became immensely rich, and the question is – where did he get his money from? When tourists come here, there is not a huge amount to see but what they do see is the church in front us which clearly had a lot of money spent on it by the priest 100 years ago – that's probably the biggest symbol in the village. Definitely the priest spent most of his money on the church. He restored it and this is the amazing thing – everything in the church is around Mary Magdalene. Everything takes you back to her."

"I have a feeling that the priest Bérenger Saunière found something, probably documents – he was asked to find them and he was paid to find them. After he found them he read them and even copied them. I have realised – because I have followed his life through his diaries – that after making his finding, he was not the same man. He was disturbed – remember he was a Catholic priest. He might have found a different version of the story. If you look at the church, he kept a secret that he was paid for. He is still trying to say something through the church, through signs on his property. The church has been dedicated to Mary Magdalene since the 11th century but there is a very special dedication to Mary Magdalene through Saunière. She is above the door of the church and inside there is a statue of her on the right and another under the altar. There is a statue of her in the stained glass window. The famous Magdalene tower at the top of his property is a reference to Mary Magdalene. The grotto where he made his discoveries is also named after her. Everything takes us back to a dualism – the basis of the Cathar religion – and to Mary Magdalene."

And many of these mystical tourists agree. It's a spiritual quest of sorts. They are flocking here, convinced Mary Magdalene took shelter here after the death of Christ. The questions they ask but can't get answers to include: Was she the wife of Christ? Did she have children? Are her descendants here?

If the books on display at the local bookstore are any guide, the tourists (more often than not female) are here to know more about Mary Magdalene. Céline Vasseur who runs the store said lots of people come here attracted by the story of the treasure, but confirmed that more and more are coming for Mary Magdalene and spiritual reasons.

Most of the visitors heading here are from Britain, Italy and Germany. Geeha from Cologne believes the Catholic Church has covered up the truth and 'just feels Mary Magdalene was here'.

There are signs throughout the village that shout out 'No digging allowed'. For years, treasure hunters have been heading here hoping to uncover the mystery for themselves or hoping to strike it rich. You might have thought the people who live here would be happy to bask in the spotlight. But they are not.

Laurent Sanchez, in his 80s, knew the priest's housekeeper as a child and says the priest was a conman and the village is now suffering. Before slamming his shutters tight he shouted at me:

"People who visit this village have no real idea of what happened here and what the priest found. Let me tell you – the priest was a crook, a hoodlum of his time who had no time for the poor of his village and hoodwinked everyone he met. We don't have the infrastructure here to handle the thousands and thousands of tourists who come. We even have Chinese visitors. What on earth are they doing here?"

And sure enough, later on I bump into a group of Chinese tourists from Hong Kong who have come here after seeing the Da Vinci Code.

The priest's home is now open to the public, there is a recording of the piano music he played in his living room. Is he trying to tell us something? He died on 22nd January 1917 and it seems in his case at least, he really did take his secret with him to his grave.

***

The End of the World – *the Doomsday Village*

As I mentioned earlier, the Corbières is achingly beautiful and I guess is the equivalent to New Mexico in terms of arid cactus landscape, big spaces and of course border country. Unlike Santa Fe, it doesn't have many super rich hippy-chic residents. But it has plenty of poor grubby hippies and traveller types who manage to live here because it's dirt cheap, the climate is pretty good and it's a place far enough away for people to come to to hide from whatever they have had to leave behind.

Some end up working in the artisan craft or jewellery making business, selling their work in the local open air markets. Others are local guides or work in cafés over the summer and in winter find jobs on the nearest ski slopes. Some grow their own vegetables or cannabis and sell some of it or exchange food for other services through a barter system.

Many are dreamers and without monthly welfare benefits, life would be perilous. They more or less fit into the local scenery, even if their lifestyles don't have much to do with the locals who were born and grew up in this tough landscape.

The arrival of these drifter newcomers has in fact helped stop the population from completely dwindling and they actually intentionally or not helped create a mini-economic boom though a conspiracy theory of their making. It takes place in the small, attractive, very out-of-the-way village of Bugarach, about 10 kilometres from Rennes-le-Château.

I got wind of this story in 2010, way before the international media shamelessly made a mockery of themselves, but I can't hide the fact that I played a small role in the build-up to that ludicrous moment when the end of the world was imminent.

Here is the first story that I did on this for the BBC back in 2011, though gosh, looking back at this and thinking of the many stories I filed on the 'Doomsday village', I should really feel embarrassed and ashamed.

From Our Own Correspondent
BBC Radio
4 July 2011

Bugarach, a tiny ancient village on the French side of the Pyrenees Mountains, is extremely hard to find and you have to make a special effort to get there. And that is apparently just what a variety of esoteric groups, 'new agers' and doomsday cults are doing or planning to do, and many of these doomsday travellers apparently come from Holland.

According to the ancient Mayan calendar, at some point towards the end of 2012, the world will come to an end. It's not clear how that will happen but apparently humanity doesn't stand a chance — except for those who seek shelter in the area surrounding Bugarach.

Just two hundred people live there all year round, but doomsday believers and spiritual groups are convinced the village has magical powers thanks to the local mountain the 'Pic de Bugarach'.

For years, rumours have circulated on the Internet that extra-

terrestrials live in the mountain and come the apocalypse, the top will open and they will emerge with spaceships and rescue the local inhabitants. Sounds ridiculous, right? But the French authorities say it's no joke. A special parliamentary committee has warned that sects may be considering mass suicides in 2012 on French territory. It has pointed the finger at some of the groups spending time around Bugarach and elsewhere in the Pyrenees.

The authorities say some individuals have bought land in the mountains with the intention of building bunkers, surrounded by their acolytes in order to survive the end of the world or even die together.

I have to admit that while I was in Bugarach I saw no space ships or mysterious priest like figures — just a painting on a wall depicting UFOs picking a human off a mountain top and some sleepy dogs basking in the sun, rather fed up at being woken up by yet another foreign journalist. A four man crew from German television was also wandering through the village looking for signs of the nearing end of the world. They too came away empty-handed.

But the local mayor, Jean Pierre Delord, told me groups that could be called sects are heading to the mountain top and taking part in strange rituals.

Other groups dressed in white outfits have also been seen holding furtive gatherings in the forest near the village. And at the nearest estate agents, about 15 kilometres from the village, Jacques Fargier says he has sold some big properties in the village to some strange types that could be characterised as sects. In fact, teasingly he said that there would be no point in all 'From Our Own Correspondent' listeners heading to the village looking for a property safe haven, because there wasn't much on the market and building permission was very hard to obtain in this stunning part of the world.

Doomsday or not, there is no question that the countryside around Bugarach has a very powerful hold on many visitors with esoteric inclinations. In the next valley is another tiny village – Rennes-le-Château – that has been swamped by tourists for several years after the hugely

successful writer Dan Brown revealed in The Da Vinci Code an ancient
rumour that the local priest became rich overnight. According to the
legend, he found proof that Mary Magdalene and Christ may have
been lovers and he was bought off by the Catholic Church to keep the
truth secret, then he buried his wealth near the village.

Every year spiritual travellers come to soak in the energy they
say comes from the mountain. They are convinced something very
strange happened here. For the local restaurants and bed and
breakfast owners, there is no doubt the strange tales and mystical
energy said to be inside the mountains are extremely good for
tourism... but they admit that too many visitors in white tunics
holding secret gatherings at night is not the kind of business they
are keen on.

That was just the beginning. Naturally as the date for the end of
the world approached, my visits to the village increased, often
for Reuters or the BBC. The mayor, a farmer who at first enjoyed
the media attention, now realised he had helped escalate a
monster he couldn't control anymore and therefore vilified and
threatened any journalist who came calling. Local residents were
furious at the number of TV cameras from around the world
criss-crossing the village looking for freaks to interview – there
aren't that many streets in Bugarach.

Many were outraged at the portrayal of their village as full
of wackos when in fact many had moved there to be forgotten
or at the very least left alone. Rumours spread that hard-core
nihilists had begun moving in, while cults got up to odd
behaviour including sexual rites and animal sacrifices on the
mountain top.

Naturally as the long awaited 'Doomsday' drew closer, the
story turned from one of oddballs in a strange setting to one
of ominous concerns about who might be heading there, how
many, and could an organised Jonestown style mass suicide

even occur. This story for BBC World News gives an idea of how the story angle shifted to security.

BBC World News
October 2012

According to some doomsday groups the end of the world will occur on December 21st. They base their calculation on the ancient Mayan Calendar. However some esoteric groups believe a village – Bugarach, in the south-west of France – could survive because its mountain has mystic powers. It might sound ridiculous, but the French authorities don't think it's a laughing matter. They fear a mass invasion of new-agers and cults and are planning to seal off the village before the dreaded date.

This region of France has always attracted spiritual groups who believe the landscape has mystical powers. But the rumours that the village will survive the end of the world and UFOs in the mountain overlooking Bugarach will rescue those who have taken shelter there have spread thanks to the internet. It sounds like a joke but the French authorities are taking the situation seriously.

Eric Freysselinard is the Prefect for the region and has the job of guaranteeing security. In his beautiful 'ancien regime' office in the centre of Carcassonne, he tells me 50 military police will be in the village and 50 others on the perimeter of the village. Others on patrol elsewhere can be brought in swiftly as backup if necessary.

Like most of the 200 residents, Valerie Austin, a retired teacher from England, came to Bugarach for the area's outstanding beauty and tranquility, and she wants that back:

"Holiday visitors in some respects have been put off by the publicity. They don't want to come to a place where they think they will be accosted by strange people in the streets. They come here for the peace and quiet, beauty and tranquility and so on, and they don't want other things happening."

Druids dressed in white gowns have been spotted on the mountain top but no-one at the moment knows whether thousands of survivalists will really turn up.

Whether you believe this village will survive the end of the world or not, the French authorities have a clear message: they don't want anyone to show up on the 21st December.

I am grateful to that English resident, Valerie, for agreeing to see me each time I came up. I think she enjoyed the attention and I was never really sure whether she believed there was something strange in the air or not, or just couldn't fathom why journalists kept making the hike up there to interview people like her.

After my visits she got called around the clock by other TV news researchers and bookers who of course just jotted down the names of the people interviewed in my various reports from the Doomsday village.

But here is the crazy thing – on the day that the end of the world was supposed to come I wasn't there. I had been asked by the BBC and Yann '*How much*' Tessier over at Reuters TV if I would go for a week! And you know what? I declined. It was coming up to Christmas, the weather wasn't great even there at that time of year, I had made some reasonable money beforehand and I couldn't face being with several hundred other journalists and TV satellite vans stuck in a village for several days waiting for, well nothing to happen. No, I was pretty sure the end of the world was not imminent and was sceptical about Bugarach's special powers.

Apart from a large police presence and one person who tried to get through a checkpoint with an axe, when the Doomsday moment finally arrived, it was a circus with several hundred journalists looking for anything, something at least, and interviewing all the odd-balls of the area who had converged on the village now that there was something fun happening out of season. They were also egged on by the tantalising possibility that a few of their own doomsday tales with journalists would trigger some free wine in the bar.

Now that you know the end of the world never came, and now the village has fallen back into comfortable anonymity, I do recommend a trip up there – it's beautiful and yes there is something very mysterious about the area, but you will discover that for yourself when you are there.

***

The Cult of the *Twelve Tribes*

This was one of the few stories that really got my girlfriend Catherine worried. It's the kind of thing you would expect to stumble across in a remote community in New Mexico or outside Waco, not in the foothills of the French Pyrenees nestled between the Basque Country and the region known as the Béarn.

A group dressed in drab medieval puritan outfits with a passing resemblance to the Amish has been living in a château in the tiny village of Sus for decades.

They call themselves *The Twelve Tribes* and their community is made up of around 100 members including nearly 20 children. The children are taught in the château, not in the local state schools because the members say they don't share the same values as the French State.

They say they live and preach the values of Christians from the 1st Century. There are similar Twelve Tribe chapters elsewhere, in Germany and the United States.

They get by growing food on their own land outside the village and selling homemade artefacts and carpentry in local markets. I suspect they also get handouts from the state but I didn't ask that when I met them. They are made up of numerous nationalities, many from Eastern and Northern Europe as well as the United States. They had come to the media's attention in 2006 because of accusations of mental and physical abuse. There were also allegations the children were more or less living in a compound run as a sect with little or no contact with the outside world, which meant they wouldn't have the emotional skills later on in life to just leave the group if they so wished.

I was pretty intrigued by all this, but of course a group with sect like tendencies doesn't exactly have a press relations department. So I wrote to them. And to my surprise I received a phone call one night from one of the so-called 'elders'. After a long conversation they warmed to the idea of allowing me in for a few days. Not to do a TV report but to meet with me first so they could 'take a look inside my soul'.

Introspection is one of my great fears (I have enough skeletons in my own cupboard as my ex-girlfriend Isabelle Cauvas likes to point out whenever I see flaws in others) and I certainly didn't want anyone – let alone a doomsday cult – examining parts of my soul that I didn't dare even look at myself.

By the way, I didn't actually use that argument, I said the BBC simply didn't have enough money to send me out there on my own for a chat before deciding whether to go ahead with the shoot or not. So I suggested I bring a camera and leave it in the car and then if you guys decide my soul is clean then we go ahead and do the report.

I went with a local Toulouse cameraman, Mathias Touzeris who is a lot more open-minded than myself and was the ideal backup. Also, friendly with a smile, he could play the good guy, who understood their way of living. But in the end he left the château just about as shell-shocked as myself[26].

The château dominates a small village that you would barely notice as you head towards the mountains. There are no locked gates preventing anyone getting in or out. They built a huge wooden yurt near the entrance.

It reminded me of the barn that was built by the Amish community in a scene in the film *Witness*. In fact as well as selling their home-grown produce, they fix local residents' roofs to raise money. Inside is where everyone gathers to eat and where speeches including the day's agenda are given by the elders.

In theory there are no bosses or chiefs, but it's clear who they are when you arrive – for a start they were the only ones allowed to use the telephone. The residents don't get to watch TV either. Actually that's not such a bad idea and it meant at least they couldn't see my report afterwards. They took me to see the classroom where the children in *Tabitha's Place* (as they call the château)are educated.

Although they assured me state school inspectors are allowed in to see what and how they are taught, I can't work out how they managed to convince the French school system to allow them to be taught from home. The day I was there, they were taught grammar by a woman by the name of Huyadah.

Guillaume Joga was clearly one of the *Twelve Tribes* leaders and he told me that their lifestyle is very close to how early Christians lived 2000 years ago and even back then they were called sects. He said the children are taught at the compound

---

26 I worked a lot with Mathias with his treacle Toulouse accent – even after the time we came back from the Basque Country where we had filmed players playing Pelote Basque (a local version of squash) and recorded in a Basque language radio station, only for me to discover when editing back home for the BBC that he had forgotten to record any sound. My journalism students think I am rather pedantic when I keep reminding them to make sure they have recorded sound and always have headphones on. Honestly, they will thank me one day.

because they can't out-source education to teachers on the outside who don't share their convictions.

Seeing the *Twelve Tribes* residents wearing outfits that could have been made literally from potato sacks, in drab blue or grey colours was weird. It seems the clothing was shaped to remove any hint of sexuality from the women members' bodies. Who said salafists had a monopoly on this idea. Yet sex must have been common from the number of young children. It seems the elders have a big say in the match-making process.

Now I have to admit no-one tried to brainwash me and no-one called me back afterwards asking me to return, but what struck Mathias and me was that anyone brought up young in that kind of environment would have real difficulty breaking out if they wanted to, as everything in their everyday lives in the château is decided for them. They grow up in a culture of dependency.

Over the years there have been numerous police raids – usually following allegations of physical abuse against kids, or paying wages under the counter – but despite all this it's still there, nearly 4 decades on, even though parliamentary committees openly call the group a sect.

***

Brainwashing and Manipulation – the Recluses of Monflanquin

This was a remarkable story in that it highlighted how vulnerable most of us are to manipulation and mind games. Monflanquin is a very pretty town between Bordeaux and Agen. An extended aristocratic family from Bordeaux had a château just outside the town and they would later be known as the Recluses of Monflanquin.

It was actually the magazine show on BBC South, *Inside Out*, that put me onto this story as there was a link with the city of Oxford. Basically this family, known as the de Vedrines, were well off, with lots of property, good jobs including senior medical positions and were well connected politically in Bordeaux[27].

But in the 1990s their lives were almost destroyed by an opportunist conman named Thierry Tilly. He had been hired as a handyman by one of the family to help run her small private school in Paris. Apparently he did a good job and she recommended him to the rest of the family. At the same time he had discovered the de Vedrines had lots of money.

Slowly over a number of years he brainwashed the family and made them entirely dependent on him. He claimed he worked for the security services, their lives were in danger and not to talk to anyone outside their circle. He even managed to force them to stay locked in the château for months at a time with the shutters closed, spending their days playing table tennis. He ordered them to remove clocks from the château and not to wear watches. The idea was to destabilise the entrenched, scared family, notably by making them lose all sense of time.

They were barely allowed to talk to each other; nearly all conversations had to go through Tilly himself because, he said, there was a traitor amongst them but he admitted he didn't know who just yet. He wasn't in the château often but would call dozens of times a day.

And of course since he knew the weaknesses of each family member, he used that information to create rivalries and a climate of suspicion. From the most elderly member of the

27 They were actually close to the mayor of Bordeaux Alain Juppé and he used his influence to get them a council flat when they had lost everything they owned.

family, who was in her 80s, to the youngest granddaughter, they were all trapped in this environment. Their lawyer Daniel Picotin who has become an expert on manipulation and cults left us stunned when he went through the whole story in his grand offices in Bordeaux. He said Tilly's behaviour was that of a spider: "He bites to sting and anaesthetises you. Once he's stung you, he will wrap you up. Afterwards he sucks the blood out of you."

Not all family members were conned but when those from ouside the château came to visit in Monflanquin to try and make the others see the light, they were evicted, as Tilly had managed to convince those trapped in the château that the visiting relatives were amongst the traitors who meant to do them harm.

Slowly, having succeeded in isolating the family from their friends and their professional world and making them totally dependent on him, he gained access to their bank accounts and property deeds.

He then split the family up, sending some off to Oxford and others to London, to live in isolation in bed-sits or crummy flats.

He said their lives were in real danger but he reassured them that their situation was temporary.

Charles-Henri de Vedrines who had been a gynaecologist in a Bordeaux hospital was now working in a public park in Oxford, his wife Christine behind the counter in a deli. They had virtually nothing to eat – everything they earned, they handed over to Tilly.

The children were kept separated from their parents. One of their sons stayed on his own for days on end in a bare flat off London's Oxford Street while Tilly drip fed him with malice about his own parents.

It was Christine's boss in the deli who sensed that something wasn't right. He took an instant dislike to Tilly when he appeared at his shop and asked her what was going on. After that, gradually their plight came to light.

Christine managed to get back to France and with her lawyer and estranged family members returned to in effect rescue her husband, cousins and children. But it wasn't easy as her loved ones and relatives had been so manipulated they even refused to open the doors of their homes, terrified. It took experts in mind manipulation to break the spell.

The family needless to say were penniless by now, the château had been sold, their property in Bordeaux as well and the bank accounts worth several million euros emptied. For the show we met several members of the family and it's actually quite remarkable that they were able to come together after a decade of psychological torture.

Some now live in grotty council flats as they have no money, but Charles-Henri has managed to go back into practice. The kids returned to university and Tilly was sentenced to a 10 year prison term though none of the money he stole has ever been found. But what is also startling is that experts say one in three of us could fall for this kind of brainwashing.

**

Seen a UFO... *Who you gonna call?*

For some reason it took me a long time to do this story. Maybe because it was difficult to do visually, after all UFOs are not frequent visitors and are reluctant to be filmed. But anyway between Bugarach and this story, I definitely made the social networks as I was now on the radar of the world of conspiracy theorists and their lot. In fact Bugarach and this UFO story were amongst the most commented and shared of any stories that I covered.

Now obviously I did this story with a lot of humour and

also a little incredulity that the French State could finance this department at a time of so-called severe budget stringency. However I have to say when I looked at the parched yellow documents dating back 60 years, with eyewitness accounts from military pilots explaining what they had encountered up there, it did send a chill through me. So I'm not taking sides on this story – here is how I reported it.

From Our Own Correspondent
November 2014
BBC Radio 4

You don't need a time machine when you visit the French Space Centre headquarters in Toulouse called the CNES. It's already a throwback to the 70s. Green lawns sweep onto wide boulevards with long, stout rectangular office blocks on either side.

It's almost Soviet style architecture in the heart of southern France. There are few signs of life even though fifteen hundred people, most of them civil servants, work in boxy offices along narrow, unappealing corridors.

France has the biggest space agency in Europe – the result of the 1960s space race and then-president de Gaulle's grand determination to keep France independent of the United States by building its own satellites and rocket launchers, and funding elite space research. An offshoot of all that is that France is the only country in Europe to maintain a full-time state-run Unidentified Flying Object department.

There used to be one in the UK and another in Denmark. They both closed down years ago due to budget cuts. France's UFO unit consists of a staff of 4 and around a dozen volunteers who look into reports of strange sightings in the skies. The team is called GEIPAN. That's a French acronym for 'Study Group and Information on Non-Identified Aerospace Phenomena'.

Its boss is Xavier Passot. Surrounded by dozens of books on UFOs, he tells me his mission is to be as transparent as possible about strange sightings and to follow up on each one that his team receives. They publish their results on their website. The team receives on average two UFO sightings a day. The department insists an eleven-page document is filled out after each sighting. The idea is to provide detail including photographs where possible, but it's also aimed at weeding out jokers and time-wasters.

If someone claims to have seen strange lights in the skies, the UFO team might go online to see whether the observation took place on a flight path – it can trace commercial air traffic going back more than a week. The team also has access to military flight paths and is in touch with the Air Force and air traffic controllers.

Xavier Passot says many of the people who report UFOs are smokers, puffing away outside bars or their own homes at night, and gazing at the stars. Sometimes, if his staff are really intrigued by photos they have seen or if there have been several witnesses to the same sighting, they will call the local police to ask whether the person reporting the sighting can be considered credible. They might even check with neighbours to see if the UFO spotter was drinking or perhaps smoking something other than cigarettes!

One of those boxy offices houses yellowing archives going back to the 1950s. The ones I look at contain eerie accounts of strange things encountered in the skies by fighter pilots on routine reconnaissance missions. For what it's worth and for those who suspect there's conspiracy afoot, Monsieur Passot tells me he has never covered-up a UFO sighting.

I see some amazing photos of strange lights and circular forms caught on camera. One, taken by a motorist, of a white ring shape above Marseille is particularly grabbing. But the team figured that one out; It wasn't invaders from Mars, just the reflection of a small interior overhead light in the car!

In fact the department can explain away nearly all these phenomena and, believe it or not, the most common culprits are

Chinese lanterns sent up at night during parties. After a sighting, the investigators often telephone the local town hall to ask if perhaps there had been a wedding going on at the time. Balloons and kites floating in the skies also get mistaken for alien craft, and space debris and falling meteorites giving off strange lights are more common than one might think.

But there are some four hundred UFO sightings going back to the 1970s that the team cannot explain. One, an alleged flying saucer landing near Aix en Provence in 1981, they take very seriously. There were landing marks and multiple witnesses.

So are there really little green men? Well, the jury's out on the colour but there are many working here, as well as others around the world, who are convinced there is some life out there. And does the use of French taxpayers' money on UFO research make sense, particularly in these times of budgetary constraint? That probably depends on whether you just saw an alien and you want to know, in the words of the Ghostbusters film, 'who you gonna call'...

**

The Temporarily Resettled Indochina Refugees *(and they're still here)*

A few years after I had set myself up officially as a registered Press Agency, I was looking for some spin-off work opportunities related to my field. One idea I had was working at the local journalism school.

The EJT or *École de Journalisme de Toulouse* had a good reputation and lots of student applications for just 30 places each year. This was partly down to the teaching but also probably due to the fact that so many students want to live in Toulouse. A bit like my old university, Newcastle, which in principle wasn't particularly for academic high flyers, but punched above its weight because so many applied to join because they knew the campus had a great reputation for student life.

Anyway, I wrote to the school and got a call back to meet the directors. They were Bertrand Thomas and Franck Demay. Expecting slightly stuffy academic types, I dressed up in a suit and went to my lunchtime meeting.

I didn't even get a chance to enter the school gates (which only later did I discover lead to a beautiful medieval quad, a throwback to my own student days) – they were waiting for me at the gates and the meeting was held in a dark tapas bar where we ate (a little) and drank (a lot of) wine.

I can't remember what my pitch was but I certainly don't remember them asking for any credentials or proof that I knew anything about journalism... but at the end of lunch they said thanks so much, and they would find some slots for me to do some English TV journalism classes[28].

And that's how it started. I've been doing that for over a decade now. Now you ask what has all this got to do with the headline about Indochina refugees. I'm getting there...

Every year the school hands out lucrative prizes for the best written article, radio and TV feature. I was invited to be one of the judges on the panel and in true music industry style, I stole one of the student's brilliant video ideas and did it myself later on for Reuters TV and the BBC (I did award the

---

28 Actually Bertrand told me that once their somewhat cavalier technique for recruiting native English speakers to the school did not work out. An American woman who'd come along talking up her journalism background was given a few teaching slots. But after just one class half the students were spooked out – she was on some sort of proselytising mission on behalf of the Jehovah Witnesses or something.

student in question the prize for best TV report[29]).

When the Reuters Paris producer Hortense de Roffignac saw the story and helped me put it together she said wow that was really depressing. And she was right. After just one day out on the story, I left feeling really glum on my long way home. And with the current massive stream of refugees to Europe rehoused in small towns and villages across France, it makes you wonder if history won't repeat itself.

Here is the story I filed for the BBC from the small town of Sainte Livrade near Cahors (also known locally as 'Vietnam-sur-Lot').

From Our Own Correspondent
BBC Radio 4
February 2012

---

29 I've been giving classes at the school for so long, some of my ex-students are now even competitors out working for rival organisations! While its fun being around the students there is one depressing fact. Most of the students are post graduates in their mid-20s. Each year that I teach, their age bracket stays the same but of course I am one year older. And the gap grows of course with each new class. Every year they invite the teachers to their Christmas party. The girls – as only the French can – mix sexy and sassy as if its in their DNA. The boys are knocking down horrible powerful cocktails and get drunk very fast and the girls are not far behind actually. As Yann Tessier at Reuters (who knows France and the UK as well as me) pointed out in dismay, binge drinking is one of the UK greatest cultural exports to French youth.The teachers are welcomed to the Christmas bash, handed a drink but then put in their own corner to speak to other adults, there is little mixing. And I now have an idea of what the very elderly in retirement homes endure. One of the teachers is another ex-pat Vanessa C. Stone – a perfectionist which meant it was a nightmare for her when she agreed to proofread this book!

First a brief history lesson. In the 1950s, like Britain, France saw its overseas colonial empire begin to unravel rapidly. France's far eastern colony Indochina or Indochine – later to become Vietnam – was no exception. In the mid 1950s the French packed their bags and left in a hurry.

However thousands of local residents who had worked for the French colonial administration or had married French citizens were considered as traitors by much of the local population and their lives were in danger. So Paris allowed some of them to come to France – they were called the French expatriates of Indochina.

1,200 of them were brought over by boat and were told they could stay in a rundown former army camp near the small town of Sainte Livrade in south-west France. The living conditions were bad – cramped, with sanitation and heating nearly non-existent, and the new residents faced severe restrictions on their movements, so as not to antagonise the local population.

It was all temporary, 'only for a few months', until something better was found… except nearly sixty years later they are still there… To be precise 30 of the original residents are still there. They are in their late 80s and 90s. The rest have died and their children have moved on and made their own lives.

The local French population referred to the camp as Vietnam-sur-Lot (Vietnam on the River Lot) – the camp had its own Asian shops and restaurants on base and while the children were taught in French, the adult refugees spoke in Vietnamese and the remaining survivors still do.

The hundreds of families lived in long, narrow, low ceilinged, grey concrete rows that resembled farm outhouses for livestock more than homes. Most are now abandoned except for those occupied by the last 30 families still there.

And when you go inside the homes you are hit by two distinct sensations – one, you are clearly somewhere in Asia, and secondly, it's a throwback to another era when France had an empire: there are photos of French soldiers parading proudly in Indochina, hats once worn by French colonial officials on the wall. It's a similar feeling to the one you get when visiting say a British expatriate club in some parts of East or Southern Africa, with pictures of spitfires on the wall and hunting trophies.

91 year old Emile Lejeune who spent 7 years in jail in Indochina for fighting alongside the French is still bitter about what happened to him. Surrounded by Buddha statues he says there was never any effort to integrate the Indochina expatriates into French life. He told me integration was a dirty word back then and the only solution for them was to adapt to the new situation and not kick up a fuss.

That view is partly confirmed by Patrick Fernand. He grew up in the camp and left when he was 24 to become a French policeman. When you ask him why the expatriates never made more of an effort to improve their living conditions, he says with dismay that it was part of the culture, not to complain, not to stand out, to lie low. The men went to work in local factories and the women in the fields nearby, but contact with the local French was kept to a minimum. Another of the original survivors is Pierre-Charles Maniquant. When I meet him he is watching Vietnamese TV thanks to a satellite dish. When he arrived he said, his family of ten were housed in two rooms and shared outdoor toilets with other families. Contact with the outside world was strictly controlled until the 1970s. He tells me the French people are no better or worse than anyone else, but the French State had let the Indochina expatriates down.

The health and safety regulations in the camp had never been a priority until 2004 when one of the elderly residents died in a house fire because of faulty electricity. The French authorities finally decided it was time to act. Some of the disused barrack homes have been knocked down and small new houses with an Asian style look are going up in their place and the last residents are now being urged to move into them.

But the irony is that most don't want to. Having lived in their homes for nearly 60 years they can't face the idea of being uprooted again. As Pierre-Charles Maniquant told me: "We have had to wait more than half a century for proper housing to be built, but all the elderly residents have died. There are just thirty of us left, all our children have moved on to make their own lives."

Many of the younger camp residents born there said they were thoroughly dissuaded by the French authorities from speaking Vietnamese, it was as if their Asian heritage had to be stamped out. That changed in the 1980s and each summer now, families remember their Asian background with a festival there. The high fence that used to surround the camp to underline the fact that the inhabitants were not locals, has disappeared and the town of Sainte Livrade has grown extensively and runs right up to the community, erasing memories of former residents that were physically cut off from the rest of the French population.

The Stereotype Stories

I was recently interviewed by a couple of young French journalists and they wanted to know if I did the typical stories about the baguette, workers on strike all the time, etc.

I replied that I was guilty and no doubt deserved nothing less than a public stoning. Forget the run-of-the-mill strikes, I have covered the unemployed who went on strike demanding Christmas bonuses just like everyone else. That's left you confused, right? Well, they said since workers get to share in the holiday spirit, why shouldn't they. And you know what? They won, getting special one-off payments after holding sit-ins in bright department stores, or job centres or the entrance to the employers confederation, the MEDEF.

I followed the post office workers who went on strike saying they had to be able to retire in their early 50s as they were in no physical state to continue to do the mail run on the standard bright yellow post office allocated bikes. I even looked at how the 35 hour working week was hitting extra-marital flings – It is a well-known French tradition that affairs are carried out between 5 and 7pm on work days – with the 35 hour week introduced by the Socialists in 2000, suddenly those excuses about having to stay late at the office went out the window.

So it goes without saying that I covered the dying traditional industries like the Beret and Espadrilles, both created in the Pyrenees. Needless to say these were stories I revisited several times for radio and TV.

***

The Near Death and the Recovery of the Espadrille

From Our Own Correspondent
BBC Radio 4
October 2012

Footwear is about far more than protecting the soles of your feet. Shoes also say a lot about a country's culture, identity and heritage. Holland has its clogs, the US its cowboy boots and the Pyrenees Mountains the espadrille.

For those unfamiliar with the espadrille, in its basic form it's a flat, rope-soled shoe made from jute with a floppy cotton canvas top stitched to it, with a life expectancy of just a few months. And certainly a lot less if you are in a rain storm with a particularly cheap pair on. Almost like slippers but with a sturdier base and made for going outside, but not too far.

Cheap and relatively easy to make, they came into fashion in the 19th century to fit peasants working the fertile land in the foothills, and later were popular amongst priests who wandered from parish to parish. Later, the espadrille found new customers in northern France amongst mine workers. Espadrilles were churned out in factories on both the Spanish and French sides of the mountains, but the world headquarters was located in the French town of Mauléon in the French Basque country.

In its heyday in the 1950s more than 2000 workers in some 20 factories across the town were churning out millions of pairs of espadrilles for French customers and fans around the world. But like much of the rest of the textile industry in Western Europe, globalisation caught up with the shoe industry – cheaper imports, mainly from Bangladesh, virtually wiped out the French espadrille industry. Until a few years ago there were just five shoe makers left in Mauléon, with a full time work force of around 120. The industry looked a smart bet for extinction. The talk in the town was not how to save the industry but how to create a museum in its memory – normally a sign that the mourning is well underway.

Today the reminders of Mauleon's industrial past are evident – massive warehouses, many derelict, wide streets built for the lorries that once clogged up the town bringing in raw materials and leaving with bundles of new shoes.

But this is not a story about yet another traditional European trade giving up the ghost, unable to survive stiff competition from emerging countries in Asia. The last espadrille manufacturers decided if they couldn't compete on price, at least focus on a different customer by offering something that the Bangladesh models couldn't – an artisan approach with a 'made in France' quality label and a high price targeted at fashion victims abroad.

Your ordinary imported espadrille costs around €5 in a supermarket – the French manufacturers are now offering elaborate shoes with colours, designer prints, buckles, and heels. Yes, things have moved on from the mine workers. The price tag – anything up to €60 or €70.

Two young entrepreneurs from the French Basque country region, Mathieu and Julien, told me they saw a gap in the market abroad where 'Made in France' still stands for something. Five years ago they started working with the last espadrille makers to export their high priced shoes to places like Hong Kong, Tokyo, and Taiwan. In five years they have sold 150,000 pairs abroad. They hope to export 100,000 next year alone as they focus on fashionistas in places like Miami with a special Spring 2012 collection. In small, dimly lit factories, women are huddled over sewing machines, busy stitching the circular canvas to the rim of thousands of newly moulded jute soles.

Close to 2 million pairs of espadrilles are still bought in France each year but few come from Mauléon. The irony is not lost on Julien Maisonnave. He told me that in France, customers have got used to buying cheap clothes from Asia and North Africa and the 'made in France' label doesn't have the same resonance at home as it does abroad. Nevertheless after years of decline, employment in the business is picking up as markets are reclaimed abroad. But finding new seamsters is proving difficult since most of the working population left the town years ago to look for jobs elsewhere in the nearby big cities like Bordeaux or Pau. The mayor of Mauléon, an entrepreneur – and full time espadrille wearer – himself, told me he intends to push ahead and build an espadrille museum to promote the shoe but definitely not to grieve its passing.

***

The Decline of the French Beret

I went to the Pyrenees several times to do stories on the woes of the beret. In fact the last time I went, the owner of Beatex, the largest French manufacturer still surviving then, wouldn't allow me to see the factory – until he heard I would also be speaking to the mayor of the town of Oloron-Sainte-Marie. He then relented, *if* he could come along to the meeting to plead his case. I can't say I loved the idea, but that gives you a feel of how tense the situation was for him.

From Our Own Correspondent
BBC Radio 4
April 2011

If the beret is one of France's most symbolic objects the world over, its roots are in the small town of Nay, deep in the Pyrenees Mountains. Its wide streets, arcades and large warehouses give away the fact that this was once an important manufacturing centre.

After the second world war, the town and surrounding region were home to 50 factories and thousands of jobs in the beret making business. Now there are just two employees left in Nay. They run the local Beret Museum in one of the former grand hat making factories.

The museum is dedicated to the history of the famous hat. It has plenty of old weaving machines that were used to make the beret from the wool of the local sheep. Faded photos on the walls underline the fact that the garment was once almost compulsory for men, a proud display of regional identity. Kids wore them to school while for farm workers they provided essential protection against the damp and cold in winter and intense sunshine in the exposed mountains in the summer.

The tide began to turn against the beret in the 1950s.

Farm labour shrunk, young people began to flock to the cities and hats in general as an essential item of clothing began to go out of style. But globalisation finished off the French beret as a mass produced item for good. Like countless other sectors of the European textile industry, production moved to Asia. Nearly all the world's berets are now stitched together in Bangladesh.

French beret manufactures, almost all based in south-west

France, were unprepared for the transformation and were unable to compete on price with their Asian counterparts. Most of the factories closed down for good in the 1980s.

Just two have survived, Béatex and Blancq-Olibet. Between them they have around 100 employees. They are less than 30 miles apart but rather than join forces, they watch each other warily and try to keep hold of whatever market share they can.

Alain Zachar runs Blancq Olibet. He used to be in the shirt making business but saw that industry vanish in France too, as low cost producers emerged in China. So he has gone into berets. But he told me he has focused this time on big buyers with financial backing. In other words, the military. The French army is buying the hats in the tens of thousands and if Alain can provide high quality, well sown hats that can handle rough terrain, then he could emerge a winner.

And not just in France. He sees a potential for military berets across the world especially for UN peacekeeping operations where the floppy hat appears far less aggressive than a helmet.

Down the road in Oloron-Sainte-Marie, Béatex is housed in an old factory that is now way too big for its current volume of production. In a warehouse, modern machines spin wool into yarn. Next door around a dozen women work behind sewing machines, threading together the trimmings that go into making the beret.

A showroom exhibits the latest garments and you quickly understand this company has a new wearer in mind. With prices as high as €70 for a beret, Béatex is targeting women looking for a 'peasant chic' look. Celebrities like Madonna and Claudia Schiffer have been spotted wearing the hat. Luxury designers Christian Dior and Hermes like the idea and have added the high quality French-made beret to their collections, hoping women not just in Paris but in Tokyo and New York will like the idea.

Béatex's owner Pierre Lemoine told me that going upmarket is the only way he can compete with cheap imports from Asia. The French-made beret only has a future as an expensive fashion accessory, he *says. It's come a long way from its traditional farm roots and it seems ironic that a garment associated with rural peasant lifestyle could have a new life thanks to urban fashionistas the world over.*

Since that report Béatex has gone bankrupt and merged with its competitor Blancq Olibert. They still provide hats for the French military... but for how long?

***

Cheapskate – *'How to cut corners and regret it'*

Before I set up on my own I worked for the Lyon-based European news channel Euronews. At the time they didn't have much money and relied heavily on subsidies from Brussels. So if you offered them anything for free, they usually jumped at it. I had just bought a small video camera, a Sony PD 150, which was sort of groundbreaking at the time as it offered quite a decent picture at a very low cost compared to the bulky traditional TV news cameras.

Needless to say old style cameramen looked at it with disdain and said small cameras would never work, no broadcaster would take that kind of quality.

Anyway to test drive the camera – and whether I had what it took to sell an offbeat story – I took a British friend of mine, Gordon Ray (an ex-cameraman based in Atlanta who runs a PBS – Public Broadcasting Service – station there) to Alaska to look at how the local Inuit community in the far north were feeling about the possibility of oil being drilled inland near their communities (they weren't very keen).

Anyway this is about a remark I made at the airport in Anchorage when we arrived. At the car rental stand, the agent asked if I would like to pay extra for snow tyres. I turned to Gordon: "We don't need snow tyres do we?" Gordon replied: "I can't believe you just said that! Do you really think we don't need snow tyres in Alaska?"

I often said stupid things in front of him, but I guess this was a new low and I have to say thank god we did get the tyres – we were a team so poorly prepared for this kind of endeavour that we should really have died in the car in the middle of nowhere – then smarter people would have said later 'well that's just darwinism for you'.

In my defence please remember I had only partly sold the report on spec and with no idea about the video quality consequently, so far I was losing money on this project – not surprising considering where I had chosen to 'launch' my independent career. Gordon had also admittedly done the filming for a pittance, but equally, he helped me eat buttery Alaska snow crab and substantially reduce my already thin profit margin on the story.

But that kind of situation would haunt me on numerous occasion. Often when I worked for broadcasters, I would work out a global fee and then it was up to me to make money, taking into account what the expenses would be. So naturally I would try and save on things like hotels or eating…

One of the most embarrassing examples was when I was commissioned to do a story for CNBC in the Spanish Basque Country, on the tourism opportunities for businesses the day the ETA violence ended.

I had fixed up a meeting with the head of tourism for San Sebastián, Ángel Álvarez who seemed to know everyone there and who thought we were some big cheese American crew coming down to his fiefdom and we needed to be treated with utmost respect.

In fact I came with a camera girl from Toulouse, Catherine Noël, in my second hand car that had lots of issues and was always touch-and-go on long trips. I didn't have much money back then and San Sebastián while of course achingly beautiful, is not cheap, so I had booked a 'hostal', just one step above a backpackers dorm, to stay at.

When we met Álvarez he was pleasant enough, keen to show us around and he introduced us as 'the American TV journalists' and took us to one of the fantastic Basque restaurants that the city is famous for. All was going fine until he asked what we were doing after we had finished filming. I said we had nothing planned and he suggested we should try the brand new spa on the crescent-shaped seafront know as the Concha.

Of course we said yes to that, and he asked where we were staying so he could send the free passes. I trembled inside and said I couldn't remember as we hadn't checked in yet. So he started reeling off a number of top palaces that we must have been booked into. When I said it was none of those and he asked what part of town we *were* staying in, he began to frown. And then his eyes lit up, of course that new place that has just opened? When I said no, it was somewhere on the cheap side as I couldn't book anywhere else, he said no problem he could get a couple of rooms freed up for us. And that's when I got scared. I said no it wouldn't be a problem staying where we were and could he just call up the spa and say we would be coming. After that, our time with the head of tourism went downhill. Lunch ended pretty quickly – I think he came to the swift conclusion we were con artists and even though we did do a genuine decent report, he made no attempt later to see it or ask for a copy which is surprising from someone in the PR game – they always usually want to see what's been said about them, it is their job after all.

He probably thought I was some low life video producer trying his luck on a story and seeing if he could sell it on afterwards, and of course he had already made up his mind that nothing I was filming would ever get broadcast anywhere.

This kind of scenario repeated itself throughout my reporting. For CNBC again I managed to persuade them to allow me to go Ghana for a *Business of Sport* story on a Dutch football club – Feyenoord – that had opened a football academy outside the capital, Accra. Having never been anywhere near the place, I asked where I should stay and everyone kept telling me 'stay at the Tulip, it's the only place there'. And of course it was outrageously expensive with its vast swimming pool and proximity to the beach.

Fortunately the local cameraman mentioned somewhere off a busy street that was within budget and used by local level NGO and UN staff. It was actually fine, had a lot of character, a few hustling prostitutes and a great local African art crafts market nearby as well as decent local restaurants. And more importantly for me at least, it was intimate enough that you got to talk to other guests so you didn't feel too lonely.

Of course everyone I interviewed for the story kept saying to me 'how is the Tulip?' When I said I wasn't staying there they frowned and appeared really confused.

One of the people I interviewed was Anthony Baffoe, a former Ghanian footballer and one of the first black overseas players to join a club in the German Bundesliga. I thought the difficult part would be getting the interview since he was now head of the players' union in Ghana and might not want to touch a sensitive subject about western clubs seeking youths on African soil.

No, the nightmare was persuading him to come to my hotel once he found out I wasn't staying at the Tulip. When he arrived his expression was one of total disdain, and he wanted to know why I had been put here. He said he didn't even know the place existed and immediately became very suspicious of my credentials. Anyway just for the record, I went for a drink at the Tulip and the swimming pool was out of order.

Every summer I was asked by the production team of the IRB or the International Rugby Board (now rebranded as 'World Rugby') to go somewhere along the coast where the organisation would be trying to promote the sport to northern French or Dutch sunbathers with little knowledge of the game, with annual events like beach rugby tournaments where anyone could sign up and play in.

One year, the show producer Martin Cross asked me to go to one in Biarritz, the upmarket and back in vogue resort in the French Basque Country. You don't skip an opportunity to stay the weekend in Biarritz, especially if someone else is picking up the tab.

Of course I pointed out that Biarritz was home to the very wealthy over summer and no hotel would cost less than €200 a night and added for good measure that restaurants would cost a fortune as the thin and beautiful haunted the resort and that meant no fast food outlets. Martin accepted this and said go ahead (these were the days before his production company had to slash their costs to keep the contract when it came up for renewal).

So I quickly called up my girlfriend Catherine and said do you want to go spend the weekend in Biarritz. Who would decline that? So I booked a hotel called *Première Classe* for about €35 a night, near the airport outside Biarritz.

'First class', well, it was a grey rectangular block close to the dual carriageway full of heavy lorry traffic travelling between Spain and northern Europe. Most of the cars in the parking lot suggested these were not travellers used to going anywhere in first class. Anyway I put a brave face on it all and went to the reception area. And to my surprise there was a very attractive, tanned woman in her thirties talking to the receptionist about her reservation. She was pretty well-dressed too and it put me in better spirits about my choice of hotel. Not so bad after all, some sophisticated guests stay here, I said to myself. Nothing to be ashamed about. And then I listened in to the conversation.

That's right, the beautiful girl with the tanned legs said, the fee includes breakfast for the whole group but they have to be finished by 9am on Sunday as they have to be back at the prison by noon. She was probably from the local county council organising the retreat for offenders allowed out for the weekend and staying, you guessed it – at the Première Classe hotel.

Of course I didn't mention any of this to Catherine and we spent as much time out of our own prison as possible. On the Sunday afternoon she checked out and I dropped her off at the train station. I then had a day and a half's free time as I only had one interview to do for the rugby show. My plan had been to spend all that time frolicking in the big waves of course with all expenses paid (albeit in a crummy hotel with convicts as neighbours). Except the weather turned appalling, the temperature plunged and when I headed to the beach I was a forlorn sight trying to make my way into the choppy sea with no-one else in view expect a lifeguard sheltering from the wind under his jacket, forced to be there on contractual grounds.

It was miserable but I was determined to swim. It goes without saying I got pretty sick a couple of days later, flu, lost my voice, you name it. After giving up on my swim I decided to go and eat. The problem is that like most coastal resorts, Biarritz is a festive town full of joyful families or young revellers (the latter in this case almost all body beautiful surfers) and I fit into neither category. So I wandered aimlessly surrounded by happy people despite the weather, while I just felt lonely and didn't dare eat anywhere in public on my own. So I got a takeaway pizza and ate it in the parking lot of my hotel which seemed to have more in common with the 'Norman Bates motel' as truckers and others came in and out of the lot. And then it began to rain hard.

It was one my most miserable experiences in a while so my Biarritz scam back-fired entirely. The next day was Monday – I did my TV interview and headed out fast, just as I was beginning to feel the early symptoms from my ill-advised swim.

Another particularly horrible experience was when I was asked by the sports TV agency SNTV (partly owned by Associated Press) to go to Montpellier to cover the beginning of their new football season. They had just won the French *Ligue 1*, even beating PSG which had already started spending millions on new stars under their new Qatari owners.

The strange thing is that the new football season starts in mid-July as players return and start training and playing friendly games, just when everyone else in Europe is in the middle of their summer holidays. Footballers get the end of May and June off.

So anyway I was asked to cover the opening of their new season as French champions. (Ephemeral title holders, they had lost their top striker Olivier Giroud over the summer to Arsenal and had a terrible Champions League outing which impacted their *Ligue 1* concentration too). Anyway I thought since it was the middle of summer and I was going to Montpellier, I should go a day early, head to the beach and eat some oysters on the Etang de Thau.

I decided to stay somewhere between Sète and Montpellier and chose the slightly more upmarket chain *Balladins* – in any case not *Première Classe*. I didn't realise it was on the edge of a sprawling, charmless shopping centre. It was one of the grimmest nights of my life. Now if offenders on weekend release went to the *Première Classe*, this *Balladins* hotel was actually a replica of a prison. In any case that was clearly where the architect had got his inspiration. The innards of jail were on the outside. The landings on the three floors looked out on the elevated motorway between Montpellier and Sète and each room had a tiny window with bars over it. Inside the room everything seemed to be bolted to the floor.

It was the middle of a heat-wave and my room walls sweated. Opening the small window was out of the question – fumes drifted in from the motorway just metres away. It reminded me of a scene from *Bullitt* where Steve McQueen tells someone under witness protection to stay away from the window in a crummy hotel in downtown San Francisco right next to a busy freeway overpass, just in case some hitman tries to shoot him from the outside.

That night I didn't sleep a second. Outside the parking lot was full of white trash holidaymakers either drunk and beating each other up, or toughs from France's North African immigrant population threatening anyone who looked at them the wrong way. Others were simply doing dodgy deals, selling on whatever they had stolen that day, dealing drugs or trying to call up a cheap local prostitute. Of course I thought I had paid a little more for my hotel and would have a slightly better class of travel companion. But since most of the rooms were seemingly filled with families of 7 sharing one room, my theory was hopeless.

Since then I have done quite a bit of crisis media training with hotel chains with my colleague Jill Thomas and ex BBC Editor and I've discovered the number of suicides in hotels is huge. It's not surprising – a depressing environment coupled with whatever issues you have weighing you down can just tip you over the edge.

The Quirky Stories

Yann '*How much*' Tessier, bureau chief at Reuters in Paris but who has since moved into the elite management stratosphere of the company at their headquarters in Canary Wharf, said he took my quirky stories as charity.

Rather than pay me a decent income for the stories that Reuters really wanted now and usually were breaking news and not much fun, he would accept my offbeat pitches and claim they didn't get the coverage that I confidently claimed they would so he was subsidising me anyway. Clever...

One of stories was about the would-be King of France. Now you have to cast your mind back to mid-term under President Sarkozy. The honeymoon had worn off very fast, his supporters had grown very disillusioned at the lack of the reforms that he had pledged to push through. And on the far left, he represented everything they hated, in particular he was flash with no guilt or shame.

So when I read that the man who stood in hereditary line to become the next King of France was touring the country to gather support and provide an alternative leadership solution if

Sarkozy's Napoleonic presidency failed, this was simply a story that I couldn't say no too.

His name is Prince Jean of Orléans and he is also known as the Duke of Vendôme. Now my good friend Vincent Joecker who is a GP in Toulouse is the real expert. He spends his free time restoring an old château near Béziers with his long suffering wife Olga, but when he periodically runs out of money for his château project or just gets fed up with it, Vincent sifts through historical French archives instead. He tells me Jean d'Orléans is not the only pretender to the French throne. There are a lot of lines claiming to be the 'real thing' so he warned me off taking the Prince's claim at face value.

As it was, the Prince didn't address any of the 'pretender' issues, but I managed to get his PR team to allow me to shadow him for a day in Toulouse as he tried to arouse a new aristocratic surge in the south.

His first stop-off was a book store in the city centre overlooking the grand Place du Capitole. He had just written a book outlining his solutions for France and what he could do if France agreed to restore a constitutional monarchy. He told me his outlook was modern, time spent in castles was over, and a new Head of State above the political fray was needed in France once more. He said that unlike elected officials, he had the well-being of all citizens at heart not just that of his own supporters. The prince, who was 44 years old at the time, was not shy but neither was he forceful or 'in your face', he was well-dressed but not regal or overbearing.

Yet the people lining up to buy his book, all middle-aged and older, were definitely light headed, giddy at the thought that their saviour might be right in front of them, signing those books. One elderly woman whispered to me that the country needs order restored and to re-discover its traditional values and pointed to him, I guess meaning he was the solution. As was often the case with my offbeat stories, there may have been one other local journalist there, I am not even sure. It's funny what interests people on the outside looking in but not the domestic media.

We caught up with him later at a speech he gave in front of an ancient literary society – *L'Academie des jeux floraux* in an amazing renaissance building, the *Hôtel d'Assezat*. Again the crowd was highly respectable, slightly younger in fact than the bookshop though some of the book purchasers had come along too. But the ones that I noticed were a number of very sexy women in their early 40s in slinky outfits. I wondered if it was some sort of late hour rendezvous for extra-martial flings. Or did they just have eyes for the next king? Another thing I noticed was that when the Prince arrived in the room to give the speech, everyone stood up as if the protocol for a royal appearance required it. Everyone stood, including opposition politician Jean-Luc Moudenc who was there in the front row to hear the speech. He is now mayor of Toulouse and it seemed a very un-republican thing to do. Anyway I have the video so if he gives me any grief…

As for the Prince himself, after his tour of France to meet his future subjects, he disappeared from the radar. He likes to point out he took part in some of the street demonstrations against the Socialist government's legislation authorising people of the same sex to marry.

But it seems he really had other more urgent things to do than worry about restoration. He has apparently been spending a lot of time with his lawyers – there is a nasty family tiff over property inheritance to sort out. That clearly comes before a royal coronation at the Elysée Palace or Versailles.

***

Crap Wine or Vin de Merde

It goes without saying that I covered the wine industry. In fact one of the very first stories I did was on a vineyard just north of Béziers. Mondavi, an American winegrower was after a local vineyard and thought it had sewn up a deal to buy it. But then it was blocked by a communist mayor with support from local growers. At first it seemed like a fight against the American capitalists who were accused by the locals of being modern day fascists, but it seems in hindsight to have been more a case of one powerful French grower who whipped up anti-American sentiment with local political support so as to buy the vineyard himself.

As I mentioned earlier, I once went to the first Bordeaux château that was bought by the Chinese. That acquisition had triggered terror and outrage amongst the French, which made no sense when you know that the Dutch and Belgians have been snapping up vineyards in far greater quantities than the Chinese. And also many Chinese have sold back their châteaux at a loss when they realised they had overpaid and couldn't turn a profit. Many French vineyards have been smart too – Chinese students have come to Bordeaux to learn how to market and sell the wine back home in China and are hired by locals in Bordeaux to do the pitching.

One night I stayed in a fantastic château in the Margaux area of Médoc where I drank great wine and had a chance to see how the world's wine merchants and graders choose the winners each year. You get a bit put off seeing them spitting it into spittoons while speaking into hand held recorders, muttering about the grape, potential price, grower and how the wine tastes.

The French – about two decades behind northern Europe – began to realise at the turn of the century (2000 that is) that drink driving was neither a good idea nor socially acceptable anymore. In fact I have often heard that on average, a driver is breathalysed in France once every 13 years. My first time came after 11 years and then another 2 years later so I am not entirely sure of that statistic. However wine consumption has fallen dramatically, especially in restaurants. So yes, I did a big story for BBC Business news on the 'doggy bag' concept developed by restaurants in Bordeaux to persuade diners to order a bottle of wine and then take away what they haven't finished in a very elegant looking bag with a rope handle. Since then I have never seen anyone carrying one of those out of a restaurant, no-one has ever offered me one, and whenever I ask for a cork to rebottle the wine I haven't used to take home, waiters are baffled and unsure what to do, like it's the first time in history they have ever been asked to do that.

No doubt most French patrons are way too embarrassed to do it and leave great wine on the table for the waiters to drink at the end of their shifts. In Bordeaux I always saw how top university labs and winegrowers threw their resources together to make the industry more high tech. They came up with robots to work autonomously in the vines driving wooden stakes into the ground, or other another which resembled the Mars Exploration Rover which was able to cut the grass and weeds in the vineyards remotely and was powered by solar energy. In hindsight despite my positive reporting on that invention I'm not sure of the market potential after all.

Just to get one fact out of the way, contrary to what you might think, filming vineyards in the height of summer is actually really an unpleasant experience because the heat is intolerable, there is very little shade and the light reflected from the grainy rocks in the soil is horrible on your eyes.

Not all experiences were that bad though. For the now cancelled low cost BBC World travel program *Fast Track,* I visited one vineyard – Château Smith Haut Lafitte in the Bordeaux region – that has hit on a highly lucrative idea: vinotherapy. It's a spinoff making full use of its own vineyard. Basically sitting next to its vines is a very pleasant spa that has gone down well with wealthy foreigners who have bought the idea that drinking wine is a healthy thing.

On top of that, bathing in it and having grape seed massages apparently reduces the ageing process on your skin. And you can stay overnight in cute wooden huts on stilts surrounded by vines. The setting is beautiful but this is not somewhere for the poor huddled masses.

It was a different story in the Languedoc region where I came across no wine spas. In that region it's not customers wearing face masks but the forlorn winegrowers. But these weren't for better skin complexion! They would take me out for lunch, complain about prices, warn they had no future and then put on those face masks and hoods at night and burn Spanish trucks carrying wine or grapes, or vandalise the offices of import merchants. For a while they would call me and using a semi-coded language (their phones no doubt tapped) invite me to see some interesting thing that would be happening at night somewhere. Many belonged to a militant group called the CRAV and when in action, they had a passing resemblance to Corsican separatists.

As I mentioned earlier, I saw the rugby players who had converted to wine growing and they wore me down repeating the similarities between the two ways of working as both are down to earth, involve toil in the soil and a fight against the elements, and produce beautiful results at the end. But there is another similarity between the rugby and wine: some of those winegrowers are extremely stocky and with accents and attitudes as hard as nails. I wouldn't want to mess with them especially in the middle of the night wearing masks and carrying firebombs.

I spent time with the estate agents who focused on trying to get Brits looking for a change of lifestyle to become wine growers and on the other hand, I met big beefy growers who could crush me with one hand yet were close to tears as they described having no choice but to accept EU conditions to rip up their vines for good in return for big one-off payments to reduce the wine lake across southern Europe. Talking of overproduction, I was stunned at how few wine growers in France were aware of new world wine and just how popular it was with drinkers not just in the UK but elsewhere. They seemed to think the enemy was Spain but they would have had heart attacks if they glanced at wine lists in restaurants in decent London pubs and saw that French wine was drowned out by choices from New Zealand, Australia and South America. Some of their lobbyists need to get them to do a tour outside of France and then maybe they will understand just what trouble they are in when over-producing mediocre or unambitious wine.

And this brings me to 'Crap wine' or literally if I had been able to translate it correctly for broadcast "Shit wine". That's what one group of wine growers in the Languedoc region decided to call their wine. It was a risky PR stunt to both highlight their frustration that wine from their region was broadly seen as crap and also a roundabout way of saying that actually they produce quite a decent wine. "Vin de merde" was printed on the wine label with a fly hovering above the words. I went to see one of the men behind the idea for France 24 and BBC World.

BBC World News
September 2011

A bunch of regulars in a local cafe near Béziers can't believe their luck. It's free drinks on the house even though they seem to have been there most of the afternoon anyway. They are being asked, well by me in fact, to test a new local rosé. So far so good. But look at the label and you might think again.

Its reads "Vin de Merde" which loosely translated means 'crap wine'. But that certainly wasn't a turn off for these daytime drinkers.

José is one:"I think it's excellent. It's fruity" while Guillaume who looks like he has emptied a few bottles in his life, agrees:"It's not bad, it's not crap like some think – for a rosé it's good."

In fact it's anything but 'merde'. At nearly €7 a bottle, it's a decent local wine. But wine growers have resorted to the public relations stunt out of frustration. Demand for their wine is sinking and it still suffers from a poor reputation even as quality has improved.

Walter Valgalier is one of the growers behind the idea. When I met him he was late and seemed to be a little worse for wear. He admitted he had a big hangover – I didn't ask if it was from his own wine.

"Of course it's a risky idea" he told me, "but in the current climate if you don't do anything, nobody will listen or pay attention to you. We had no choice but to make a dramatic gesture because we have a good product but we are unable to sell it."

'Crap wine' may be a good publicity stunt but it's nevertheless a symbol of desperation down here because hundreds of winegrowers are giving up and ripping up their vineyards for good. But an irony of sorts is that distributors have sold out of the 'vin de merde' and are waiting for more.

***

Sir Alfred

When I first set up in the south of France I sent written letters by regular post (how very 20th century!) to TV stations around the world telling them that I was here in case something ever happened and they were looking for a TV journalist in the neighbourhood

Now you might think making contact with a channel in Australia, New Zealand or Singapore ridiculous, but over the years stations in all those places have got back in touch asking me to do stuff.

In Singapore I developed a good relationship with Channel News Asia – a rolling news outfit – and provided coverage on a wide variety of stories. One of them was actually based in Charles de Gaulle Airport outside Paris which of course was a long way from my beat but it was such a weird one I figured I had to include it too.

A film with Tom Hanks called *The Terminal* was being premiered in Singapore and it was loosely based on a real person who had been living in a sort of no-man's land at the Paris airport for more than a decade. Sir Alfred (you will understand later) bore little resemblance to Tom Hanks and it was even harder to find anyone resembling the love interest, Catherine Zeta-Jones, when I trekked around the airport with him. Here's the story though.

Channel News Asia
August 2004

50 million passengers travel through Paris's Charles de Gaulle airport each year. In fact it's one of the busiest hubs in Europe. However there is one passenger who isn't just passing through, in fact he has made the airport his home. That person is Mehran Karimi Nasseri.

This is where he works, eats and sleeps – a space of around 15 m2 located next to the food halls and stores at Terminal 1 of France's busiest airport. Sixteen years ago he tried getting into Britain, saying he was a political refugee from Iran. Britain sent him back to France because he didn't have the right visa to enter the country.

The French weren't sure of his claim either so he was kept waiting while they checked his background. One and a half decades

on, he's still here. He calls himself Sir Alfred Mehran, and now says he isn't from Iran or anywhere else. Conversation with him is not easy.

Q : Where are you from?

A : I have no country.

Q : Where were you born?

A : I have no country.

Most days, Alfred Mehran just sits at his table and gazes into empty space or he reads or writes. He's accumulated enough luggage and personal belongings to fill a small plane, but for now he has no intention of leaving this spot he calls home. Alfred breaks up the monotony by taking short strolls, some as far as the terminal entrance but that's the nearest he will get to visiting the 'City of Lights'.

Q : So this is the furthest you will go outside?

A : Yes not further, just one time I went to a hospital for X-rays.

Alfred has become such a fixture here that frequent travellers make a point of greeting him when they pass through, like one businessman from Sri Lanka, Mr Rajakaruna who has bumped into him several times while transferring between flights. He tells me: "It's really great that a person could stay in a limited area for so many years without going out. That is a great achievement."

News of Alfred's long airport wait caught the attention of Hollywood Production company DreamWorks. And that's how Academy award winning director Steven Spielberg ended up sending a team over to buy the rights to the story of his life.

Unlike in the film though, no stunning air hostess – a role played by Catherine Zeta-Jones in 'The Terminal' – has fallen in love with Alfred. But he's just maybe one of the richest homeless people in the world now.

DreamWorks paid him handsomely. He made half a million US dollars from the film but he didn't have his own bank account. So a lawyer had to open one for him at the airport post office. But he only takes money out to buy newspapers, books or something for lunch.

Nobody can say that money has changed this man's life. Lunch is usually a burger or pizza but takeaway only. Alfred says he never 'dines in' because he fears thieves may steal his luggage in his absence.

In fact, he rarely even leaves the first floor of the terminal. The floor above is bustling – packed with check-in counters and people arriving from around the world, but it's not a place Alfred cares to venture to.

Alfred was offered asylum by the Belgian government 5 years ago. He turned it down. He says he's become conditioned to living in a bubble – the unnatural environment of a busy airport hub as home.

If there's one person who knows Alfred better than anyone, it's the airport doctor Philippe Bargain who has been treating him for 16 years, free of charge. He told me: "His physical health is fine but his psychological state of mind is not as good because there is nothing normal about staying in an airport terminal for 16 years. He is on the same record of life as the rest of us but he's not on the same track."

Another person who has been watching over Alfred is Martin Youenang, the pharmacist from the store just a few metres from Alfred's lodgings. He hopes the movie will prompt the authorities to finally sort out Alfred's case.

"He needs to get out of this situation. First of all, he has to sort out the legal paperwork. I think he needs to go somewhere where he will be looked after, where he won't have to do his own cooking, pay the electricity bills or rent. He needs somewhere where he can slowly break out of the isolation that has closed in around him over the past 16 years."

Alfred tells me he has no idea whether he'll ever get to watch the movie based on his life but the film appears to have given him fresh impetus to eventually leave this place.

Q: Are you happy with the way your life has gone or not?

A: Yes, its fine, its fine.

Q: Is it a good life?

A:The life I don't talk about. My ending my time here and moving to another country or city is still possible.

Q:You still want to do that?

A: Of course, yes.

Q:And where?

A:America.

Q:Where in America?

A: Hollywood or New York.

Of course, that dream is unlikely to be fulfilled while he refuses to say what his real name is, where he was born or whether he has a family somewhere. After several hours at Charles de Gaulle, I, like the many people around me, was more than ready to leave for home[30].

***

Bears in the wild

When the French government decided in the 1990s to re-introduce wild bears into the Pyrenees it unleashed a not entirely surprising backlash from many backward, reactionary farmers. They claimed school children would be at risk (presumably from bears waiting outside schools),walkers would be abducted and taken into caves and held during hibernation just in case the bears woke up hungry and felt peckish.

They claimed their flocks were being devoured by the bears

---

30 When I wrote my script an editor at Channel News Asia asked me to change one thing – not to refer to Sir Alfred's constant smoking and to take those pictures out. Apparently smoking on camera in Singapore is a bit like sex before the TV watershed in Europe.As for Sir Alfred, I never saw him again but I have read that he was finally taken to a home in France for the psychologically unstable.

when in fact the vast majority of sheep were attacked by stray dogs. They also liked to say if Parisians (i.e. well-off tourists) wanted to see bears they should be released on the Champs Elysées. Of course what they didn't say was that without huge subsidies from Parisians and other taxpayers, their own very existence in the Pyrenees as farmers would have disappeared long ago, well before the bears.

Not all farmers were opposed to the re-introduction of the bears (from Slovenia) and no human has been attacked. One particularly enlightened farmer near the mountain village of Seix in the Ariège (France's equivalent to hillbilly northern Georgia in the US south) once pointed out to me that there are thousands of bears in Canada and everyone seems to get by, so why so much outrage over 20 bears along the French-Spanish border?

As it is, most of the mother bears and their cubs chose to migrate to the Spanish side, where it's sunnier (and maybe a little more tolerant of their presence).

Some farmers do see the financial positives to having bears in the wild again. Think of all those tourists in Scotland who flock to Loch Ness in the hope of seeing the monster! Well, it's the same thing in the Pyrenees for urban families with small kids. They will never stumble across a bear but they like the idea that they might, or at least to imagine that a bear may be watching them from behind a tree as they walk past. And of course mercantile farmers have succeeded in selling their produce at local markets at highly inflated prices to the same tourists.

Apart from a rise in ecotourism helping the local economy, one other positive side effect has been the resurrection of the job of shepherd to look after the flocks.

***

Shepherd School

To placate the rural community, central and local government have funnelled extra money into schemes to train a new generation of shepherds to keep the bears at bay.

At the same time a local race of dog that had also almost disappeared – the beautiful but fierce looking *white patou* has made a huge comeback. The patou is just about the only indigenous animal that the bear won't pick a fight with. The patou is left with his or her sheep day and night and if a bear appears won't take fright and will stand between the bear and the flock. I'm told the bear isn't actually scared of the dog but figures why bother, and will go elsewhere to find food.

So some farmers and breeders have got into the lucrative act of breeding patous (subsidised of course by those urban taxpayers again) and are sending them back into the fields.

Patous are adorable if raised at home and domesticated but that makes them entirely useless for standing up to wildlife. All the same, it's kind of sad seeing them living in isolation from man – out on their own with their flock all the time with no human contact – but that's just me.

Anyway it was a great excuse for me to go and spend a few days at shepherd school for the BBC and Reuters. As you can imagine, a story like this got lots of mileage.

BBC World News
September 2007

In the French Pyrenees there used to be thousands of shepherds to look after the livestock. But the skill is being lost. So the French government has set up shepherd schools. It's proving popular but not everyone who signs on is cut out to become a shepherd. Christian Aynto however clearly is. He is shivering and soaked. He used to run a bar; now he is learning to become a shepherd. Christian tells me: "I have always loved animals and the mountains, so I wanted to work with both, so this is perfect. My job is to watch over the flock and check which animals are limping or sick and to provide first aid. That's really my key role."

Christian comes from the French Basque country and shouts his orders in his local language. His sheepdog must be one of the few that rounds up sheep in Basque. A local farmer, Jean Arrous, is teaching Christian the tricks of the trade and makes it clear: "When you decide to do this job, you have to enjoy being out in the wild, stuck on a mountain. If someone can't handle that, they can forget about being a shepherd."

Shepherds are needed to protect sheep and cattle from stray dogs, the raw weather and even the odd bear. There used to be thousands of shepherds in this mountain range; now there are just a few hundred left, but the profession is going through a revival. But those who join shepherd school because they think there is something romantic about becoming a shepherd quickly drop out. Jean Bernard Castéran has invited us to his summer home. It's a hut in a valley with a gurgling stream going past. He has been doing the job for 10 years. He admits that thanks to the mobile phone he is less cutoff than others were in the past, but it's still a tough job.

He says: "I get the feeling there are lot of unhappy people living in towns working in factories or in front of a computer all day who think this job is about freedom and wide open spaces and sunny weather. But it's not that, for a start you have to get up at 5am to find your flock."

The shepherd school managers meet weekly with the farmers to see how the trainees are doing. Sandrine Verdier is a shepherd school co-ordinator. She can't be accused of overselling the job.

"It's a difficult job physically and psychologically and the mountains are not always pleasant to be in. Having to spend several days looking for your flock in the fog and rain when you are soaked and exhausted is not fun."

But Christian was upbeat. He left us and headed up into the fog in good spirits. His coaches tell me he has what it takes to become a very good shepherd.

I did another story on shepherd school for business programmes too. Proof that you can turn anything into a business story. In fact I was always amazed more freelancers didn't offer stories to business news commissioning editors, after all they have to churn out stories for business bulletins every hour.

I guess it's because most think they will have to talk about the bond market or gold futures, and to be honest I don't understand any of that either, but business reporting became a long term lucrative niche for me and I never had to talk about things like derivatives.

BBC World Business Report
March 2003

Due to the mad cow scare across Europe and the foot and mouth outbreak in Britain, consumers are switching more than ever to lamb, especially French lamb. Now in theory, French farmers should be happy, but the only problem is that there aren't enough shepherds to look after the flocks. But that's changing thanks to new recruits like Romain Touzet.

He already looks like a pro and he only started his nine month long shepherding course a few weeks ago. The farmer he is working with shouts out instructions on how to steer the animals forward and how to make sure the sheepdog is doing her job too.

If Romain makes the grade he can look forward to months of solitude and exposure to the raw elements in the unforgiving Pyrenees, which is just what he wants: "It's mainly a love of the mountains. Thanks to this job I can work in the mountains five months a year. I am not made for working in a city with a computer, but out in nature, with animals. Once we have finished our training we will have to work on our own for a long period of between 3 and 5 months. People who can't handle a solitary existence can't do this work. You have to like being alone just with your dog and herd and in the mountains."

In all, eight people out of more than 40 who applied have been accepted on the shepherding course. The state is paying for the training and it's not cheap, costing several thousand euros. While most of the course is spent outside in the fields, every few months the trainees gather in a remote mountain lodge to learn about legal, medical and other farming issues.

The trainees include a former electrician, a laid off factory worker, locals who need regular work outside the ski season and one woman, 29 year old Christine who wants to go back to nature. She told me that after sometime living in a city she wants to return to her roots – her grandparents were farmers.

With other state subsidies, the pay for being a shepherd is also up. Monthly salaries are as much as €1,500 a month – well above average in this economic blackspot. But it takes passion to want to spend more time with farm animals than humans. Nicolas de Munnik runs the Shepherd school and told me what's required to look after a flock. Daydreamers beware!

"A good shepherd is a person that succeeds in uniting several aspects. They must be very attentive to their herd that they are keeping in good health. Their herd must eat well because the fatter the animals are, the better it is for the farmer. Physically it's very difficult because often they have to get up at 4 or 5 in the morning to climb to a mountain top where maybe the herd is sleeping. You have to arrive while they are asleep because they are quickly on the move once they wake up and catching up with them is very difficult."

The shepherd's goal is to find the best pastures so the sheep end up fat and happy. And of course to protect them from wild animals including bears. A shepherd's accommodation is likely to be a rundown cottage, possibly with an outdoor well for water. Romantics need not apply. But for those of you living in towns and cities and thinking of moving down here to become a shepherd, bear in mind you will probably have to take a pay cut and it's freezing in winter, scorching in summer. On the other hand, there aren't many traffic jams and you're the boss.

BBC World News focuses these days on what social media is reporting as opposed to generating its own stories. I exaggerate a little and radio still thankfully bucks the trend, but it's a common tendency across the industry, as monitoring social media is a lot cheaper than providing complex news gathering films. But then I could just be getting old and talking about social media on rolling news channels may be just what younger people want.

I only mention this in passing because so many stories that I did would never get on air today. One fun one that comes to mind instantly was a profile of the Brazilian writer Paulo Coelho.

Having just written his best seller, *The Alchemist*, Paulo Coelho, I discovered, was living part of the year in an anonymous hotel opposite the train station in the rather ugly town of Tarbes, a former communist stronghold that used to be a centre of the French tank building industry before that closed down. You get the idea.

No-one could really figure out what Coelho was doing in Tarbes but the mayor gave him the symbolic key to the city. I went around the town with Paulo to try and understand what an international writer at the top of his game was doing there. He wasn't really sure either, and while he eventually gave up the hotel for a farmhouse in the Pyrenees, it seems he had a lot of fun in Tarbes. Just about the only local resident celebrity not from the rugby world, he was certainly the centre of some flattering attention – the number of attractive women who came running up to him throughout our day's filming certainly provided me and my cameraman Michel Bousquet (an avid skirt chaser himself) with the main answer to why he chose to live there.

***

The Modern day Cure for Travelling Anxiety

The other day as I finally got through security and long queues at Toulouse airport – in other words a normal day at any airport – I stumbled across someone playing a piano in an atrium sandwiched between lots of glitzy duty free shops. And the person playing was a passenger waiting for his plane just like everyone else. He wasn't playing classical music but a jazzy tune; he was good and it definitely had a positive effect, on me at least. Flying for me is an ordeal, I imagine a whole bunch of scenarios taking place in the cockpit when turbulence hits and now of course you have a new fear factor, a suicide bomber striking in the departure hall before you even take off. Like you need that to add to the list.

Anyway, the open-to-all piano in stressful environments has caught on everywhere. It provides something soothing and triggers a little more empathy in most of us, a bit like the pet cat in a hospital for the seriously ill. (Maybe that is why 10 Downing Street always has a cat milling around there... I know a little about that because in pre-9/11 days I had to do a story for GMTV on Humphrey, the cat reunited with his political masters after he had done a runner from the Prime Minister's home in a van that had come to pick up dirty laundry). Anyway, Toulouse train station was one of the first to put a piano in the arrival hall. And I thought it made a nice story for BBC radio.

From Our Own Correspondent
BBC World Service
April 2014

The train from Marseille is late. But there isn't the usual seething-but-resigned, resentful atmosphere that spreads every time the SNCF French rail network announces bad news. No, a surprising and unfamiliar calm reigns on the arrival concourse of Toulouse train station this Friday afternoon.

In fact passengers and those waiting for friends and loved ones aren't anxiously glancing at the arrivals board every 10 seconds, they're watching — or more precisely listening to — a young man around 20 years old playing classical music on a piano nudged in a corner of the hall, between the waiting room and the automatic ticket machines.

His name is Paul. He is waiting for a train for Bordeaux where he's heading for the weekend. A sign above the piano reads 'It's your turn to play' and that's just what the one-time music student is doing.

The piano was installed in December. With 40,000 passengers passing through every day, the idea behind the instrument was to calm people down a little and give them something to focus on during the waiting time.

The many fears of the station manager Thierry Danton were, in no particular order, that the sound would be terrible, the players hopeless, commuters uninterested, or worse, the instrument vandalised.

But the performers are diverse — old, young, talented or not so — and their repertoire wide, from classical music, to 70s French romantic ballads to theme music from contemporary American TV series.

With 150,000 students in Toulouse, many players are music undergraduates passing through, sometimes in a group with one playing the piano, another on saxophone or even a singer. Occasionally while someone is playing, a total stranger offers to join in and do a duet.

The piano was bought second hand and cost €5000. Some of the players come to the station on a regular basis to practice like Dorian, in his mid 20s who can't afford to buy a piano and doesn't have the space at home to install one anyway.

He admits he also enjoys the attention he receives when he starts playing. The audience can be made up of just a few passers-by but sometimes the crowd is far bigger and there is applause at the end.

Richard, one dapperly dressed elderly man, said he was pleasantly surprised at how many young players knew classical music. Growing up I was told women couldn't resist for long a man who knew how to cook or play a musical instrument. I wish I had listened. Several times I saw women cooing over the musicians, hovering far closer to the piano than seemed necessary.

One asked if she could put her mobile phone next to the keyboard to record the music. If that wasn't a chat up line...!

Like any big city train station, with 12 million passengers a year, Toulouse Gare Matabiau has its fair share of young pickpockets and aggressive looking drifters with beer cans and sad dogs in tow. I'd like to say the music changes their wayward ways, but of course it doesn't. It does however give the heavily armed 'seen it all' police who spend their days watching over them all and/or chasing them out of the station, some respite. Often you can see a police officer pause to soak in the music and think of something else for a few minutes. The station is open every day, only closing from 1am to 5am. Rush hour is when the piano is in biggest demand. But one Sunday morning when the station was nearly empty I saw a middle-aged blind man playing *what I think was Bach, with his labrador sleeping at his side. It was a very moving scene.*

The piano rules are pretty simple: anyone can play but you can't ask for money in return. Someone comes by once a month to tune up the strings and repair any broken keys. Not everyone is a fan. Sound absorbers were installed after complaints from a couple of in-station stores that some of the performers were too noisy.

The station manager told me he was very sceptical when the idea of 'installing a piano to calm nerves' was first raised. Now he is a believer and says the idea is spreading to dozens of stations across France.

***

French Farmers paid to go on Holiday

There is a long standing view in the UK that French farmers in a cabal with EU elite are subsidised to the maximum – and on top of that mainly by the UK taxpayer – and then they go on to grow crops or food that will get thrown away due to oversupply.

According to the *Daily Mail* etc., the French farmer will go on strike, tip fresh manure or tonnes of tomatoes on pretty town centres or blockade key intersections with their tractors at the first sign of reforms that would ask them to consider working in a free market.

Of course no-one seems to notice the hugely successful large scale farmers in East Anglia living very well partly down to Brussels and terrified of what Brexit may mean for them.

French farmers actually get unfairly bad press. Their numbers have been dwindling rapidly over the past two decades, many barely make a living wage and their capacity to negotiate prices with large rapacious supermarket chains is close to zero.

With some of the highest social security charges in the world, they can't compete with cheaper imports.

Among the depressing stories I covered in rural departments like the Gers was the suicide rate for farmers. It's amongst the highest of any profession in France, often because they have run up huge debts, are physically and emotionally cut off from the rest of the population and don't know who to turn to for help. Asking for counselling is not part of their culture.

If there was one person they could turn to for support and who did back them, it was Jacques Chirac. On paper at least the former president was an unlikely ally. Just like Donald Trump, the urban billionaire surprisingly drew much of his support from blue collar minimum wage voters, Chirac, with his background as mayor of Paris, was an unlikely candidate for defender of rural France and its traditions. So when he passed legislation giving French farmers financial support so they too could go on holiday just like the rest of the French, it was a golden opportunity I couldn't let slip by.

World Business Report
BBC World News
August 2006

The French take on average between five and nine weeks of holiday a year. That's especially thanks to the 35 hour working week. Farmers however take only around 3 or 4 days a year. But that is beginning to change because the government is now paying them to take a break. It's down to a new law giving farmers a financial incentive to go on holiday as they will be able to pay workers to fill in while they are away. The idea is two-fold: to create jobs and make the profession more attractive.
In the Lot region, late August is traditionally one of the quietest periods on farms. The tobacco plants don't have to be cut yet and the corn

still has a couple of weeks before it's ripe. Only dairy animals need constant attention. So Marie-Claire Rougié, a farmer all her life, is going on holiday.

First of all she has to show a replacement worker where everything is and what to do. And this month for the first time ever, the state will give farmers like her a €900 tax break to pay for staff while she is away. She is taking up the offer. With her suitcase sitting on her bed, she told me giddily that holidays are expensive and until now, she has always had to pay someone for eight hours of work a day in her absence, just to keep the farm ticking. Thanks to this new tax break maybe she will be able to leave twice a year and for longer periods.

But first, farmers like Marie-Claire have to find someone to replace them. They meet in a small village hall. They are working out how to find temporary workers for the dozens of farmers now thinking of taking time off. As Dominique Bertrand who runs a sort of temping agency for farm workers pointed out, it's also about preserving relationships on farms:

"There are lots of women married to farmers who don't work on the farm themselves and have jobs with long holidays, but their husbands don't. So if they don't take some time off together there could be trouble within the family."

I meet Laurent Donnadieu, who is now working on seven different farms in the area. He is more or less the rural equivalent to a city temp, often called out at short notice. But he is not complaining: "It's more interesting because there is less routine and when the owners go on holiday we are on our own with more responsibility – it's like we are the farm owners when they are gone."

Meanwhile Marie-Claire and her husband have just finished packing their suitcases, said goodbye to the dogs and are headed off for a walking tour in the Alps. Their timing is perfect, where they live, rain and windy conditions are expected for the next few days.

I didn't cover politics in France that much. Sure I had to go to vote counts, film and interview the odd politician when they were campaigning in the Southwest, whether it be Alain Juppé, Segolène Royal or Jean-Luc Melenchon (whose speeches very much had an undertone of 'bring back the guillotine for the bourgeoisie'), but overall it wasn't really part of my beat. The only politician with national stature in the region apart from Philippe Douse-Blazy was the former Prime Minister Lionel Jospin. But in 2002 he lost in the first round of the presidential election, triggering the sensational run-off between Jacques Chirac and Front National candidate, Jean-Marie Le Pen.

But I did find a lovely angle from which to cover the US presidential elections in 2004 when Democratic Party candidate John Kerry was running against the incumbent, George W. Bush.

I was particularly happy to do this story as the American TV networks had been circling the village of Saint Briac in Brittany for weeks trying to get the mayor to speak (without success) and expose Kerry's gallic ties.

It wasn't in the Southwest but I think it's worth including as a special add to this quirky section.

BBC World News
Sept 2004

Anti-French feelings in the United States are still running high after Jacques Chirac's government refused to back the invasion of Iraq last year. So most American voters would probably be surprised to know John Kerry has extensive family ties in France. And it's no accident that his campaign advisers are trying to keep his French connections under wraps.

St Briac appears to be like any other small town in Brittany, but look more closely and this French scene has an important American connection. This is John Kerry country.

Kerry's grandfather, James Forbes, an international banker, bought an imposing coastal property here at the turn of the last century. He had eleven children, some of whom married into French families, and French relatives still live here. As a child, John Kerry spent many of his summers here where he studied French culture and he even learnt to speak French – the very things his campaign team are now eager to downplay.

Brice Lalonde is the mayor of St Briac. He's also John Kerry's first cousin. He spoke to the BBC despite pressure from Kerry's election staff to avoid publicity in the hope that the French connection might remain unknown. He is sure that is not his US cousin's idea.

He laughed as he told me: "You know how it is. The candidates are quite ok. 'Bienvenue (welcome) Brice'… but all the staff terrible."

Mr Lalonde has also run for higher office. He ran for President of France as a Green candidate although he suffered a heavy defeat. He hopes his American cousin fares better but admits his intellectual honesty could be a handicap against Bush.

"He is not a very good speaker to the crowd. He is a guy who thinks a lot, yes and he's deeply concerned and he knows reality is complicated, that you don't have black and white. You don't have the good and the bad."

The Bretons – like the local oysters – don't open up easily. But after the fishing boats have come in and the wine has started to flow, they admit to some excitement about Mr Kerry's French links if he becomes president, but they don't really think he will have time to visit if he gets to the White House.

There is a monument to three US soldiers who died liberating St Briac in 1944. But today, the two countries are separated by more than the Atlantic. The town hopes the Mayor's cousin is the one who can patch up that drifting relationship.

***

Celebrities *(don't get excited – it's not what it seems)*

One time I got a brief chance to interview Arnold Schwarzenegger as he was following the Tour de France via helicopter and since one of the day's stages ended in Toulouse, he chose to premiere his latest Terminator film in the city too[31].

Other than that, most of the time the nearest I usually came to brushes with celebrities was interviewing the assistant deputy mayor in charge of sports facilities or the head of the regional chamber of commerce, that kind of thing – you get the idea.

So when a panicked call came through from a production company that made the Channel 4 program *The F Word,* I was intrigued.

What I really should have done is told them to never call me again, slammed the phone down, changed my number, and then made it unlisted for ever. But I didn't (or else I wouldn't be telling this sad tale).

You see the frantic call was because one of the producers on the team – who was also the only one who spoke French – had forgotten his passport and only realised at the airport.

Now any normally sane person would have picked up the clues pretty fast that you shouldn't have anything to do with an outfit like that. But what hooked me in was that the 'talent' was coming down too and I would have to work with her. The talent in question was Janet Street-Porter. Ok you feel let down – it

---

31 It was at a time when the actor was considering a run for governor for California so anything he said publicly about politics at the time was considered of vital interest. It will come as no surprise that he said nothing of interest to me though.

wasn't Cameron Diaz or Gemma Arterton, but like I said I was starting from a low level.

Janet Street-Porter had been in the news a few months earlier accused of using racial slurs against a black neighbour – that news had even reached me. I had heard she could be difficult but after her recent unneighbourly behaviour I was sure she was contrite and would now be doing her best to get along and fit in.

It was one of the worst assignments I ever did. For a start, the subject matter pretty grim: *'The French eat foie gras and horse meat – surely the Brits are missing a trick and should do so too'*[32]. So the filming assignment took us to horse butchers and cold, damp and rundown farms in central France in November where ducks were force-fed.

Janet was absolutely charming to all her fans as she stepped off the plane in Limoges, and totally vile with her camera team.

Apart from complaining about the subject matter, she didn't like the long drive, the money she was being paid, the way the shoot was being organised, the on-camera sequence she was supposed to ad-lib… The poorly paid team were humiliated at regular intervals, but they couldn't answer back as they were on contract with a production company and therefore terrified of her calling the bosses and telling them she couldn't work with this crew ever again.

In fact at one stage on the first day she did storm off saying she had had enough – and I had to take her to the nearest village café to calm her down.

In fact she more or less ignored me but looked at her blackberry non-stop, giving running commentary on the various TV commitments she had accepted or turned down because there wasn't enough money in them. Or when some other well known star had been chosen instead of her for some

---

32 I did like one plot in the episode I admit. Janet opened a barbecued horse meat stand outside the Cheltenham race track and tried to convince punters to eat it.

new pilot or series, she then gave me the reasons why they had been picked - it never had anything to do with talent, it was always sex in some shape or form.

Her vocal ranting took place in a small village where probably the whole community was on minimum wage or dire state retirement levels. Yet oblivious, she muttered out loud she was only being paid around £12,000 or something for this episode of *F Word* and what a stupid mistake she had made and was just doing a favour to Gordon who is a wanker anyway, etc.

In any case she decided she had enough filming that day and wanted to be taken to her hotel. So the crew of 4 split up - one taking her back while the others soldiered on - which was a bit difficult since the whole show is built around the 'talent'.

Around 11pm we finally reached our hotel in a small out of the way town called Aubusson. Janet had gone to bed hours earlier and we managed to persuade a small restaurant to stay open just for us. Anyone familiar with the French countryside will know that finding a restaurant in the Massif Central in November open after 8:30pm is a small achievement - that this one stayed open and waited just for us was incredible gallantry.

The hotel owner had also made a special effort to ensure someone was there to greet us and the hotel was renovated, extremely comfortable and very welcoming. Or at least so I thought… until I discovered it was a killing machine.

Around midnight, the harried director Tim Whitwell's phone goes off as we are eating. Who would be calling him here of all places at this time of night? And as he takes the call he goes pale - all the rest of us can think is that someone close to him has just died in terrible circumstances and he is being told the details. And then the conversation changes: "A lawyer? Here? Now? Where am I going to find a lawyer now?"

And then I hear Janet yell out 'pass me the translator!' - yep me. She had apparently slipped in the shower and was now in extreme pain with severe back injuries that might leave her entirely crippled – not enough to require an ambulance mind you, or a doctor, but enough that she required a lawyer on the spot so she could sue the hotel owners for running a dangerous outfit, and she wanted one now.

I can't quite remember how I managed to get her to hold off until the morning, but the next day it seemed her back had made a miraculous recovery. But not her team spirit. Shortly after going to a horse farm she decided she had had enough and demanded she be taken to the nearest airport – she was leaving – she didn't like the story, hated the crew and she had to head back to try and salvage her spot on a new programme.

The crew were left adrift unsure what to do, then a call came from the BBC asking me to do something at Airbus and I quit too.

The funny thing is, a few months later the production company called me again, Gordon Ramsay wanted to do a new episode in southern France looking at a British-run restaurant that was: 'absolutely crap, they were fucking hopeless and he would tell them they were and then he would sort it out. Chris could you find us such a restaurant?'…

On occasion I do actually learn from my mistakes and so having learned my lesson with the Janet Street-Porter nightmare, I turned this one down.

The Border Stories

I've always been fascinated by borders and living so near Spain I often had a chance to criss-cross the border on foot. In fact if you go cross-country skiing in the French resort of Somport, one of the pistes takes you on a loop across the Spanish side before returning to France. And there are marked footpaths along the aching beautiful rocky shoreline of the Côte Vermeille south of Perpignan that dip in and out of Spain. On the other side, in the Basque country, there is a superb trip by boat from Hendaye to the gorgeous Spanish Basque town of Hondarribia. It takes less than 10 minutes and you are in a whole new world, even though both are in the Basque Country. Many people jog between the two towns along a coastal path. Others row in beautiful long boats in teams in the middle of a channel which is also the international border between France and Spain. Amazing when you think what that border was like 50 years ago when General Franco was around[33].

33 My friend Cathy Ragland started as a journalist in Texas where she grew up, and later became a professor of ethnomusicology at various universities, studying Tex-Mex culture and Tejano music along the Texas border and on the Mexican side. I can understand, it's a fascinating field. She hopes to do similar work in the Basque country one day if, she gets the funding – I hope she pulls it off.

I ended up doing lots of stories involving the French-Spanish border. One involved the last cigarette seller on the French side of the border in Le Perthus – he was about to close down as he could no longer compete with his counterparts on the Spanish side where tobacco products were about 30% cheaper.

I crossed the border on foot with my cameraman to see the day tourists in their masses getting their supplies along with cheap petrol before heading home. Some (men) stay to pick up prostitutes in nearby La Jonquera where the girls perch on the roadsides in large numbers wearing next to nothing in broad daylight. High heels and underwear as day wear is not an uncommon sight. Brothels are banned in France (although prostitutes can be self-employed) but not in Spain, so massive ones have popped up on the border, but most of the customers are French.

I managed to convince the then head of TV features at BBC World, Simon Smith to let me do a story on the prostitution business on the border. A former church had even been converted into a brothel and the owner had invited us in for an interview. I can assure you the number of French cameramen who volunteered to do that story virtually for free is truly remarkable and a real sign of altruism. And then a couple of days before we were going to set out, the BBC called back and said it was off, they were worried about our safety.

It was true that we had been briefly taken into custody by Spanish police when we did the cigarette story as Spanish and Andorran shop owners doing a roaring trade had no interest in media coverage on how the French were losing out on business. Something similar happened in Andorra – police questioned us in their border post when they saw us filming lines of French cars loaded up with their goods heading down the hill back home. Andorra makes a lot of money from duty free goods so it has little interest in seeing that showcased either[34].

In theory there is a limit to how much alcohol and cigarettes you can bring from Spain and Andorra to France, but the number of French customs officers out on the beat has been slashed for budget reasons and they are now so focused on terrorism that you have to be really unlucky to get caught with your boot full of booze and fags. And the Spanish and Andorran authorities certainly aren't going to remind you of the rules.

Talking of Andorra, it had become the winter equivalent of the Costa del Sol. Thousands of British skiers on cheap package holidays arrived in Toulouse from airports in the UK that I didn't even know existed, to be whisked straight to their winter resorts in Andorra. Of course these all-inclusive holidays included free and constant booze and there were a series of fatalities involving blind drunk Brits out on the mountains.

I remember being asked by the then British Consulate in Bordeaux to get a message across on Radio 5 Live and elsewhere that drinking at high altitude and outside in the snow can be dangerous for your health. I often gave stories about Brits in France to Sébastien Marti one of the editors of the local newspaper La Dépêche. Every time I bump into him he still chuckles at that one.

Looking back on my earlier story on shepherds, there is one that got away. I always wanted to do a story about how shepherds on both sides of the border between France and Spain had ancient access rights to each other's pastures. I was never able to get that off the ground, mainly because those areas with rights of passage are very far from any roads and very difficult to reach.

A moving border story I did cover was the *Chemins de la Liberté*. I spent a day out with British soldiers and ex-military from both France and the UK who spend nearly a week each summer

34 Andorra also makes money from French owned secret bank accounts but doesn't like to talk about that either. And anyway likes to say it's all in the past now.

tracing the routes used by escaping World War II allied pilots who had been shot down and were helped by 'passeurs' over the mountains to relative safety in Spain, using various 'chemins de la liberté' or 'freedom trails'. The groups I did part of the hike with did it in broad daylight, with no safety fears of running into Germans, with lots of food, a drink at each stage, well equipped and in July. In other words with none of the fear and hardship fleeing service men faced back then. Each year a *chemin de la liberté* journey is undertaken and in the past some of the last remaining French passeurs would join them at various points for moving ceremonies in memory of those who didn't get through alive.

I took part in sections of the *Chemins de la Liberté* re-enactments several times. Here is one story I did for France 24.

The Freedom Trail
France 24
July 2009

It's an unusual scene. Around forty walkers and local officials standing in silence at the crack of dawn on a wide bridge in the town of St Girons in the foothills of the French Pyrenees. They listen to resistance era music playing on a record player plugged into a van. Very old French war veterans hold flags. Most of the walkers are British men and a few women from army backgrounds who are retracing the dangerous 'Chemins de la Liberté' or 'freedom trails' taken by Second World War pilots shot down by the Germans. Their aim was to flee to safety through the mountains into Spain.

To get there they had to rely on local 'passeurs' or people smugglers, who knew the way at night – and how to avoid the enemy. Colonel Guy Séris is one of the guides for this trip and helps keep the Freedom Trail history alive. He told me the rendezvous point between the people smugglers and the fleeing pilots was under the bridge. And ever since, the bridge has been the symbolic starting point for the annual walk. The climb through the mountains takes 4 days. It's gruelling at the best of times – but for the escapees it was a question of life and death. Around 3000 tried to get through enemy lines; many never made it. One of those taking part is Keith James, formerly with the British army. He puts their experience into context:

"The real thing was so different but this is the nearest we can do nowadays. We don't walk at night and we are not pursued by people with guns. We are reasonably well-equipped and fairly fit. We are obviously a lot older but we know what to expect… For the guys who did it for real it must have been a nightmare. People died doing it."

During the trek there are numerous reminders of the dangers escaping pilots and their local helpers faced. There was a moving memorial service for local passeurs who were shot dead here on this mountainside for helping British pilots.

One man, Paul Broue now 86 years old, knew them. As a young boy he entrusted himself to the 'smugglers' to get through the mountains into Spain then join French forces in North Africa. He has helped set up a local museum in memory of those who risked their lives on the 'Chemin de la Liberté.' In a soft, very quiet voice, he says schools and young people need to be made aware of what happened back then and we don't want what we faced ever to be forgotten.

Four days later this group arrived exhausted but safe on the Spanish side of the mountains. There, local Spaniards had organised a party in their honour. That of course, is the least historically accurate part of the reenactment – most of the original pilots who managed to get into Spain, rather than finding freedom, were captured by General Franco's forces and put into concentration camps. But their chances of survival in the camps were at least greater than on the run.

When I began scaling back the journalism side of my work and taking on corporate media assignments, one of my clients was ATR, the Toulouse-based plane maker that makes aircraft for up to 70 passengers that stand out because they fly using turbopropellors.

Working there I met one of the contract negotiators in the finance department, Gilles Colaveri who in his spare time was part of a group that spent its days looking for wreckage of old aircraft.

This is a story I did that got a lot of coverage possibly because the photos that were taken from the scene were quite remarkable too.

The Plane Wreckage Investigators
From Our Own Correspondent
BBC Radio 4
September 2013

It's a long drive up gravel and dirt roads in the Pyrenees through the mist, and finally, over 1000 metres up, I reach my destination and I feel I have either joined the flickering embers of an illicit all night rave party or a group of hard core forest environmentalists.

The men look haggard, bundled up against the early morning cold, shabby tents bunched on the rare dry earth, lots of heavy machinery on the ground, while coffee brews on a makeshift stove and the remains of a cassoulet sit in the bottom of a large pan.

I have just entered the select French world of Second World War plane wreckage investigators.

They number around 50 in all, and their mission this time is retrieving the remains of a German bomber, the dreaded Dornier 217. 1,700 were built and none are intact today.

This particular salvage operation is intriguing. The Germans had stationed many of the Dorniers outside the French city of Toulouse and they conducted bombing runs from there on allied forces at sea. With radio-guided technology they were able to accurately target ships in the Channel. However, in July 1944, two of the bombers got lost on their return to base and collided over the Pyrenees Mountains.

The 8 crew members were killed instantly but the mountains were also home to 'passeurs' who helped smuggle allied troops over the peaks and into relative safety in Spain, and the local residents feared reprisals from the Germans who would come looking for the bodies. So they decided to throw the wreckage down a nearby 100 metre cave hole to hide the evidence. And then a collective unofficial silence descended on the local community. It became almost taboo… until very recently.

Today's plane wreckage hunters are a mixed bag, including archaeologists and historians, but many come from the aerospace industry themselves, working for manufacturers like Airbus or the turboprop maker ATR. You could say they have aviation in their blood. One of their most recent discoveries was a highly rare French seaplane, the Latécoère 298.

Gilles Colaveri is one of the most determined members of the group. It was word of mouth and long forgotten rumours that sent him trekking through the forest last year in search of this remote cave.

The cave's location matched eyewitness accounts about the crash, but it was inaccessible. So he asked a local speleologist group to help him discover what might be at the bottom of the cave, and sure enough they stumbled on large charred metal sections of one of the lost Dorniers.

Like most things in France, it took months of haggling and bureaucratic paperwork with the French state before they received permission to start retrieving the wreckage – a complex affair requiring makeshift cranes, harnesses and muscle power. Many of the parts weigh more than 50 kilos each and pulling that up a narrow 100 metre shaft is a daunting task. Out in the open air, much of the wreckage looks like mundane scrap metal, but other parts bring the history to life, whether wing sections, the remains of an oxygen tank, ammunition or a part with the German instructions still intact. The team say what they have found is relatively well preserved. It will all end up in a museum in Berlin and another in southern France, but there are nothing like enough remains to re-construct the aircraft. In fact one reason no Dorniers remain to this day is because after the war, their metal fuselage was retrieved for other industrial needs.

The team celebrated with a makeshift lunch provided by the owner of an aviation-themed restaurant near the control tower in the nearby city of Toulouse. The chef, an amateur pilot, too old to go down a cave on ropes himself, rustled up a beef stew with mustard sauce, followed by brownies all washed down with red wine for everyone.

But not everyone is happy to see this history brought to light. The mayor of the nearby village of Sacoué, Yvette Campan has lived there all her life and she remembers her grandparents talking about how scared they were when the two bombers crashed and seeing the crew's bodies scattered over a wide area. The last thing they wanted was to attract attention.

And even now, there was no local ceremony to mark the recovery of the wreckage – in her own words, 'the Germans were the enemy' after all, if it had been a British plane that was being salvaged, it would have been a different story. The local hunters out searching for wild boar also seemed uncomfortable at the sight of these plane hunters, digging up the past.

But one of the elderly plane hunters, Georges Jauzion a former pilot in the French Air force and former test pilot for Airbus says he wants to put himself in the place of the German pilots and understand what happened in the skies over this mountain range nearly 70 years ago.

***

The Enclave of Llívia

Finding and knowing a good story is a crucial skill of course in this business but another is knowing when to pitch the story to the newsroom. I never managed to get the one about Llívia off the ground at the right time. But I finally found a 'buyer', *From Our Own Correspondent*. I wish I had done a TV piece there at some point and boy did I try. Anyway you can't get closer to a story on borders than this one.

From Our Own Correspondent
BBC Radio 4
March 2016

To begin, a brief history lesson is needed. After a long war, the Spanish and the French reached a peace agreement in 1659 called the Treaty of the Pyrenees. Under the settlement, Spain handed over 33 villages in a region called Cerdagne or Cerdanya, on the northern side of the mountain range, to France. But Spain held on to one, called Llívia, because it had the status of a town, not a village.

It wasn't until the early 19th century that a border was actually traced between the countries and that is when the 'Enclave of Llivia' as it is officially known, all 12km of it, found itself completely surrounded by France.

Its 1,500 residents have been entirely physically cut off from the Spanish 'mainland' ever since.

To get to the town which is about two hours inland from Perpignan you have to drive along what is called the 'Neutral Road' maintained by both the French and Spanish authorities.

It's less than 7 km from the enclave to the Spanish border town Puigcerdà and before the Schengen agreement, French motorists needed to show passports at customs before joining the road. The local residents had right of way between their enclave and Spain.

However 83 year old Valentin Súria who has lived here all his life told me that in the 1940s and 50s under Franco, only Spaniards with special stamped permits were allowed into Llívia – the last thing the regime wanted was opponents being able to flee or even set up a stronghold there.

Despite the border controls, under the original treaty agreement, farmers in Llívia were allowed to bring their cattle and horses to graze on higher ground on French territory from April to October each year and they still do, with a big ceremony at Easter.

The French also have to guarantee the town's water supply but that is a bone of contention as mild winters and very hot summers have led to rationing and grumbling in Llívia that they are being hit way too hard compared to their French counterparts.

The local school basketball and football teams play all their weekend games in Spain, not against local French clubs, and surprisingly few residents speak French considering they are in a tiny landlocked haven, surrounded by France. The local shops have dried ham hanging in the windows and the yellow 'Correos' mail boxes mounted on walls are just the same as those elsewhere in Spain.

The French police have to coordinate with their Spanish counterparts if they want to chase a criminal heading to the enclave.

One of the first things that strikes you when you arrive at the entrance to the town is an official sign stating: "The enclave of Llívia is for independence". At the recent national and regional elections, 80% here voted for independence from Spain, along with the rest of Catalonia – the autonomous region Llívia is administratively attached to. Why? After all, the residents of the UK colony Gibraltar are said to be more British than the Brits.

If I said the turn towards independence was due to a road stop sign, that would be over-doing it. But Elies Nova, the mayor of Llívia, in his grand office with a huge terrace overlooking the snowy Pyrenees and the Spanish border, told me there is a link.

That neutral road I told you about earlier is supposed to provide unhindered direct access between the town and the Spanish border. But the French regional council decided to create its own bigger bypass that cuts across the neutral road, so they put stop signs up. The signs kept disappearing overnight so they built a roundabout instead.

The mayor told me the Llívia council complained to Madrid but nothing happened, and that, in his mind, sums up the attitude of the Spanish. Most don't even know the enclave exists, and local residents feel much closer in spirt and geography to policy makers in Barcelona. He also raised a familiar argument – they give far more money to Madrid in taxes than they get in return. But not everyone in Llívia is ready to rock the boat. While Spain has an unemployment rate of over 20%, it's less than 7% here thanks to tourism. Llívia's novelty status draws in more than 15,000 visitors a year from both France and Spain. They are drawn by this historical oddity and the extraordinary sun-blessed ski slopes nearby in Font Romeu. The tourism has created jobs in the French resorts and triggered a holiday home housing boom in the enclave.

The mayor admitted that under the current arrangement, Llívia is probably the most well-protected town in Europe, since it can count on the French gendarmes and their Spanish counterparts the Guardia Civil, but also if really necessary they can call in the Spanish national and local police units in nearby Puigcerdà – although flashing lights or not, they still have to go through a roundabout these days.

***

Ghost Train

Remember that remote hotel on a mountain side in the Stanley Kubrick horror film *The Shining* where Jack Nicholson well… suffers from writer's block?

Now take that hotel and place it on the French-Spanish border along the Pyrenees mountain range and you get the idea.

The building in mind is Canfranc international train station – once considered the second biggest rail station in Europe after Leipzig and definitely now the biggest ghost station in the world.

When I heard about it and saw some photos in *Le Monde* magazine I just figured I had to go and see it. And is it worth it! You wonder what it's doing there and what was the vision of those who decided to launch the project in the first place.

Here is a story that I did for BBC Radio 4

From Our Own Correspondent
BBC Radio 4
October 2017

To give you an idea of its size, there are 365 windows – one for each day of the year – hundreds of doors and the platforms are more than 200 metres in length. It was an architect's dream come true, built with iron and glass. It included a hospital, restaurant and living quarters for customs officers from both France and Spain. No expense spared, it had to be bold and modern and at the time it was nicknamed the 'The Titanic of the Mountains'.

The question is: how did such a grand train station, 1,200 metres up a mountainside in a village with a population of 500, ever see the light of day? And more importantly, how did it end up having next to no passengers and how is that it might now be on the cusp of a new lease of life?

At the turn of the 20th century, the Spanish and French authorities had a grand project to open up their border through the mountains to trigger international trade and travel. It was a remarkably ambitious scheme involving a series of tunnels drilled through the mountains and dozens of bridges. Needless to say a highly expensive and challenging engineering feat at the time. At one point, the French workers were pulled off the project and sent to the northern trenches during the First World War and were replaced by Spanish counterparts.

The station was located in Canfranc, just over the border on the Spanish side, but one of the platforms was under French control, similar to a foreign embassy. French police and customs staff sent their children to a French speaking school installed in the village.

But the day the station was opened in 1928 by the French President Gaston Doumergue and Spanish King Alfonso XIII, flaws quickly became apparent.

The track sizes were different so passengers had to change trains and for freight it meant transporting goods was too slow. And then the Wall Street Crash of 1929 reduced international trade substantially anyway.

As few as 50 passengers a day were using Europe's second biggest train station. And then things got worse.

With the Spanish civil war, Franco ordered the tunnels on the Spanish side to be sealed to prevent rebels from smuggling weapons in.

When the international line re-opened during the Second World War, it was used by thousands of Jews and allied soldiers to escape into Spain. The mayor of Canfranc is Fernando Sánchez. His father was a customs officer at the station. He told me the station became a spy hub for allied forces and was even involved in the planning for the Dunkirk evacuation. But when the Germans occupied the station they used the rail line to transport stolen gold.

After the war, the French lost interest in the line and allowed it to deteriorate... When a train derailed on the French side in 1970, that signalled the end of the adventure. The French abandoned the line and it's been that way for nearly 50 years.

The Spanish were furious according to Fernando Sánchez, as there was an international agreement to maintain the line and the French were accused of breaking the deal. Canfranc's population which had risen to 2,000 thanks to the station has dwindled to 500 today.

The grand station went to rot, the tracks rusted, the ceilings fell in with the harsh winter weather and vandalism did the rest.

But a few years ago the local government in Aragón decided to buy the station and restore it, claiming it was a major part of Spanish history. You can now visit it in a hard hat and in the past 4 years 120,000 people have done just that – ironically far more than ever actually used the line when it was in service. The tourists, nearly all

Spanish, are fascinated by its size, a little proud too at the symbolism and image the station was supposed to project to the world.

On the Spanish side there are now even two trains a day between Zaragoza and Canfranc. The journey takes 4 hours – the same time as when the station opened back in 1928. The freight trains that went from Portugal through Valencia and up to northern Europe however, remain a nearly forgotten memory.

But now the Aragón government wants to not just restore the station as a hotel but build a new one next to it, to relaunch rail travel through the Pyrenees, and the French regional government based in Bordeaux has agreed to re-open the line on its side too. Its President Alain Rousset told me the rail line which goes through the achingly beautiful Valley of Aspe will be branded 'The Western Trans-Pyreneen Line' when it opens. He has vowed to find €200 million and says Brussels will offer matching funds. He says he has made a lot of enemies by pushing ahead with the plan, pointing out that politicians in Paris had envisaged a motorway in the place of the track to link the French capital to Aragón. Graffiti scrawled on walls in the valley reads: "Long live Canfranc" – the line is back in favour.

If all goes to plan, the Titanic of the Pyrenees could be back in business within 5 years. I noticed the massive wooden ticket counters at the station have already been restored.

The Banlieues:

from Gangsters to Terrorism

A decade ago the overseas impression of life in France was heavily influenced by what tourists experienced while on holiday here. They visited the picture postcard centre of Paris, or they skied in the Alps or swam, camped out and flirted along the Côte d'Azur in their youth on their first overseas holidays away from parents. And as adults, they stayed in beautiful gîtes or chambres d'hôtes with pools in lively, beautiful countryside.

In other words, they experienced the best of France and that stayed with them. Hence the pull and attraction of the place.

When I first moved here, I could say I came with much of the same idealism, but quickly I discovered another side to life here. Days are quite different in the far-flung suburbs where the police are often involved in skirmishes at the bottom of grim tower blocks with kids from mainly North African immigrant backgrounds and to lesser extent West African. Often it's over drugs, but equally often the drug sellers are poorly paid foot soldiers, reporting to shadowy ruthless operators who invest their drug money in property, arms dealing and other violent gangster activity that can be highly lucrative – which explains the relentless rate of casualties in turf wars. Of course only later was the link made between urban violent delinquents and their transition to Islamic fanaticism, often while in jail.

It was in 2004 that I went out with the police for the first time in the banlieues of Toulouse for BBC News, having got permission from the French Interior Ministry. In one sense there was nothing unique about my report, except that back in the UK, it was a whole new look at France. Within the BBC, Simon Smith, my commissioning editor (a frequent summer holiday-maker in France) and his team said it was an eye-opener, they had no idea this kind of thing occurred in France.

Toulouse's Crime-ridden Banlieues
BBC World News
April 2004

The French centre-right government has pledged a major 'get tough on crime' campaign this year. To prove it can get the job done, it's even singled out 23 of what it says are the most violent housing estates in France, where it has vowed to turn around soaring crime rates. On this Monday morning on the Bellefontaine estate on the outskirts of Toulouse, while the nearby ring road is jammed with commuters, there is little sign here of rush hour activity. With unemployment on this sprawling estate at 32% and double that for the under 25s, residents have few jobs to rush to.

The only real sign of life is council workers cleaning up last weekend's debris. But the scars run deep here. This concrete jungle housing 9000 mainly North African immigrants has all the hallmarks of urban poverty and the social problems associated with it. Violent crime is on the rise here and that's why the hardline French Interior Minister, Nicolas Sarkozy, has ordered the police to crack down hard here... and they certainly have a lot of work on their hands. Just last weekend, 10 cars were set alight on this estate.

The police have been told to root out the tiny minority making life a misery for the rest. The kind of violence they face goes far beyond random vandalism. One police officer on patrol who doesn't want to be named tells me there is a lot of cannabis and cocaine dealing here as well as stealing of cars and he added, we have noticed recently a large number of armed carjackings.

But the youths who live on this estate, many whom have had run-ins with the authorities in the past, say the politicians are simply out to make a name for themselves. They add ruefully that they will have more trouble than ever trying to find work because they are linked to this now-notorious 'Bellefontaine' estate. One told me: "When I look for a job and try to get ahead, I get rejection slips because employers say they don't want people from this neighbourhood."

Dalia, another youngster, added: "Automatically when outsiders speak of this neighbourhood it's about the negative things, nothing positive, nobody really wants to listen to us."

One of the biggest problems is that there are simply too many restless youths with too little to do. A gym in the basement of one tower block was created to help keep young toughs off the streets, but it's going to take more than that.

At a café on the outskirts of Bellefontaine, the district mayor Françoise de Veyrinas admits a crime crackdown on its own won't solve anything so long as poor immigrant families are excluded from the rest of French society.

She tells me: "It was a monumental failure to have 73% of the social housing put aside just for families on the poverty line – that's created a ghetto effect which makes integration difficult and we have to break that."

There are some positive signs: money has been provided to equip one council-funded association with brand new computers for young kids to play and learn on. And later this year, three of the estate's *squalid tower blocks will be knocked down to try and create more green spaces and encourage more prosperous families to move in. In the meantime, the police have a more immediate task – to restore order. The number of arrests has doubled this year.*

***

The Three week long Riot in 2005

In October 2005, France experienced some of its worst prolonged civil disorder in decades, with more than three weeks of rioting in hundreds of cities and towns up and down the country.

I won't pretend that I was expecting or predicted it, but about a year before then, something which might seem innocuous had disturbed me and seemed ominous. I was reporting on a court case in Pau over several days and there was a lot of downtime when I would sit outside on the steps of the court basking in the sun.

At one point, there were a bunch of kids between the ages of 13 and 15 of Arab immigrant background hanging around there on the steps too.

They asked why I was there and I explained and they were not impolite or anything. But they kept saying – to themselves almost – 'France en feu', or 'France on fire'. I don't know if they were waiting for their own court case on some sort of delinquent charge or to support one of their friends in court. But on a regular basis in that half an hour they would say 'France is burning' to no-one in particular. I thought it was very strange to mutter that all the time somewhere that sunny day where there was no particular tension either, and to me it suggested even then that things were looking ugly.

Pau, like so many other small cities in France, has a highly prosperous community but on its outskirts a small but particularly sensitive and at times highly violent *banlieue*, maybe because it feels so cut off from the more genteel population. I know several journalists who have been attacked there and lost much of their TV equipment, which is hard to believe when you stroll through central Pau.

The autumn riots were triggered by what was initially a routine police chase. When two kids died, electrocuted while hiding in an electricity generator cubicle after running away from the police in a particularly tough Paris suburb – Clichy-sous-Bois, riots were inevitable. But they quickly spread to other impoverished estates in the Paris suburbs that had nothing to do with Clichy. Within days they even reached similar neighbourhoods in Belgium.

I was actually on an assignment in Israel when the rioting spread. I remember going to a newspaper kiosk and the seller, seeing me pick up a French newspaper said to me: "Now you see for yourself Arabs are not that nice after all."

I was in Israel for a week and each day in my hotel room I watched, mesmerised, as the riot fever spread south. So naturally the call came through from the bureau chief at Reuters in Paris – at the time Marina Gaillard – to hit the ground running as soon as I returned to Toulouse. I can't say the idea thrilled me. And when my plane approached Toulouse airport at dusk, the flight path was as usual just above (no surprise here) the sink estates where most of the rioting was occurring.

It may have been something else, but from the air I saw lots of small fires, and I think they were cars and rubbish bins set alight. Not the kind of sight you want to welcome you home especially when you know you have to head to that zone too.

Anyway over the next two weeks, every night I would be out with a cameraman in the bad neighbourhoods, on the look out for trouble. We would take shelter behind the 'robocop' dressed

CRS police. Some wiser journalists and photographers had bike helmets to wear, I chose simply to dress as hoodie-like as possible but then it meant the police couldn't really distinguish between the likes of me and the rioters.

One image I still have is of a middle-aged Arabic man, crying in front of his van parked close to a row of tower blocks, a crowd watching nearby in shock. His vehicle had just been set alight indiscriminately on an estate called Bagatelle. He told me his van was all he had to work and his equipment was inside it, charred. That was to be a routine scene over the coming days.

Every night a police helicopter would emerge with its powerful search beam and that both indicated where the disturbances were taking place and added to the tension with its powerful engine throb.

I was the only international TV journalist in Toulouse initially and the strong pictures I was sending back nightly sparked a decision by Reuters' main competitor APTN to send a crew down too.

Their desks back in London hate each other but on the ground it's a different story. You have to try and work together so that no-one gets screwed if the other finds a great story or pictures that you don't have.

So we agreed to shadow each other and leave together in the evening – the pact being that we would have drinks later on (in the pleasant centre of Toulouse) and if either desk called saying they or we had to return to the field, we would all go. It worked well.

What was amusing about APTN is that when they arrived at Toulouse airport and picked up their hire car, what they wanted wasn't available but they were given an upgrade, a top of the range sleek black Mercedes instead.

It was hardly undercover – the police looked with disdain and suspicion at the crew and it wasn't the kind of car you wanted driving into a riot zone – but having said that maybe yes it was – because it could have been associated with successful dealers and they would have been untouchable as they drove through the hood.

Except they messed up – while running away from one battlefield scene, the sound man with the APTN crew dropped the car keys and of course couldn't go back to pick them up. Their Mercedes spent the night in the riot zone before being towed to a garage the next morning, but you know what, no-one touched that car overnight whereas rioters didn't hesitate to torch the car dealerships nearby...

Despite all the nonsense by the likes of CNN saying there was civil war in France and getting its cities all mixed up and in the wrong locations on maps of the country, one thing that struck me was that it was indeed a riot for the TV age. The trouble kicked off early around 6pm and was usually over by 8 or 9pm which meant the rioters, many very young, not even out of their teens, could head home to see what chaos they had caused, on TV, within hours of committing it.

During the third week of rioting, there was rarely trouble late into the night. But still it struck me that there was a bizarre competition to see how many cars could be set alight and the arsonists would try and see if their estate could emerge top that night.

Sadly both Reuters and APTN played provocative roles because under pressure from the French government, the French media stopped filming burning car scenes so broadcasters at home and abroad counted on agency reporters like me to provide those images. It was not my proudest moment and I remember giving an interview to the local newspaper *La Dépêche* explaining that both Reuters and APTN were spending fortunes providing the same evening pictures of garbage bins and cars on fire – coverage which only prolonged the nightly disturbances – but neither would give up and pull out as they feared leaving the scene to the competition. The newspaper editor appeared genuinely appalled.

One Saturday night while we were out looking for trouble to film, one of the local journalists received an alert that a fire had broken out at a huge store in Blagnac, near the airport.

I said it was far from where we were and it made no sense to cover it as it clearly couldn't be linked to the rioting. But APTN said they were going and we followed. In front of the huge warehouse store, employees were crying. They had come to see what had happened – already probably on minimum wages they were now about to go on unemployment benefit.

I said we should film the store (called GIFI, a low cost chain that sells a bit of everything from cheap kitchen furniture to garden tools) but hold onto the video and not distribute it. However the Paris bureau said the rolling radio news channel *France Info* was already reporting that the store had been burnt down by rioters and that meant Reuters needed to run the video. Many weeks later investigators said the fire had been caused accidentally.

I kept telling the desk that we should bail out and only at the beginning of the fourth week did we call it quits and stop covering the urban guerrilla war that had already burnt itself out.

While the rioting occurred at night, during daylight hours the atmosphere was feverish at the prefecture which has responsibility to maintain law and order and is under direct orders from the Interior Ministry in Paris. There was never any real threat of the state being overwhelmed but it did look at times like it was wavering and the one winner was of course the Interior Minister at the time, Nicolas Sarkozy.

He had been pretty much abandoned by the Prime Minister, Dominique de Villepin and by President Chirac during the disturbances, almost intentionally it seemed, to leave him in the lurch and see him fail to restore order so that they could then take control of the situation themselves. But it was a role he excelled in, jumping into the void – both promising that order would be restored and helping create an 'us versus them' atmosphere that worked in his favour... a trick that he would go on to use time and time again.

One of the most poignant and electric moments of this whole episode was when rumours started swirling one night as cars burnt and we filmed them, that Sarkozy was going to making a flying visit to Toulouse to see for himself the police reaction against the young rioters.

He had already made a name for himself in the city a few months earlier inviting the national press to the police headquarters with hints he would have something interesting to say. And he did. In a packed courtyard, in front of everyone including ranks of uniformed police, he said to the police chief: "Your job is to arrest criminals, not play rugby with them!" in reference to a once a year game that rank and file police played against locals from the housing projects.

The police chief in question was dismissed on the spot... Except that since in true French style (it's nearly impossible to fire *fonctionnaires* or civil servants), he was put in charge of a police sports academy near Paris. French police humour you might say.

As the rumours continued to agitate everyone that Sarkozy was coming down, we received texts on our phones to go to police headquarters around 11pm. I've never seen so much firepower packed so densely into the same place. Maybe 80 burly police officers from various units, many undercover, lined the four walls of an overheated, windowless room which resembled a bunker. And that was the atmosphere, of an entrenched group. Sarkozy walked in and in a very similar kind of speech that the former Mayor of New York Rudolph Giuliani gave to police officers at a graduation ceremony I went to once in Madison Square Garden, made it clear they were all that stood between order and anarchy.

I have to say it was a very powerful moment and at the late hour as he walked through the room slowly greeting each police officer individually, there was such a remarkable silence you could hear the neon lighting in the room buzzing.

I was dressed particularly slobbishly that evening – unshaven, in jeans, big boots and with a woolly hat on, to try and fit in as much as possible on the streets as I said. Many of the police officers wore the same, and Sarkozy stopped in front of me and said: "good job".

After the three weeks of rioting, lots of expats in Toulouse told me they were getting calls from worried family members who thought the city was on fire. It wasn't the first time I flinched at some of my work.

After that episode, foreigners' views of France changed, but it nevertheless continues to be most the visited country in the world… Most tourists continued to climb the Eiffel Tower or head to the south-west or to campsites near Nice for their holidays and rarely saw any further evidence of the social exclusion that was exposed to the outside world throughout that autumn in 2005.

In fact many French people in prosperous city centres never saw it either. The French government did a lot of public soul searching on what was wrong on the estates and vowed to plough billions of euros into renovating them. But the maths didn't add up – the money needed to rebuild hundreds of sprawling estates up and down the country didn't match the intention. Soon the ambitious energy ran out too and of course renovating tower blocks but leaving the same people in them without a lifeline from the outside to help them changes nothing anyway.

However one positive local initiative in Toulouse that emerged after the riots did grab my attention. I have participated with the organisers several times and over a decade on, their 'tour' or 'riot tourism' as I called it, is still going strong. This was the idea: after the disturbances a couple of women decided to show another side to life in the banlieues and also offer a chance for outsiders and the curious to meet some of the residents.

I did this story many times, for BBC World and France 24. Here is one of the stories at the time for the travel program *Fast Track*.

BBC World
November 2006

Last November hundreds of cities and towns across France were hit by urban rioting which lasted for several weeks. The violence focused attention on the little known decrepit, poor housing estates or projects, far from the beautiful, wealthy city centres.

One of the worst hit cities was Toulouse in south-west France, more known for good food and being home to the aeroplane manufacturer Airbus. Every night over a three week period I was on this estate in Toulouse covering the riots. The police were in front of me and on the other side of the street were violent youths throwing fire bombs over our heads. A year on and city officials are trying to project another image of this neighbourhood by showing a different side to the people who live here.

Regional and city officials had a plan. Since so few tourists head out to the suburban high rise estates, get someone from the area to show them around. On a bright spring morning, a group of Spanish tourists and French social workers were taken out for the day by the local guide Catherine.

Their first stop: a vibrant market in the heart of one of the biggest housing estates in southern France, in an area called La Reynerie. Most of the shoppers and the stall owners are first and second generation immigrants from North Africa but also from France's former colonies in West Africa. These groups now make up the majority of the residents so it's no surprise that the group stops for lunch at a Moroccan restaurant in the middle of the estate.

The owner, Abdellah Malzi shares with the group what life is like here but believes initiatives like this could go even further:

"People should visit this area and why not even live here a bit, let's say a neighbourhood swap scheme, those here move out for a while and outsiders come in and see what it's like. That would be a far richer experience, but what they are doing already is pretty good because they get a glimpse of this neighbourhood and what's here."

After lunch we head to the notorious tower blocks which were ringed by the police during the riots. Catherine shows us a model of what urban planners are hoping the estate will look like in a few years. Many of the towers are being knocked down and residents will be rehoused.

High up on the 13th floor of one of the tower blocks you can see just what an isolated urban sprawl this is, with the lush countryside on one side and the prosperous, dynamic city centre in the distance. Occasionally the group come across residents like Jacques who are only too happy to stop and talk about their area and with a certain pride.

"It's important to see the positive side of a neighbourhood or a country as well as the negative side. There are residents here with their good side and their bad side and that's what makes our neighbourhood vibrant."

40 years ago this estate was farm land – the animals have long gone but there is one big surprise in store, the local château is still here, hemmed-in but an oasis in the middle of an urban jungle. And we get a chance to see it up close. It's now for sale and the city is likely to take it over for community projects. It's a side to the housing estate that few outsiders know about.

Catherine Deauville, the housing estate tour guide says that this is the purpose of her tours: "The negative side of life here, everyone knows about all that even if I think the problems are exaggerated. However it's true there are problems here and you know them – so I want to show you what you don't know."

And the members of this group, like Spanish tourist Yurena Perez, say it's been worthwhile seeing another side to what it's like *on one of France's most impoverished estates: "It was a real eye-opener because during the riots in November, on Spanish TV we saw lot of violence – cars on fire and so on – and it was every day. Now I know it does happen but it's a minority behind the trouble and most people here want to improve things."*

Whether the riots actually changed anything for the better in the long term, who knows? But what is certain is that the estates involved are now at the heart of more intense long term media focus whereas previously they were of interest to TV crews only when there were violent disturbances and the media usually moved on quickly once the last embers had been extinguished. So I guess you could say that was positive development.

Since *les banlieues* had become a hot topic, the French rolling news channel France 24, broadcasting in both French and English and later in Arabic also, was very keen on anything from the troubled estates.

So I looked at the situation from many different angles, for example how sports charities and social workers using rugby in particular tried to keep kids out of trouble by focusing their aggression on the pitch and showing respect for the opposition, shaking their hands after being tackled, encouraging girls, often from Muslim background, to play too and often in mixed teams – an initiative I really applauded.

What saddened me though was how few parents ever turned up to see their kids playing rugby in their spare time on pitches ill equipped for the game. Social workers told me parents showed in fact very little interest in their children.

I'd also see young and eager entrepreneurs from the estates who wanted to 'give it a go' but didn't have a clue how to get financial help or who to turn to for simple advice on setting up a business. Occasionally I came with successful entrepreneurs to meetings on dingy estates late at night to see them explain what they do and how they could provide seed money to help these estate-dwelling, wide-eyed, would-be entrepreneurs launch their own ideas.

I went several times to see a former French boxing champion, Christophe Tiozzo, who, with backing from local businesses, opened a ring for kids in the heart of one notorious estate in Toulouse called *Le Mirail*. Those who really took the sport seriously, turned up on time, listened to the coaches and showed discipline were then offered a lifeline – a full-time job opportunity.

Business of Sport
CNBC
June 2010

This is not someone you want to mess with. Christophe Tiozzo is a former middleweight World Boxing Champion. His boxing career is over but he's picked a new fight. His mission is to help today's kids from France's rough housing estates get ahead through the noble art. In 2005 France was rocked by weeks of rioting on housing estates in hundreds of cities and towns across the country. Tiozzo is convinced they could erupt again soon: "It's getting worse and worse and an urgent plan is needed. The state needs to help these kids. I hope I am wrong and that things are fine but I think there is a real emergency out there because the situation is explosive in France's housing estates again."

With financial backing from big business, Christophe has set up two boxing gyms in the heart of two of France's roughest estates in Paris and Toulouse. Several more are planned.

The idea is simple: the youths who train in the rings get a workout and maybe even land a job. Boxing, as I am discovering, is hard work and that's the whole idea. If big businesses are sponsoring this project it's because they have been told boxing is a good way of finding new talent. But the companies who have poured around half million dollars into this club don't promise a job to just anyone who turns up in the ring. What the instructors are looking for is regular attendance, punctuality, hard work, team building and a positive attitude. In other words everything a future employer would expect from a model employee. Bernard Continsouzas is regional director of the Casino supermarket chain:

"The aim is not to attract youths to take up boxing and say we will find you a job. It's definitely not that – it's come and box. Do some sport and then maybe with the structure that has been put in place here, some of those youths will stand out and their talent get noticed. They can be pointed in a new direction or given career advice."

Thomas Piquemal, chief financial officer for EDF and a boxing fan is also involved in the project[35]:

"Personally, I am convinced that these young people are really very positive for our country, but sometimes it's extremely difficult for them to find the link, to have the contacts to get out of the suburbs where they live."

Fathi Belmekki is one of those they have in mind. He has no job but plenty of determination. Spotted by his instructor, he said he was interested in getting work experience in security and fire prevention. And that is what he is doing now during the day – getting trained up. It costs around €1,100 and that is underwritten by the firms who have put money into the boxing academies. That doesn't mean he is guaranteed a job at the end of it, but he's almost there.

"I started work at the age of 16 and worked in carpentry. But with the economic crisis I had real trouble finding work. I have been in the club for five months and they helped get me on this training scheme and finance the qualifications. Maybe down the road, I'll get to work for this firm if an opening comes up."

The estates that most of these youths come from suffer from all

---

35 Thomas Piquemal later resigned from EDF after the French giant agreed to finance and build two new nuclear reactors in the UK. He said the deal put the company's future at stake.

the problems associated with poverty: poorly integrated minorities, high crime and unemployment at around 40%. In other words a turn-off to employers. And companies have indeed been accused of discriminating against youths from these housing projects.

So is this new involvement of captains of industry in this boxing project simply a way for them to buy themselves a clear conscience?

Thomas Piquemal says he feels no guilt: "I have nothing to blame myself for. So I don't have to ease my conscience. But it's true that doing business all day, personally I felt the need to do a project which has nothing to do with financial values, which is only dedicated to people and sport."

The reality is that most of these young boxers won't get a job by sparring. But that misses the point say the instructors. One of their key aims says their coach Philippe Kaminsky, is trying to provide some sense of order and respect in these kids' lives, which is so often absent out on the street.

"There are rival gangs in this neighbourhood who will behave differently towards each other when they are here and show more respect towards each other thanks to the discipline we try to give them."

Faith, one of the young boxers agrees: "You are so tired that you don't think about anything. Your daily problems? You don't even think about that — all that goes away when you are here and the atmosphere is good — everyone gets along and that's why, even after a hard day I come here — it's what motivates me."

Meanwhile Christophe Tiozzo, now aged 46, says he can't expect the kids turning up at his gym to put in lot of effort while he just watches. Despite health problems, he says he will continue to workout to show that he is in this project for the long term too.

As a footnote to that story, I even joined the boxing club. It was new, airy, clean, the training was fantastic, the coaches genuine and hardworking. The only reason I stopped was because my shoulder began to give me lots of pain – it may or may not have had anything to do with sparring, but sadly I had to call it quits.

Those more 'positive' stories were great to work on but in the end what really sold – to no great surprise – were the hardcore 'this is a violent ghetto' ones. But they were also a reality too, so I suppose as long as you didn't focus on just that...

Two years after some of the worst urban rioting France had known since the second world war, came the stunning declaration from the fire crews in Toulouse and elsewhere that they would no longer go into rough neighbourhoods to put out blazes unless they had police protection on their arrival.

As shops, banks and other businesses pulled out of those ghettos, what remained of the 'state' were often unemployment offices and child support agencies providing financial help for single mothers and big families on the bread line. Hardly positive symbols but essential for the local population.

But not welcome were the police and the fire engines, seen as intruders by violent younger residents who would set traps for both and then attack them.

Again it was the kind of story that was difficult to comprehend in newsrooms back in the UK and when I got permission to spend the night with a team at a fire station, the coverage got big exposure back home because it just didn't sync with their vision of the France that they thought they knew.

BBC World News
November 2007

Another emergency call-out for the team on the weekend overnight shift at the city's main fire station. The atmosphere is heavy. The job is difficult enough but something else is weighing on the minds of the several hundred men and women who make up the Toulouse city fire service. Increasingly they are coming under physical attack from youths in some of the city's isolated, troubled housing estates.

In one incident I witness someone's tried to set fire to one of the few remaining stores on this sprawling estate. But only two fireman actually put out the blaze, the rest of the team act as cover, making sure no-one attacks them or throws chunks of concrete from the top floors of the tower blocks.

And this time they have armed police protection too. In fact if the fire teams arrive before the police, they won't intervene to put out the blaze until they get the backup because it could be a trap or ambush.

French housing estates with double digit youth unemployment have become no-go areas for businesses, banks and some state services. The firemen are seen by some gangs as one of the last symbols of the state still prepared to enter these neighbourhoods.

The violence towards the fire fighters surfaced two years ago during the urban riots that flared up across France. The rioting is over but not the nightly attacks. They are easy targets – if there is a fire, they have to put it out.

Back at the fire station morale is low amongst the team. They have pushed their own alarm button warning – unless their own lives are protected they will stop going into some housing estates.

Julien Vignancour is angry: "We feel a certain bitterness because we are there to help people but instead we set out on our missions scared, not because of the fire but because of what kind of reaction we can expect from some of the people when we get there."

Another fireman, Julien Frédéric, looks at it from a philosophical point of view: "They may not have anything against us personally but we represent the system or the state... But it's still us going out there so it's us who are being targeted regardless."

At 5am we come across a car on fire on a ring road near an estate with a bad reputation. There is no sign of trouble but the emergency crews have to be wary – the week before, another car *on fire also contained a booby trap, gas canisters in the boot... Amazingly they didn't explode. If they had, someone would have been killed.*

Eric Segura is fire chief and he's exasperated:"Unfortunately my team are attacked frequently and that without question challenges how we put out fires and there is the question of how well we can do our job now."

It's 6am on Sunday morning. It's nearly the end of the shift. The team were called out 11 times – but overall it's been a quiet night.

At the time I didn't think much about it, but during one of the fire incidents we went to a grimy sprawling estate, *Empalot,* on the banks of the Garonne River. While there, one of the police officers said there weren't just your usual violent criminals and young delinquents here, it also housed homegrown Islamic fanatics who could well go on to commit atrocities against their own country at some point. This was back in 2007.

I continued to do 'police in the hood' stories, and I remember going out with the BAC, which translates as the anti-criminality brigade. They are a special unit of police officers who go out in groups of 3, they don't wear uniforms and they drive unmarked cars. They are often in the front line in the French banlieues, and car chases (which is their favourite part of the job) when trying to catch bank robbers – or more likely teens who have just held up a tobacconist or stolen a car.

I came out of that experience shaken up and so did my cameraman Xavier Marchand[36].

No, we weren't shaken up just because we came under attack

---

36 Xavier Marchand was my occasional cameraman. A tall, well-built former French swimming champion and as soon as he was at my side in front of any women, I can sadly tell you I was made instantly invisible. When he would turn up on his massive Harley Davidson motorbike and shake his hair free after removing his helmet, pile-ups involving female drivers were imminent.

from people throwing huge rocks off a high rise roof in the bad neighbourhood of Mirail when I was trying to do a stand-up, with the police right next to us... no, it was the BAC units themselves.

There seemed to be a tacit agreement that the gangsters on the grimy housing estates should stick to where they were and not head out elsewhere. In other words keep their trouble to their home turf. If they didn't play by the 'rules' they would be crushed by the BAC. It seemed to be a sort of cat-and-mouse game and at times I couldn't really figure out who was on the right side of the law or who was provoking who. Like I said, after heading home in the early dawn hours after spending some time in the highly virile ambiance of these police teams, working out the goodies from the baddies was very tricky.

At the police headquarters, when I joined the night teams at the beginning of their shift as they loaded up their weapons, strapped them to their waists and you could hear the clicks of their handguns being cocked and prepared for service, you could feel a testosterone-fuelled drive. And yet the lights in the corridors didn't work or flickered, the toilet seats were broken, the rooms were bare and totally bleak, so I guess the buzz comes from the power they know they have once behind the steering wheels of their powerful unmarked cars carrying loaded weapons.

What also amazed me was the control room in the police headquarters: a massive screen – like something in a Pentagon war room film. It displayed a map of the city and the exact location of every single police car on night duty in real time and at the first sign of an incident, the control room could send the nearest police car to a crime scene or guide them during a rapidly moving scenario like a stolen car chase, all of course remotely. At the time it was mesmerising, and I am sure the technology has moved well forward since then.

The Merah Affair

When I travelled abroad, I liked to read the local newspaper *La Dépêche du Midi* online just to see what was going on and what I might be missing.

That was what I was doing in Seattle in March 2012 where I had been invited by the French Chamber of Commerce to cover a visit by French aerospace suppliers working with Airbus but now being encouraged to wean themselves off their single client model and branch out and look for work with Boeing and its suppliers.

One prominent story in the paper that day was about a soldier who had been shot dead in a suburb of Toulouse on his day off, his motorbike was found next to his body. The police couldn't find a motive. They were looking at his private life, was he having an affair and shot by a jealous husband, or was he buying or selling drugs on the side and had unpaid debts... It didn't really go beyond that. And didn't really register with me either.

The day before I returned from Seattle, three more soldiers were shot while lining up at a cash point machine outside their barracks in the town of Montauban about 50 km north of Toulouse. Witnesses said they had been shot by a lone gunman on a moped in broad daylight. Two of the men died and a third is paralysed and has been hospital-bound ever since.

Again there was a lot of speculation, was it the work of Basque terrorists, or an extreme right wing faction? The soldiers came from ethic minority backgrounds. On my return from the US on the Sunday, the story had taken a dramatic step forward. The same gun had been used in both shooting incidents.

On the Monday morning I was still suffering from a bad dose of jet-lag and was pretty weary when I woke up. A few minutes later came the sound of a police siren and then another and then another. It was relentless and soon helicopters were circling. I didn't know anything at this stage but I just felt it had something to do with the previous shootings.

Catherine left for work and called me quickly to say she had heard on the radio there had been a shooting at a nearby school for Jewish children. 4 people had been shot including three children at the entrance. Witnesses said a lone gunman on a scooter shot them at close range as they were filing into school and had a camera on his helmet filming the scene. The city was on the verge of being in total lockdown. A few minutes later the Today Programme called to put me on air.

This was to be known as *the Merah affair*. For the next 10 days my life was to be focused on the manhunt to find the 23 year old of Algerian background brought up on the troubled estates of the city, and then on the long standoff as the police tried to capture him alive, and finally the craziness about what to do with his body.

My coverage of the Merah shootings was doubled-edged – it was traumatic and depressing but it gave me enormous personal publicity as I was on air virtually the whole time, and this came after a period where my on air presence had been waning substantially (I was doing more corporate coverage and media training and with big cut-backs at broadcasters like the BBC and shows disappearing entirely whether rugby or business related, it meant there were far less outlets to get on). Merah in a way gave a whole new boost to my on air journalism career as I sort of showed that having stringers outside big capitals had plenty of benefits.

In fact at one point I had that terrible dilemma where two key channels wanted me on air at the same time, both the BBC

6pm domestic news and France 24. Since France 24 had been loyal to me throughout the few years of its existence, I chose to go on air at that timeslot with them.

Apparently in the BBC television news world, no broadcast journalist declines the 6pm program and certainly never an opportunity to go live on it. When I did, a senior executive called up and said my profile was low in the UK this was my chance to boost it. Well, I guess I blew that one. As I say, Merah was double-edged because while it gave my journalism side a new lease of life, it also left a bitter taste, as I saw mass broadcast journalism at its worst.

Within hours of the blood being cleaned from the school entrance, both President Sarkozy and his key opponent François Hollande had made their way here to pay their respects.

This was at the height of the presidential election campaign. After their respective visits, both said they were suspending campaigning… then of course did no such thing. It was more about navigating their campaigns during a national tragedy.

The media as a huddled mass did little to question their opportunism, and during the Merah standoff acted as lemmings, providing the young man – possibly on drugs throughout the siege – with worldwide live coverage for hours on end that he probably never dreamt of obtaining when he planned his shooting spree.

And he no doubt triggered the same suicidal wishes amongst many others who in the years since then have chosen to copy him. After all he died in a hail of bullets, jumping over his flat balcony while firing a gun at one of the most well-trained police units in the world…

The same evening the Jewish children had been killed, their bodies had been taken away in coffins to be flown to Israel for burial the next day.

To my surprise much of the international media that had descended on to the streets near the school began to pack up the next day and leave – on to the next story. News desks figured it would be too costly to keep their reporters in the city while the gunman was tracked down. After all it was widely believed from the various briefings from the state prosecutors in both Paris and Toulouse that they were far from finding the gunman. But the city was on 'scarlet' alert which I had never heard of before – it meant another attack in the city was imminent.

Residents were uneasy, some told me later they were really frightened especially those who were in relationships with foreigners, thinking they could be targets. Because I lived so close to the school, I got there pretty quickly. Fortunately I didn't see bodies or large pools of blood – I came well after that, but I was struck by harrowing sounds of muffled whimpering from within the school courtyard – shell shocked families grieving and barely able to speak. A week later when parents dropped their kids off at the school for the first time since the shootings, again the tears in their eyes were wrenching to see.

But what also struck me during those few hours after the shooting was the number of CCTV cameras along the high perimeter wall of the school. I quickly understood just as the police clearly did, that the gunman knew he would be caught, it was just a question of how many more people he could kill before that moment came.

The proof is that after the shootings he went straight back home to his small flat less than 15 minutes away, to upload his video, rather than flee the city.

The sound of police cars wailing non-stop was unsettling and I have to admit for several years afterwards the sounds of several police cars hurtling down a street would shake me up.

The day after the shootings, after another string of live stand-ups for the BBC, France 24 and other broadcasters including ABC in Australia and Deutsche Welle, I said I needed to take a break as I had meeting that had been scheduled since well before the attacks, near the airport.

As I left the city centre there were numerous police checkpoints. Two hours later when I returned they seemed to have been lifted. I don't know if it was a coincidence or not but I wonder if that was a clue the authorities had located Merah already. I was shattered from all the live coverage but didn't manage to get to sleep until around 11pm. At about 4am I recall my phone going off but I was so tired that I didn't react. And then it went off again and again.

I know some journalists are used to this and probably thrive on middle of the night call-outs. Thankfully it's happened to me extremely rarely and is not something I look forward to ever.

The last time it occurred in the middle of the night was the truck massacre on Bastille Day night in Nice in 2016. Fortunately I was working at the Farnborough Airshow at the time and got out of that. The thing is, callers at that time of night are rarely bringing good news.

So when I finally answered that 4am phone call, someone from France 24 said to my confused and half awake self that the rolling news channel BFM was reporting the gunman had been located and there was a standoff.

Over the next few days the media kept reporting that the gunman, Mohammed Merah, was holed up in a well-to-do neighbourhood.

Now the police kept the media in their hundreds well back from the scene and indeed where we were all camped out during the siege was rather nice, with turn-of-the-century attractive brick homes and gardens, but the actual neighbourhood Merah was living in was grotty.

How could it be otherwise? He was a revolving door delinquent, in other words in and out of jail all his young life. Except that unlike other delinquents his age, he had travelled far, spending time in the Middle East as well as Pakistan and Afghanistan, where he learnt how to fire weapons before returning to France.

That triggered the Fox News correspondent standing next to me to say in one of his live broadcasts "French president Nicolas Sarkozy turned a blind eye as Al Qaeda was allowed to open a local chapter in this well-to-do leafy neighbourhood"[37].

That phone call was disturbing enough for me but equally or even more so for my girlfriend Catherine. It's pretty frightening for your partner, seeing you slip out in the middle the night to meet up with a killer. Of course it happens in police families all the time but not to us.

When I arrived at the scene it was still very dark and there were other journalists who had just arrived. The security perimeter was just going up, and then suddenly came the sound of grenades and bursts of machine gun fire. Flashes of light reflected across the tower block windows, I had never witnessed anything like it.

And then something surreal occurred. The rubbish collectors were out early as usual, doing their round even as we heard the blasts as the police tried to dislodge Merah from his small ground floor flat. When they saw us and the barriers I heard one say 'I suppose we can't pick up those ones'... it was such a strange scene, the ordinary routine life of a city juxtaposed with that of the abnormality and anarchy of guerrilla warfare just a few streets away.

The interior minister at the time Claude Guéant emerged

---

37 When police had identified Mohammed Merah as the gunman and had established what neighbourhood he'd grown up in – Les Izards – a lot of foreign journalists asked me how far it was and how to get there. I said it was a small rundown suburb north of Toulouse that had a lot of drug dealers who wouldn't be too happy to see cameras pointing in their direction disrupting their lucrative trade. Not for the first time, CNN's sneering team said to me, the country bumpkin, that they were used to heading to flash points the world over. Needless to say they went then left very quickly after their car was pelted with rocks and they said they were lucky not to be ripped out of their vehicle and torn apart. When they came back a year later to do an anniversary piece, they asked me to set everything up and come with them.

from the shadows with a small entourage to explain what was going on. He didn't leave the scene throughout the siege and from my vantage point, if Merah wasn't captured alive it was simply because Guéant and his boss, Sarkozy, the president put pressure on the police to get him quickly.

Their argument was that there was way too much worldwide publicity being generated by Merah as he held out and this had to be finished quickly.

But since he hadn't slept for days, had had his electricity and water cut off and was entirely surrounded, the waiting game or even sending sleeping gas canisters into his flat would have been enough and would have allowed the authorities to resolve once and for all whether he had acted alone, in other words whether he was a 'lone wolf' to use the French terminology.

But at the same time, French presidential elections were just around the corner and Sarkozy didn't want this polluting the campaign, or at least he hoped a swift and successful end would boost his. He spent time in and out of the city with his large motorcade clogging the streets and consuming massive police resources – getting updates on the siege, speaking to the Jewish community, meeting families who had managed to escape from the same block of flats where Merah was holed up... But the president's patience – not one of his strong points throughout his time in office – wore thin fast.

The police were ordered to storm Merah's flat when it was assumed he was asleep. In fact he was waiting for them and shot and injured several of the best trained police officers in the country when they broke into his dingy apartment. He continued firing rounds at them while simultaneously leaping off his balcony. His body was riddled with bullets, his gun by his side, turning him instantly into a martyr, the Butch Cassidy of banlieue delinquents-turned Islamic fanatics.

I heard that gun battle from where I was and it went on for several long minutes. I had my mobile phone pointed in the direction of the gunshots and BBC World carried that live (I'm not sure they actually heard anything) and then there would be a lull before it resumed. It was a horrific sound for anyone, including myself, a journalist not used to the sounds of war. A friend of mine chose a bad day to get dental work. He said he could hear the blasts as his teeth were being examined making what is at the best of times a jumpy situation, an anguishing ordeal[38].

The French authorities to this day are still unable to determine what kind of support network Merah had or whether he had simply made up his savage week of killings as he went along.

Merah's older brother was arrested soon after the killer was located. At his later trial he was found guilty of turning his young brother into a fanatic but not of participating in the killing scheme itself.

During the siege Merah held long phone conversations with a hostage mediator and he apparently said that it hadn't been his initial plan to target the school – he had been planning to kill a police officer but didn't stumble across any that day. He also said that he had intended to kill the agent from one of the French security agencies whom he had several meetings with when he returned from Afghanistan. They had called him in for debriefings precisely because they were concerned about what he might do next after his paramilitary pilgrimages abroad.

---

38 One of the few amusing moments throughout the Merah affair concerned my very laid back and smooth colleague Lucien Libert who is a Reuters producer in Paris. When he rushed down from Paris with his team, he hired a very big Volvo type estate car at the airport. He didn't bother negotiating mileage or anything. Throughout the Merah standoff the car didn't move. Instead the engine turned around the clock, acting as the generator for the Reuters live camera focused on the housing block where Merah was entrenched. When he returned the car to the hire company the engine was close to explosion from over-heating and I think he said the car had done around 10 kilometers but the motor had run for a week non-stop

In the week that followed, unsurprisingly a lot of navel-gazing went on in France, as both the media and the establishment tried to understand how someone like Merah, a petty criminal for sure but one who was born in France and liked to go out to nightclubs, drink and chat up women – in other words nothing out of the ordinary – could turn to Islamic extremism and film his killings.

Sadly in the years since then it's a question that has been asked again and again with each new attack by French born citizens. I think it was President Macron who answered it the most succinctly well before he was even candidate for the presidency, when he said France has simply created the conditions and space on French territory for people to grow up hating their country and everything it stands for.

Remember earlier when I mentioned those kids of North African background casually muttering "France on fire". I don't think you are born a terrorist, but faced with bleak prospects, the weakest of the bunch are ripe pickings for fanatics who convince them they can become heroes and masters of the universe in their own right while subtly turning them into killing machines.

Incidentally, I find it extraordinary that many commentators, especially in the UK, like to say it's a French problem and the outcome of decades of racism and failure to integrate its minorities. I've even heard so-called serious commentators in the UK media try to suggest it can't happen back home because far more efforts have been made over a long period in a far more open society like Britain's to be inclusive. It was clearly stupid thinking from the beginning, as the Brexit referendum result has since shown, and of course required amnesia or total denial about the root causes of what happened in London on July 7th 2005, or I suppose dismissing it as mere aberration.

In any case the various foiled attacks on planes between the UK and US underlined the fact that the massacres in Paris and Nice would have been dwarfed by atrocities committed in the air from the UK. The Westminster bridge attack and Manchester Arena suicide bombing have hopefully extinguished the last voices that think young kids from immigrant backgrounds turning to fanaticism is still just a French or continental problem.

In fact although European (including British) terrorist groups in the 70s and 80s never envisaged killing *themselves* in their outrages, their recruits were often facing similar 'no future' lives to those faced by today's islamist extremists and becoming gunmen and bombers gave them too a feeling of pride, swagger in their communities and a reason to live.

During the week after Merah's death, the debate swayed between why he did it to why wasn't he captured alive and how come the warning signs had not been detected beforehand. That discussion isn't over but so many other cases since then have diluted the focus on Merah.

But there was still the urgent and pressing issue to resolve: what to do with his body. His mother wanted to send her son's body to Algeria but people in the 'know' told me there was no way the Algerian authorities would allow his coffin to be sent there with their own civil war with islamist extremists in the 1990s still very raw and not entirely over.

As it is, a week after his death Merah's family were determined to fly his body across the Mediterranean.

This was one of those moments when I actually learnt something new on the job – that there is a competitive, lucrative business in transporting corpses. There is a special entrance to the airport where hearses pull up with bodies to be sent elsewhere, or indeed to pick up the dead from somewhere else to be buried in the region.

That is how I found myself on a macabre job for Reuters that very early Friday morning, scrutinising long black or dark brown cars carrying coffins near the freight entrance to the airport.

When I flagged one down asking if they knew the whereabouts of Merah's body, the two pall bearers inside replied they didn't get the job from the hospital morgue where his body was, it had been given to a rival company. And they seemed pretty annoyed about it too. A couple of hours monitoring the traffic in the dead certainly showed there is big business in industries you had no idea existed.

Then came the news alert from the French wire service AFP that the Algerian government had denied permission for Merah's family to bury his body on their soil. So it remained stuck at the morgue.

What followed was an electric and frantic 8 or so hours as from Merah's family to the Mayor of Toulouse and all the way up to Sarkozy, people scrambled to find a solution and burial site for the gunman's body.

After Algeria had declined to take his body, the then Mayor of Toulouse, Pierre Cohen also quickly refused to bury him within city limits, fearing it would become a pilgrimage site for fanatics. He also no doubt had in mind his own re-election campaign and the promised backlash from his constituents if he had freely volunteered to provide a burial plot.

And so there unfolded a standoff over several hours about what to do with a terrorist's body in a city still numbed by what had occurred a week earlier. Merah's family and friends (more on that later) waited at the hospital morgue, a hearse on standby. Then news came from the Elysée in Paris – Sarkozy hard ordered the mayor to resolve the problem. He said it was a legal requirement for the mayor to sort it out as Merah had died in his city. But Cohen refused to budge.

At the same time the Imam of the main mosque in Paris also sent down a special envoy to speak to the family and the mayor and find an urgent solution. I managed to track him down outside the Algerian consulate.

He told me there was a small Muslim plot at a graveyard just outside the city where Merah would be buried in an unmarked grave.

I quickly made my way there and as I was the first, the municipal gate keepers looking after the quiet graveyard were totally unaware of the tornado that was about to descend on them.

Sure enough, within a couple of hours panicked police units were scrambling, sealing off the graveyard as news emerged that Merah's family were on their way from the morgue.

A massive police convoy followed the beat up brown van, you knew they were coming because you could hear and then see a police helicopter following the procession. The atmosphere was electric, as youths with their faces covered, some in white Islamic gowns, pulled up in cars at the cemetery gate. They were the entourage Merah had hung out with. The gendarmes were scrambling to intercept them and get their identities. Merah's mother didn't come to the funeral.

From outside a perimeter fence we were able to see them pray, their voices drowned out by the helicopter, except for their shouting out in unison: "Allahu Akbar" – 'God is great' – and then they began digging. The imam's envoy was with them. He told me afterwards that some in the group were salafists, others friends from Merah's neighbourhood. Very soon after they had buried his body they slipped away.

Five years later, of the dozen or so who dug that grave, nearly all are either in prison or dead after joining the jihad in Syria.

***

Post Merah

The Merah affair raised my profile and sparked a surge in new work commissions. But it also heralded the beginning of my withdrawal from daily broadcast news journalism.

Filming and interviewing a weeping, terrified father dropping off his kids at the Jewish school the day it re-opened was depressing and the whole way the media had swooped on Toulouse and turned a tragedy into a spectator event was inevitable but not something I really wanted to be part of anymore.

But the media wasn't the only culprit. There were many, including the Israeli Prime Minister Benjamin Netanyahu. He even unashamedly came to Toulouse and led a memorial service in the school that quickly turned into a political campaign rally, broadcast live back home with elections just weeks away. President Hollande was there and looked extremely uncomfortable as Bibi urged France's Jewish population to move to Israel, claiming they were no longer safe where they were.

As the wave of terrorism attacks picked up in France in the years after Merah, the story was constantly about the lack of integration – could Muslims integrate into western society or was it doomed from the start.

Not long after the Charlie Hebdo and Jewish supermarket attacks, both in Paris, I got invited to the Prefecture in Toulouse for a swearing in service for new French citizens. They wanted to show that there was a positive message about social cohesion and immigration to get across. It was a rare moment of emotional and uplifting news in an otherwise gloomy climate.

From Our Own Correspondent
BBC Radio 4
February 2015

In France, prefects are modern day regional governors and are the eyes and ears of the government outside of Paris.

They live and work in grand gated mansions with huge manicured gardens in city centres, with permanent police protection. Not many people get a chance to penetrate these secretive fortresses apart from local grandees, politicians and journalists for special events.

But once a month the gates open wide for a group of people who until then couldn't ever be sure they wouldn't at some point be deported.

For 144 men and women from 42 different countries, this was a very special day.

Their long desire to obtain French nationality officially became reality. In ordinary circumstances a ceremony like this would always be an emotional moment for any of these new French citizens, but today there was an added poignancy. It was the first naturalization process since the terrible terror attacks in Paris in January and I was invited along by the Prefect to see it happen.

Algerians and Moroccans made up the largest proportion of the group. Some of the women wore short skirts, others head scarfs, the men had dressed smartly. All had come with cameras. Young children chased each other under the grand chandelier-lit hall, oblivious to protocol.

Some of the new French citizens had spent years battling for a French passport, for others it was far simpler. Many like 28 year old Leila, had come over from Morocco as engineering students and then found work in the aerospace industry.

One couple were long term political refugees from Iran.

Others had come on holiday or short term work contracts, fallen in love and married French locals, and were able to stay with residency papers but until today had had nothing that said officially they were anything but temporary visitors.

The ceremony started with a short video highlighting the history of France and how it had become a republic.

The Prefect then took to the stage and addressed the attacks that had occurred in Paris in January. He said it was up to these newly French citizens to show they could integrate into French life and in a rather bold move for an elite French civil servant, he reminded them of John F. Kennedy's famous line: "Ask not what your country can do for you – ask what you can do for your country."

Every new French citizen-to-be had been handed a sheet of paper with the words to La Marseillaise – the French national anthem – and then an honour guard of military veterans with draped flags in hand led the room in collective song. There was spontaneous applause and the first tears began to run.

Within the next 50 minutes 144 people were about to become French citizens. Each one was called up to the front to receive a solemn handshake from the Prefect and a folder containing the official documents confirming they were French, a copy of the French Constitution and a charter spelling out rights and obligations under French law.

Many of the new citizens had been accompanied to the ceremony by local mayors, councillors and the odd MP, who knowing the system, had battled France's overwhelming bureaucracy to help their constituents overcome the numerous hurdles along the path to citizenship.

To get French citizenship all these candidates had had to prove they spoke French and had no criminal record and to show proof of financial independence and commitment to assimilating into French life.

Later the Prefect, Pascal Mailhos (who by the way once ran the equivalent of MI5, the French Domestic Intelligence Service) told me that after the attacks in Paris, it was more important than ever for new citizens to show their willingness to belong, live together and become part of French society. He used the word 'fraternity' several times.

One of the new French citizens, Bashif, an Algerian-born truck driver, said that life had become harder for him in recent weeks as the attacks in Paris had thrown suspicion on his Muslim faith. Another, a Moroccan woman, said she didn't even want to think about what had happened during that terrible week in January, especially on a day like this.

After the last new citizen had been applauded, everyone moved next door for a brief reception.

The whole ceremony had taken less than two hours. As the final guests filed through the Prefecture gates towards the bustling, snarled up medieval streets to start the rest of their lives as French citizens, the population of France had just swelled by 144.

Even without Merah, my daily journalism output would have diminished with time, but maybe more gradually. When you see that there are more and more of your very young ex-students from the journalism school out in the field, reporting; and you notice your own insolence on the phone with news editors that a decade before you had feared, you know it's probably time to bow out.

And so I began to switch increasingly to corporate video coverage, helping big companies with crisis communications and media training, or providing them with video news releases – otherwise known as VNRs – for newsrooms to use.

As broadcasters have slashed costs and reduced staff and especially overseas travel, they may not like to admit it, but when they receive video and interview clips on a decent story with a suggested guideline script in an easy to use format that can be downloaded in seconds, there is a good chance they will use it.

Anything to do with Planes

Remember when I said there were three people I had to stay on the right side of when I moved to Toulouse if I wanted to make a living from journalism? One was Guy Novès, who had been manager of the Stade Toulousain before moving up to Paris as rugby coach for the *Bleus*, another was the ex-mayor Philippe Douste-Blazy, and the third was the long time head of the Press Office at Airbus, Barbara Kracht.

I had been warned by many that she was well 'a little difficult'.

She was the first female press officer I ever met entirely impervious to male charm or flattery. Or maybe just to mine… But nevertheless I had to go through her to gain any access to the plane manufacturer. And we didn't hit it off from the start either. Since Airbus makes around half of the world's big aircraft and employs up to 50,000 people locally directly or through suppliers, that was going to be an issue for me.

Often my conversations with her would start like this… "Barbara I really need an interview with the new CEO/Head of Sales/Chief Engineer or visiting airline boss."

"No."

"But Barbara the BBC is hounding me – they say what is the point in having someone down here if he can't even get an interview at Airbus?"

"Well Chris that is really not my problem."[39]

I had moved to Toulouse just as Airbus had challenged the United States by launching the world's biggest ever passenger plane, the A380. Boeing had considered a similar project but then backed out, considering there wasn't a large enough market for it. So the European partners behind the *super jumbo* (as Airbus's project was nicknamed) were taking a big risk, and for once (in the industrial landscape at least) being more bold than the Americans and taking the lead.

Of course Boeing said the A380 wouldn't fly – not in the real sense, but financially. They said there were not enough airlines out there prepared to pay for a double decker aeroplane with seating for more than 800 passengers as there weren't enough routes where they could turn a profit with a plane that size, equipped with four engines.

And more than 10 years on, that debate still hasn't really been settled.

Just like rugby I knew absolutely nothing about aeroplanes – I'm even scared of flying and unlike most 'real' aviation correspondents, I am not a frustrated wannabe pilot nor do I harbour any secret desire to cosy up to throbbing engines or coo over complex circuit boards. But what that meant was that I had a very steep learning curve if I was to understand anything

---

39   Barbara has since then retired and now provides courses on media awareness to aviation students. She invited me along with a defence publication editor and a New York Times reporter to speak about what I do when there is a plane crash. Funnily enough, many of the video reports I showed seemed to have me speaking into a microphone standing in front of perimeter fences. We laughed about it as I pointed out she had played a key role in the culture of Airbus keeping people like me away as far as possible whenever an incident occurred. Things have fortunately changed slightly since.

to do with planes. The media's fascination with the A380 was impressive and to be honest so was the public's. In fact aviation stories in general seem to get some of the most hits on the BBC website on a regular basis.

On June 27th 2003 the last flight of an Air France owned Concorde occurred. It took off from Paris and as it landed in Toulouse to be grounded for good, it was incredibly moving to see so many middle-aged aviation engineers near the runway with tears rolling down their cheeks. That's the kind of emotional bond and passion people who work in the aviation industry tend to have about their field. Alas I didn't have that...

Plane spotters gave me a lot of trouble – whenever a new plane was about to be launched on its first test flight, they would circulate conspiracy theories that the plane would carry out its first flight secretly in the middle of the night, and I would have to chase up whether there was even the slightest chance of that happening. With the A380's first flight imminent but not yet scheduled, night and day for weeks plane spotters converged on a hill overlooking the runways, convinced that was exactly what would happen – a secret first flight before the break of dawn on a Sunday etc. And they weren't actually nutcases after all – I discovered later that some of Airbus management did in fact argue for a 'clandestine' first flight because of what was at stake – only calmer executives said any secret mission like that would wreck the company's credibility for a decade.

Plane crashes were always a pain to cover – in one case literally. When the Germanwings plane was flown into the Alps by a psychotic/depressive pilot, killing all 144 passengers and all 6 crew members, I had to do lots of live pieces to camera outside the Airbus gates (again) for the BBC and France 24. But the evening before, I had broken my foot playing squash. I didn't know yet I had snapped a bone (I hadn't had time to get an x-ray) but I sure knew it hurt and other reporters seeing me wincing and hobbling from my car to the broadcast van were appalled – it just went to confirm their suspicion that Brits have no medical care, have to work even when they're on their death bed etc. No, I was just eager to be on TV!

Crashes are a pain for other reasons – you are asked immediately by whoever the researcher/booker is in the studio to give 'your take' on what might be the cause of a crash… and being live TV you have to say something. Of course you rarely know anything – and when a plane goes missing for years like Malaysia Airlines Flight 370, any instant running commentary is exposed for what it is…

Sometimes the BBC Foreign desk would call me to do an Airbus story, especially if there was a UK link. After all, the wings and many of the engines were built in Britain. One time a lovely colleague on the desk called asking me to do live two-ways all day in front of the factory with an Airbus behind me, starting at 6.30am. I said great but it didn't make sense starting so early as you wouldn't see anything in the background, just me – rabbit in the headlight, you get the idea.

She sighed and replied: "Chris nice thinking, but you are really going to have to take your common sense and logic and leave it all behind if you want to work for the News Channel."

Business news loves aviation stories – how many sales, why a new plane is behind schedule or why a major airline cancelled an order. Or like when Sir Richard Branson whipped himself up enormous publicity with his comment about his Virgin A380s – that you could get lucky twice: once in the on-board casino and secondly in the first class luxury suites. It was a great line and he got great coverage (as usual for him)… especially as he never actually bought the plane. Toulouse won the battle against Hamburg to be the city where the A380 should be assembled, thanks to massive government lobbying. But the parts are so big that a special road had to be created outside Bordeaux to bring them down to Toulouse. First the huge parts are carried on ships to an unloading dock just outside Bordeaux from the various factories across Europe, then they're put on barges before being unloaded again, this time onto trucks in a town called Langon. The night-time convoys became a tourist attraction. I went along for one of the first. Here was a story I did for BBC business news back in 2004.

BBC World Business Report
April 2004

People in south-west France last night got an exclusive glimpse of the A380 which will be the world's biggest passenger plane when it's built. Just getting the parts to the Airbus factory in Toulouse has proven a major feat of its own.

If it wasn't for the temperature – around 2°C – and the hour – close to midnight – this could be the same crowd waiting for the Tour de France to pass.

But in many ways the first A380 is making a tour de France of its own, albeit a very slow one. As the first convoy headed off towards the brand new assembly lines in Toulouse, there was a ripple of applause from the crowd. Locals emerged from their village homes and marvelled at the colossus rumbling through.

The A380, with seating for 550 passengers, will be the world's biggest passenger plane when it goes into service in 2006. Just getting the parts to fit widthways along 240 kilometres of winding, narrow roads was a major challenge of its own. It has cost the taxpayer more than €120 million to widen roads, demolish a few houses, cut down trees (and re-plant them elsewhere).

There are still some pockets of resistance to the convoys, some residents fear the parts – more than 14 metres in height, in other words roof level – are a recipe for disaster. But they are a distinct minority. The trucks have been equipped with special engines and are remarkably quiet.

Gilbert Raust is the chief engineer in charge of studying and *planning the A380 route. He told me the work that has been achieved showed that the environmental problems that were feared had not been as difficult to resolve as concerned residents had first thought.*

The trickiest part of the journey may in fact be the sea journey. All the parts – including the wings – arrive by sea from factories around Europe.

They are then placed on a special barge outside Bordeaux before having to inch their way under the city's historic bridges. What's more, it's a tidal river. A sudden change in the water level could jeopardise everything.

Back on land, the first A380 convoy was slightly behind schedule but it has three days to do 240km. It will soon become routine and the local residents are going to have to get used to it because Airbus is planning to run one night convoy a week along this road... Although of course that depends on whether the A380 proves popular with its clients.[40]

There were dozens of stories about the A380 including of course the obvious one – who was responsible for the long and costly delays before it went into service – but there were more off-beat angles to take...

I preferred stories about the lifers in the maximum security jail south of Toulouse in Seysses who worked in prison workshops making parts including the air conditioning for the super jumbo, on behalf of Airbus suppliers. They told me sometimes they used to run out of their factory (but behind secure walls) and wave at the plane when it was doing a test flight overhead.

And which is more interesting? A story about an airline

---

40 Of course the A380 didn't sell well and those who have profited the most from the new route are truckers who choose to use it rather than pay toll fees on the motorway – in the end they have been far more disruptive to the residents who live along the convoy route than the A380 itself.

which might order new planes or one about an airport like Châteauroux in the centre of France that is an exposed graveyard for the broken dreams of would-be airline owners, forced to ground their fleets for good when they realise running an airline is, like opening a restaurant, one of the quickest ways to go broke.

You often wonder what is actually happening in the company board room at times of total crisis, for example when it's on the verge of declaring bankruptcy, like Lehman Brothers.

Well, I can't speak for bankers but I had a fascinating insight with Air Lib. At one time it was France's second biggest airline after Air France, with more than 3000 employees and routes around the world.

But it couldn't compete despite massive cash injections from the government, and in a desperate throw of the dice, opened new low cost routes to the exotic French overseas territories like Guadeloupe and Martinique. I headed up to see the new CEO, Jean-Charles Corbet, at the airline's headquarters near Orly. He was already announcing massive job cuts. I said to myself it was remarkable that he had time to see me – as it turns out, the company's closure was imminent. My friend Anthony Jeffers, a sports journalist, came along to help me out with the camera work. The atmosphere in the long corridors was calm, serene even, despite the death sentence that hung over the company.

I found Corbet huddled with a few of his staffers examining Air Lib spreadsheets, but no sooner had he discovered that I lived in Toulouse than the conversation turned to anything but Air Lib's failing fortunes... It turns out he is a massive rugby fan and a former player in Perpignan before the game turned professional. Le Stade Toulousain was dominating French rugby at the time. So he asked me question after question about the 'Stade'. It took a long time to get him off the subject of rugby and to talk about his airline, and when he finally did, it was with a lot of reluctance, accusing me of being a real killjoy. Even after the interview we went back to the subject of rugby. Maybe he knew then the game was up for his airline. Anthony, as staggered as myself, couldn't quite bring himself to believe that a company CEO struggling to keep his company afloat wanted to talk just about sport. Corbet was a former Air France pilot and he would have had a wonderful pension if he had stuck with that – instead when Air Lib folded he was put on trial for embezzlement – accused of taking emergency funds and funnelling them into offshore accounts. He was acquitted on appeal 7 years later but was left virtually broke. Anyway I don't know what the atmosphere was like in the Lehman boardroom when they announced they were broke – maybe they were talking about renewing baseball season tickets before they lost all their perks.

One of my worst moments and biggest mistakes involved a plane crash in 2008. An Air New Zealand plane had come to southern France for routine maintenance. In the hangar it had received a new coat of paint but apparently the paint had clogged up the sensors near the cockpit which provide important data for the pilots.

The crew picked up the plane and took off and then unable to read the information, flew too low and straight into the Mediterranean, killing all 7 people on board.

The foreign editor of New Zealand's state broadcaster (who had a great name – Max Hayton) got in touch and asked me to cover the story for them. So far so good, but much later when the bodies had been retrieved and the families flown over by Air New Zealand and its CEO to pick them up and bring them home, a rival network had also sent over a team to cover the event.

I knew the French state prosecutor investigating the crash (he once prosecuted ETA suspects in the Basque Country) and he gave me an interview which I naturally used, although he didn't say anything earth shattering to me. But the next day my rival, a beautiful, ambitious blonde Kiwi journalist, begged me for his contact details, so I called the prosecutor asking if he could see her too, and he agreed. Except she asked far more interesting questions than me and got a real scoop about the last moments and conversation in the cockpit before the crash...

The families were outraged, the airline CEO and his press officer livid, so they then tried to smear me, saying that I had been paid by the reporter to set up the interview for her AND that I'd colluded with the judicial authorities.

No, it was a lot simpler than that – I'd fallen for an attractive blonde who'd pleaded and batted her eyelids... and who then asked better questions than me.

That doomed Air New Zealand aircraft had taken off on its last flight from the airport in Perpignan. Perpignan airport – or to be exact the maintenance side of the runway field – has become a favourite of plane spotters in recent times thanks to one exotic looking aircraft: the late Colonel Gaddafi's.

How did it end up here? I thought I would end with this little tale.

From Our Own Correspondent
BBC Radio 4
October 2016

Motorists heading south along the A9 near Perpignan in southern France are often in a hurry after being stuck in long tailbacks on steamy days.

But a strange thing has happened over the past year. People have been adding to their journey time by coming off the motorway to visit a new tourist attraction – it's a fenced-in aviation maintenance and repair centre on one corner of Perpignan's sprawling airfield.

What they've come to see is a four engine Airbus, an A340 that belonged to Colonel Gaddafi. Its tail is now painted in the new colours of the Libyan flag. When the colonel was alive it had a very understated look with the simple name Afriqiyah Airways (the national Libyan airline) so as not to give away the fact that the Libyan leader was in town.

The question is how did the aircraft end up in Perpignan? Well, it all comes down to debt and power struggles.

Five years ago, as rebel forces overran the Libyan capital, the airport came under attack. Gaddafi's plane was damaged. The new administration in Tripoli got a French team which specialises in repossessing aircraft to patch it up well enough to fly to the northern side of the Mediterranean and be fixed in Perpignan.

And it was. The newly appointed Libyan Prime Minister, Ali Zedian flew around Europe in it to various summits but when the plane needed servicing it was taken back to Perpignan. And it hasn't flown since.

The reason is that lawyers for a Kuwaiti property conglomerate asked a French judge to impound the aircraft. They claimed the conglomerate was owed €900 million by Gaddafi for work on a new holiday resort that was never finished. How did they even know the plane was on French soil? One of the lawyers representing the Kuwaitis, Rémi Barousse, told me that thanks to an app on his mobile alerting him to news about Libya, he discovered that the plane had just landed in Perpignan. He asked a French judge to stop it from leaving – the judge agreed to his request.

The Kuwaitis wanted to sell the plane for more than €100 million.

That had aviation specialists chuckling. Several told me the Kuwaitis would be lucky to get a quarter of that amount. Four-engine aircraft dating from the early 1990s are much less fuel efficient and have higher running costs than today's aircraft. But it seems Gaddafi didn't have the Libyan taxpayer's purse in mind when he bought it. He was scared of flying and thought a four engine plane was safer than one with just two.

And whoever bought the plane would have to do a costly refit unless they wanted to keep the onboard jacuzzi, gold taps, double bed and other accoutrements that the Libyan leader had had installed.

Over the summer, a French judge in Montpellier lifted the no-fly ban on the aircraft saying it was the property of the Libyan State not of one leader, and the Kuwaitis could not lay claim to it.

Carole Sportes, a Paris based aviation lawyer representing the Libyan State in this affair told me that in principle, a crew can come over anytime and pick up the aircraft: "But there is a snag," she pointed out, "actually several snags. Who actually has sovereignty over the airbus? With Libya still in chaos, who represents the official government in Tripoli? And at a practical level, just how good are the runways and airport infrastructure back in Libya?"

She told me there is more chance of the plane staying intact while it's on French soil. That's not all.

Every few weeks maintenance teams turn over the engines of the aircraft and check that it's in proper working order for the day that it takes to the skies again. Except the maintenance company is a subsidiary of Air France and looking after the plane has already cost €3 million. They too want to get paid by someone in Libya.

As for the Kuwaitis and their €900 million bill that the Colonel never honoured, another court said their claim is valid. They must now try to find the money in one of the former leader's offshore accounts. You may not be surprised to hear that they told me THAT is proving very difficult too.

***

December 2017 – Ile des Faisans

Recently I spent a long weekend at the Serge Blanco Spa hotel in the Basque beach resort of Hendaye.

It's the last town before you hit the border and the hotel is actually incredibly well situated along the estuary which acts as the natural border between France and Spain. The view across the water to Spain is beautiful and sitting on a breakwater you can see rowers in colourful Basque outfits training and just make out the cox shouting out instructions in Basque. It's a very soothing spectacle. But what I have really come to see is the Île des Faisans or Isla de los Faisanes in Spanish. It's an island just over 200m in length and 40m in width in the middle of the River Bidassoa which flows out into the estuary.

Finding it is not easy – as you head upstream from the coast, the imposing and colourful Basque buildings give way to industrial warehouses on the French side and to unappealing residential tower blocks on the Spanish side.

When I ask for directions nobody understands why I want to go there. They tell me there is nothing to see and warn me you can't visit it – it's not like Mont St Michel…

But there it is – a peaceful, inaccessible island with trees and trimmed grass, sandwiched in the middle of the river with an old monument on it paying tribute to a remarkable moment of history that took place here in 1659.

Over a three month period, the Spanish and the French negotiated the end to the Franco-Spanish war which has lasted nearly 3 decades. They signed the peace on this island having built wooden bridges from both sides and amassed armies next to their respective negotiators. The agreement was called the The Treaty of the Pyrenees (the same treaty that established Llivia as an enclave). Land was swapped and the border drawn. The deal was sealed with a royal wedding – the king of France, Louis XIV married the Infanta María Teresa, daughter of the king of Spain, Felipe IV.

One spin-off was that from that moment on, the island was to be shared between the two countries. For six months from February 1st until July 31st, it's under Spanish rule, and for the following six months it's French. The joint sovereignty is called a 'condominium' and it's the oldest arrangement of its kind in existence.

I speak to the mayor of Hendaye. He tells me that in theory, the naval commanders in the Spanish town of San Sebastián and his own counterpart in Bayonne act as governors or viceroys of the island. In reality they have bigger fish to fry... so it's up to the mayors of Irún and Hendaye to look after the island during their on-off six month sovereignty.

Nowadays, they keep the tree branches trimmed and the grass cut and that's about it. On the Spanish side, since the river is tidal, you can sometimes reach the island on foot, so the Spanish police also occasionally chase illegal campers off... But under Franco, it was a different story – there were sentry points facing the island to prevent opponents getting into or out of Spain via the island.

When the Île des Faisans is next handed over to Spain on February 1st, it will be done without a shot being fired, and barely anyone will notice. In fact the island has shrunk by half over the centuries due to erosion, but apparently neither country has the money to restore the island's defences...

This will be the subject of my next *From Our Own Correspondent*.

A few weeks ago I got one of those calls I dreaded from the Reuters bureau chief in Paris Marc Detemple ...a driver had deliberately run over Chinese students in a suburb of Toulouse. And then of course all the other channels got in touch too – a sense of déjà vu. The French police were quickly on the scene and the authorities were quick to add it wasn't terrorism – he was just unstable – sure he had radicalised Islamist brother but sheer coincidence. So are new guidelines from above to keep us calm if fanatics strike again to refer to them as loons who simply haven't taken their medication? While terrorists of course are not unhinged?

Bernard Laporte the new bad boy of French rugby is under

investigation for corruption. To keep things simple as President of the French Rugby Federation or FFR, he is accused of putting pressure on an impartial « ethics panel » to sweeten the sanctions on Montpellier Rugby Club. The fines were imposed for bad behaviour on the pitch and by fans in the stadium.

It just turns out that Laporte also had a lucrative contract with the owner of Montpellier Mohed Altrad to do... well thats not really clear. But the billionaire also in a branding marketing coup now has his company's name and logo on the French national side's rugby shirts thanks to Laporte but all that is a coincidence too.

Laporte has now dropped that nice contract to show there is no conflict of interest... and never inactive has just settled other scores firing the current manager of the French team Guy Noves. When they were both mere club rugby managers there was no love between them. He hasn't been allowed to finish his 4 year mandate a first for a French national rugby coach and just a few weeks from the start of the Six Nations tournament. French rugby sloshing with cash, clubs owned by tycoons using them as toys, and now riddled with open political infighting looks set to become as unpopular as the French national football team when it went on a stroppy mutiny refusing to their leave their bus for a training session during the World Cup in South Africa in 2010.

But for me of course all this means there is plenty to keep me occupied for the foreseeable future.

Acknowledgements

There are a lot of people to thank.

Anthony Jeffers, (a Yorkshireman trapped in a Brummie's body) for pushing me to write this book and reminding me of some of the stories that I had done and kept saying 'Put it in the book!' Vanessa Stone and Flore Negroni for taking my book and elevating the grammar and punctuation from 11+ level to something a little more adult.

There are a lot of commissioning editors over the years who accepted, tolerated or even encouraged my offbeat stories. I can't mention them all but in no particular order I would like to especially thank Yann Tessier at Reuters. At the BBC Neil Heathcote, Simon Smith, Mike London, Tony Grant, Polly Hope, Joe Kent and Ed Horton. From the world of rugby production a special mention to Martin Cross and Bob Wayte. From the murky world of independent production companies Jon Lamberton and Eckart Sager. At France 24 Albert Ripamonti, Loick Berrou, Francoise Champey and Remy Gabala for the photographs..